Debating
Anarchism

DEBATES IN WORLD HISTORY

Series Editor: Peter N. Stearns, George Mason University, USA

Editorial Board: Marc Jason Gilbert (Hawaii Pacific University, USA), Heather Streets-Salter (Northeastern University, USA), Sadiah Qureshi (University of Birmingham, UK)

Bloomsbury's *Debates in World History* series presents students with accessible primers to the key debates in the field of world history, from classic debates, such as the great divergence, through to cutting-edge current developments. These are short, argumentative texts that will encourage undergraduate level history students to engage in the practice of doing history.

Published:

Debating the Industrial Revolution, Peter N. Stearns
Debating Modern Revolution, Jack R. Censer
Debating Genocide, Lisa Pine
Debating Nationalism, Florian Bieber

Forthcoming:

Debating Gender, April Haynes
Debating the Great Divergence, Shami Ghosh
Debating Populism, Anthony Taylor

Debating Anarchism

A History of Action, Ideas and Movements

MIKE FINN

BLOOMSBURY ACADEMIC
LONDON • NEW YORK • OXFORD • NEW DELHI • SYDNEY

BLOOMSBURY ACADEMIC
Bloomsbury Publishing Plc
50 Bedford Square, London, WC1B 3DP, UK
1385 Broadway, New York, NY 10018, USA
29 Earlsfort Terrace, Dublin 2, Ireland

BLOOMSBURY, BLOOMSBURY ACADEMIC and the Diana logo are
trademarks of Bloomsbury Publishing Plc

First published in Great Britain 2021

Cover image: Terry Woodley
Cover image © Igor Stevanovic/Alamy Stock Photo

A catalogue record for this book is available from the British Library.

A catalog record for this book is available from the Library of Congress.

Library of Congress Cataloging-in-Publication Data
Names: Finn, Mike (Michael Thomas) author.
Title: Debating anarchism : a history of action, ideas and movements / Mike Finn.
Description: 1 Edition. | New York : Bloomsbury Academic, 2021. |
Series: Debates in world history | Includes bibliographical references and index. |
Identifiers: LCCN 2021006791 (print) | LCCN 2021006792 (ebook) | ISBN 9781350118119
(hardback) | ISBN 9781350118102 (paperback) | ISBN 9781350118126 (epub) |
ISBN 9781350118133 (ebook)
Subjects: LCSH: Anarchism–History. | Social movements–History.
Classification: LCC HX828 .F56 2021 (print) | LCC HX828 (ebook) | DDC 335/.83–dc23
LC record available at https://lccn.loc.gov/2021006791
LC ebook record available at https://lccn.loc.gov/2021006792

ISBN: HB: 978-1-3501-1811-9
PB: 978-1-3501-1810-2
ePDF: 978-1-3501-1813-3
eBook: 978-1-3501-1812-6

Typeset by Deanta Global Publishing Services, Chennai, India
Printed and bound in Great Britain

To find out more about our authors and books visit www.bloomsbury.com
and sign up for our newsletters.

For
Nicola, Rhian, Vicky,
Gavin, Robyn, Sol and Josh,
comrades

History, at its best ... is the most subversive discipline ...

JAMES C. SCOTT, political scientist

Nothing ever burns down by itself,
every fire needs a little bit of help ...

CHUMBAWAMBA, anarcho-communist rock band
Give the Anarchist a Cigarette (1994)

Contents

Acknowledgements

In writing a book of this nature it is inevitable that the author will be hugely indebted to the vast range of scholars whose work they have attempted to summarize and synthesize; their names are listed in the references, but to all of them I owe sincere thanks both in terms of this book and for my wider education as an historian and an anarchist.

As I translated personal politics and activism into a research interest, I have been grateful for the support of friends, comrades and colleagues from across activism and academia. Some belong to both camps but amongst the anarchists I would like to mention Thomas Swann, Jack Saunders and Alex Prichard in particular. More widely in the activist arena thanks are due to Nicola Northcott, Steven Shakespeare, Elena Boschi, Vicky Blake, Robyn Orfitelli, Josh Robinson, Gary Anderson, Lena Simic, Dana Mills, Peter Riley, Sunday Blake, Leon Sealey-Huggins, Craig Black, Tor Krever, Stan Papoulias, Jane Elliott, Myka Tucker-Abramson and Aimée Lê. Amongst the academics at my home in the History Department at the University of Exeter, I owe particular thanks to Henry Knight Lozano, Richard Toye, Martin Thomas, Gajendra Singh, Gemma Clark, Sarah Hamilton and Rhian Keyse. A special mention is reserved for my friend and colleague Jon Lawrence, who has been a mentor for over twenty years and who I'm now privileged to teach with. Also at Exeter I should like to thank Morwenna Ludlow, Susannah Cornwall, Jon Morgan, Louise Lawrence, David Tollerton, David Horrell and Susan Margetts. Colleagues away from Exeter have contributed hugely too – thanks go to Matthew Adams, Pippa Catterall, David Goodway, Brendan Burchell, Gavin Schwartz-Leeper, Constance Bantman, Ruth Kinna, Jim Yeoman, Danny Evans, and Evan Smith. A special mention goes to my old friend Mike Gledhill, who has shared many political conversations over the years and is a brother to me. Grateful thanks are extended to Maddie Holder and Abigail Lane, the editorial team at Bloomsbury, for their patience and support throughout the life of this project. Thanks too to Joseph Gautham for rigorous editing of the text. In this connection I would like to note the fine work of the three anonymous reviewers who looked at the original manuscript with clear eyes and provided insightful comments. Any mistakes or errors which remain are my own.

Thanks to Freedom Press for permission to quote from José Peirats, *Anarchists in the Spanish Revolution* and to Prickly Paradigm to quote from David Graeber, *Fragments of an Anarchist Anthropology*. Thanks too to Boff Whalley and Chumbawamba for permission to use the quote from *Give the Anarchist a Cigarette*, to James C. Scott for permission to use the quote from *Against the Grain,* and to Andrew M. Koch for permission to quote from 'Post-structuralism and the epistemological basis of anarchism'.

I would like to add a special note of thanks to the people who have done most to educate me on anarchism, namely my students at Exeter on HIH2034A Anarchism: Theory, Practice, History and HIH1136 'Dangerous Woman': The lives and afterlives of Emma Goldman.

My final thanks are to my family, my parents Rita and Tom Finn, who have endured so much over the years and have always been generous with their love and support.

Mike Finn
Lincolnshire, 2020

Abbreviations

AFED Anarchist Federation

APOC Anarchist Peoples of Color

CNT Confederación Nacional del Trabajo

DAM Direct Action Movement (later SolFed)

EZLN Ejército Zapatista de Liberación Nacional

FAI Federacion Anarquista Iberica

FRE Federación Regional Española

FTRE Federacion de Trajabadores de la Region Espanola

IGO Intergovernmental organization

IMF International Monetary Fund

IWA International Workers' Association (anarcho-syndicalist international)

IWMA International Workingmen's Association (First International)

IWPA International Working People's Association

IWW Industrial Workers of the World

PGA People's Global Action

SI Situationist International

SolFed Solidarity Federation

WMD Weapon of Mass Destruction

WTO World Trade Organization

XR Extinction Rebellion

Introduction

Everywhere and nowhere: The problem of anarchist historiography

Anarchism is not a Utopia, but a faith based on the scientific observation of social phenomena.

– CHARLOTTE WILSON, in Fabian Society, *What Socialism Is* (1886)[1]

A tale of two 'moments': Anarchism in the past and the present

In 1884, a series of articles by 'An English Anarchist' appeared in *Justice*, the newspaper of the Social Democratic Federation (SDF), a British socialist organization.[2] Appropriately entitled 'Anarchism', the series sought to explain anarchism, 'a word . . . open to such grievous misconstruction from English readers' to a British audience.[3] The author's real name was Charlotte Wilson.[4] Wilson was, in the words of her posthumous editor Nicolas Walter, 'the best known of the small group of middle-class intellectuals who played an important part in the emergence of the British anarchist movement in the 1880s'.[5] A member of the SDF herself, in addition to the Fabian Society, she was unequivocally a socialist but of the anarchist kind.[6] As Wilson put it:

Anarchism . . . means simply 'without a ruler'. Anarchist, therefore, is the name assumed by a certain school of socialists, who . . . believe that 'the time has come to teach the people to do without government', as well as teaching them the advantages of common property. They believe that, in the present stage of progress, social union can only be stable when it is based on absolute economic equality, and perfect individual freedom.[7]

Few scholars working in anarchist studies today – as opposed to the public at large – would quibble with Wilson's definition of anarchism. For Ruth Kinna, writing recently, anarchism is not chaos or disorder but the 'government of no-one'.[8] For Colin Ward, writing in the 1970s, anarchism was a 'theory of spontaneous order', the theory and practice of a society which self-organized in the absence of authority.[9] Yet it is equally true that today, just as in the late nineteenth century, anarchism is still – as all anarchists and scholars of anarchism know – a term 'open . . . to such grievous misconstruction', as Wilson claimed. Then anarchism was popularly associated with violence; today the same connection subsists in popular and political culture, and when politicians today seek to demonize protest movements, a term often reached for to conjure fear in the minds of electorates is that of 'anarchy'.[10] Whilst anarchists decry this, their voices largely go unheard. During the anti-austerity movement that mobilized in Britain after the financial crisis of 2008, the Metropolitan Police informed businesses in London that 'any information relating to anarchists should be reported to your local police'.[11] Though the call was rescinded, in 2019 – following the Extinction Rebellion (XR) protests in central London against government inaction on climate change – a former head of the Metropolitan Police Counter-Terrorism Command called for extended surveillance of 'far-left, anarchist, and environmental extremism'.[12] Tellingly, XR distanced themselves from anarchism as quickly as possible, with one XR member writing in the *Guardian* newspaper that 'to [his] mind, anarchists are destructive in their aims, and are not afraid to use violence'.[13] Anarchism's 'image problem', as it is often described, has stuck.[14]

And yet, in this vignette of two 'moments' – the late nineteenth century and the present – with which I open this book, I wish to argue that anarchism as a *practice* was and remains not merely a reality in both time periods but is also increasingly recognized as such. This framing is borrowed from Andrej Grubacic, in whose essay 'The Anarchist Moment' explicit parallels are drawn between the late nineteenth century and the present, which he regards potentially as a 'second anarchist moment'.[15] Whilst anarchism is often recognized as an influence on the anti (or alter) globalization movement in the 1990s and then again in the Occupy movement (not least due to the work of David Graeber in and on both), I concur with Colin Ward that as a form of anti-authoritarian 'self-help socialism' anarchism is far more prevalent than merely this.[16] This is the anarchist socialism described by the Russian theorist Peter Kropotkin, the chief advocate of anarchist communism: the practice of self-organization without hierarchy which characterizes human social relationships absent the authoritarianism of the state.

Ward's theory of spontaneous order – his 'self-help socialism' – found its echo in the recent coronavirus pandemic, when mutual aid groups sprang up to meet the needs of communities without the state.[17] In the Occupy movement which developed following the 2008 financial crisis, participants embraced non-hierarchical principles in their activism, with popular assemblies reliant on direct democracy.[18] For Graeber and a number of other scholars, Occupy – and anarchism – was part of a broader 'democracy project' that had found its 'moment' in the opening decades of the twenty-first century.[19] The arrival of prominent media spokespeople for anarchism, such as Graeber, Kinna and most recently Carne Ross (not to mention the enduring influence of Noam Chomsky), has ensured that – for all the demonization – anarchism is, at least some of the time, in some quarters, being taken increasingly seriously. When reflecting on the Metropolitan Police's renewed interest in anarchism after 2010, it's worth considering the words of one London-based anarchist in the mid-1960s: 'it would be a sign of revival if we were being watched by the police today.'[20]

Even in popular culture, depictions of anarchism – which since the time of Joseph Conrad's The Secret Agent have cast the anarchist as terrorist – have become increasingly contested.[21] The ubiquity of the Guy Fawkes mask popularized by the film adaptation of the anarchist Alan Moore's graphic novel V for Vendetta on street protests worldwide has offered up a vision of the anarchist as rebel, yes, but one whose rebellion is aimed at a repressive state apparatus in an age of high-tech surveillance. In the contemporary moment, the synthesis of technology and oppression as a trope in popular culture has become ever more prevalent, exemplified in the USA Network series *Mr. Robot*, which follows the story of a 'hacktivist' who joins what purports to be a digital anarchist group, 'FSociety', clearly based on the rise of the hacktivist collective Anonymous.[22] The series is distributed internationally by Amazon; it is an irony, however, that Amazon is commodifying the wider critique of its own business model and practices in a way Karl Marx would have found telling.[23] Nonetheless, the shifting perceptions and articulations of anarchism in popular culture represent resonances – meanings shared and understood by broader publics – even if they do not explain them.

This is true too of academia and university settings more broadly, which are the assumed primary audiences for this book. 'The anarchist turn', to cite one (controversial) title on the rise of anarchism as a mode and object of analysis within the humanities and social sciences, is real.[24] Anarchist studies, a multidisciplinary field uniting scholars across the globe, is growing – with a number of academic journals dedicated to it and an ever-increasing range of scholarly publications on different aspects of anarchism as a set of ideas, a set of practices and a set of social movements, and new 'postanarchist' epistemologies stirring much scholarly debate.[25]

One discipline where anarchism is increasingly making a significant impact within scholarly work is history. At a methodological level, James C. Scott has emerged as a major figure advocating for – and demonstrating – an 'anarchist squint' in his historical analyses,[26] and historians such as Arif Dirlik, Ilham Khuri-Makdisi, Dongyoun Hwang, Constance Bantman, Carissa Honeywell, Matthew S. Adams, Maia Ramnath, Ole Birk Laursen and Kinna (to name but a few) have offered recent historical studies of anarchism in China, the Eastern Mediterranean, Korea, France, Britain, India and elsewhere, broadening the perspectives of Anglophone narratives of anarchism's development which have too often obscured as much as they have revealed.[27] Anarchism – simultaneously understood as a school of ideologies, a series of practices and a(n) (anti)political movement – may have been defined in Europe in the mid-late nineteenth centuries, but its development was a global phenomenon. And it was in the global space that anarchism – across all these categories –

was made, remade, formulated and reformulated. Whilst historians such as Dirlik and Maia Ramnath have sought to get anarchist studies to grapple with anarchism's Eurocentricity, others such as Grubacic, Sho Konishi and Benedict Anderson have asserted the global nature of anarchism as an anti-authoritarian set of practices, distinct from, though at times relating to, and in dialogue with what began as a European movement.[28] Konishi and Grubacic have paid particular attention to the question of modernity, arguing separately that the post-Enlightenment modernity of the nineteenth century which acted as a hegemonic cultural and political imaginary in Europe and much of the Americas was distinct from at times anarchic modernities or political imaginaries which prevailed elsewhere. From Grubacic's perspective, drawing on 'one of the vital differences between the anarchist and Marxist traditions was that the former was a project of the South, while the latter was a project of European Modernity'.[29] For Konishi, the attempt following the Mejji Restoration to impose 'Western' ideas of modernity and modernization met resistance through

> the rise of a distinct temporality that developed throughout the second half of the nineteenth and the early twentieth century in Japan, which was structured by the terms of anarchist progress and civilization. This temporality, based on a concept of progress toward an imagined future, coexisted with and simultaneously countered the temporality of Western modernity.[30]

Given the historical discipline's own 'modernist' legacy – rooted as it was traditionally in the search for objective 'truth' and 'facts', though few historians would articulate such views unproblematically today – such challenges to understandings of modernity challenge the premises of the historical discipline itself.[31] Such challenges at times correspond and overlap with challenges posed by shifts in epistemological thinking such as poststructuralism or the linguistic turn, but they also have their own distinct emphases. They in part both explain anarchism's marginalization in historical debate and offer new ways of writing history. For Scott, an 'anarchist squint' means looking for silences, absences and resistance beyond the formal structures with which history as a discipline has often been concerned.[32] It also offers a nuanced way of approaching anarchism's mortal enemy – the state – within historical analysis. As such, there is good cause to agree with Adams that anarchist historiography has moved on a good deal in terms of scope and methodology since David Goodway lamented the lack of such an historiography in 1989.[33]

But the emergence of this new anarchist historiography has, as yet, been unmatched by an introduction to anarchism's place in specifically *historical* debate, which the present volume seeks to offer. This book is on one level an introductory history of anarchism, in that it is not unique. But it is also an attempt to draw out the new debates on anarchism which have been opened up by the new scholarly literatures, and to differentiate between the hagiography and demonization which often characterize partisan political accounts, instead offering the student a broader assessment of anarchism's significance in different spaces and places in the historical period since the mid-nineteenth century. The central problems of anarchist historiography as it stands presently lie in the fact – as many historians have acknowledged – that it is a historiography which until recently was rooted in mythology and partisanship. For historians in the 'liberal' tradition, as defined by Noam Chomsky, anarchism was simply invisible in the historical record.[34] Anarchist 'realities' were inconceivable, too antithetical to their political sensibilities and the norms of a discipline which had grown from the study of nation-states and leaders. This discipline could not countenance analysis of a movement which not merely rejected the state but promoted a vision of a non-hierarchical, spontaneously organizing society wholly distinct from the liberal state model. In a recent intervention arguing for an anarchist approach to history, the medievalist Ian Forrest has noted that 'a tacit belief in the rightness and naturalness of states is an almost indelible element in much history writing'.[35] Criticizing 'constitutional history', Forrest states:

> It is a manner of writing about the state that is highly teleological and blinkered: state growth is treated as a 'good' not warranting critical examination because in most liberal historiography and social science writing modern states are considered as – on balance – good, or better than the alternatives, whatever wrongs they may do . . . Teleologies of the state are rarely investigations

into the capacity for surveillance, normalisation or genocide . . . We often allow our attention to be caught by the deeds *and records* of the powerful to the exclusion of other perspectives.[36]

Forrest argues powerfully for an 'anarchist history', that is an anarchist approach to historical investigation, which ranges beyond simply a history of anarchism (as offered in this volume). In his words:

It is notable that there is today very little anarchist history as opposed to histories of anarchism. As a result of its marginalisation from academic history writing, anarchism has not been developed as a mode of historical enquiry in the way that feminist history involves much more than the history of feminism, or that Marxist history encompasses more than just the history of Marxism.[37]

But Forrest's intervention is only an important beginning. His reference to Marxism is a poignant one; Marxism's influence on historical writing has been profound for the fate of the history of anarchism as a topic. For historians in the Marxist tradition, which dominated much of social history in the post-1945 period in Europe and the United States, anarchism was a subject to be demonized and even ridiculed. This perspective was for its part rooted in the 'socialist schism' between Marx and Bakunin which took place in the 1860s, which as Robert Graham shows gave rise to the anarchist *movement* as opposed to anarchist *ideas* (which had a longer history).[38] The mythologized histories of Marxism and anarchism, with their 'sites of memory' from the expulsion of Bakunin and Guillaume from the First International, to the Red Army's crushing of the Kronstadt Commune, to Stalin's attacks on anarchists in Spain during the Spanish Civil War, were read differently by both sides. For Marxists, anarchism was – in Eric Hobsbawm's words – a political movement suited to 'backward peasants' – a statement echoing Marx's contempt for the peasantry and the overarching Hobsbawm thesis that anarchism was a movement of 'primitive rebels', anti-modern, unscientific, utopian – whatever anarchism might claim for itself.[39]

But whilst some historians may have demonized anarchism and others written it out of history, anarchist partisans have played their part in the mythologization of anarchism too. The search for 'proto-anarchisms' – forerunners of the 'canonical' anarchism of the nineteenth and early twentieth centuries – by anarchists, and the developments of grand narratives of anarchism's immanence, taken together with the marginalization of anarchism by liberal historians and Marxists, has made the job of the historian of anarchism more difficult than it might have been. The problem of anarchist historiography is that anarchism is either everywhere – an immanent, naturally occurring reality that is universal and eternal, as argued for by its partisans, or nowhere – an inconceivable entity erased from the pages of scholarly literature.

The task then of the historian of anarchism is (apart from the straightforward tasks of identifying anarchism as ideas, actions and social movements) to demythologize anarchism and relate it to broader historical debates. This has profound implications not just for the study of anarchism for itself but also for the study of history more generally. To return to Wilson, her story is a case in point of how anarchism has been treated by history, but also the 'possibilities' an historical approach offers for anarchist studies and the opportunities an anarchist approach offers for history.[40] Wilson was, until fairly recently, characterized as a 'forgotten anarchist'.[41] Yet in her own time she had been a person of real significance: a pivotal figure in the anarchist wing of the British socialist movement, founder of the *Freedom* newspaper, a friend and colleague of Peter Kropotkin, a friend and ultimately a critic of the Liberal Prime Minister H. H. Asquith, a campaigner for women's suffrage, a founder of the Fabian Women's Group, a believer – along with her friend William Morris – in anti-parliamentary socialism.[42] As Hinely notes, she withdrew from public advocacy for anarchism in 1895, though she did not 'renounce' it.[43] Wilson's writings of the 1880s illustrate a moment in history when – so anarchists at the time believed – revolution was in the air and a world of possibility lay before them. As Kropotkin put it at the time, the poor 'feel the necessity of a social revolution; and both rich and poor recognize that this revolution is imminent, that it may break out in a few years'.[44] This was the spirit of Grubacic's 'first anarchist moment', a time when anarchists and anarchism played a key role in the development of socialist practice and organization.[45] The Britain Wilson and Kropotkin were writing in was not yet a representative democracy, with millions still beyond the franchise and where women could not vote at all. Yet it was also, as E. H. H. Green put it, 'an age of transition', where from the 1860s onwards elites began to believe in the inevitability of *some* form of democracy.[46]

In 1867 the Second Reform Act had brought some working-class men within the franchise; in 1870 W. E. Forster's Education Bill passed Parliament, introducing state-sponsored elementary education for all children for the first time. Addressing the House of Commons, Forster made part of the rationale for the Bill clear, stating that 'now that we have given them political power we must not wait any longer to give them education'.[47] As Geoff Eley notes, the process of democratization in Europe before 1914 was uneven and incomplete, but most of all it was a 'conflict':

> In Europe, democracy did not result from natural evolution or economic prosperity. It certainly did not emerge as an inevitable byproduct of individualism or the market. It developed because people organised collectively to demand it.[48]

In Wilson's time, political imaginaries were in flux. Anarchism – and anarchist propagandizing – had not yet attained the mythologies of defeat, doctrinal purity and futility which would – at times – characterize the movement in the twentieth century. Wilson's interventions – like those of Kropotkin in her own time and Bakunin and Proudhon before her – were made in the sincere belief that an anarchist society was a meaningful possibility in the short term. She wrote, spoke and advocated for a self-organizing society without government organized on a principle of equality during an era Bantman has called 'the first globalization' and living in a city – London – at the centre of it.[49] For anarchists like Wilson, the revolution was not merely imminent; in some places it had already arrived. The centrality of the memory of the Paris Commune of 1871 to anarchist and socialist mythology is well documented in scholarly literature.[50] For two months in the spring of 1871 the citizens of Paris seized control of their city from the Republican government following the conclusion of the Franco-Prussian War and sought to implement a socialist society. For Marx, this was his theory of communism vindicated, in the Commune's failures as well as its successes; for his anarchist opponent Mikhail

Bakunin, it was his vision of an anarchist – stateless – socialism which the experience of the Commune had borne out.[51]

But for Wilson, the legacy of the Commune and other revolutionary upheavals in the 1870s and 1880s lay as much in the people she met as a consequence of it as the ideas and practices these events were taken to represent. Louise Michel, the legendary French anarchist, was exiled to New Caledonia in the wake of the repression of the Commune by the French government. Already a Communard, a socialist and a revolutionary, it was during her voyage into exile in New Caledonia that Michel became an anarchist.[52] Amnestied in 1880, she was jailed again in France for revolutionary activity and ultimately arrived in London in 1890, when she became friends with Wilson and worked with her in the foundation of an anarchist school.[53] Wilson had earlier persuaded Kropotkin – also in exile – to join her in the founding of her anarchist newspaper, *Freedom*.[54]

Wilson described herself explicitly as an 'anarchist communist' (*Freedom* billed itself a 'journal of anarchist communism') and echoed much of Kropotkin's thought in her writings. She also explicitly referenced Bakunin and in her 1884 articles cited him on education, noting the 'fine passages' in *God and the State* where 'Michael Bakounine outlines the Anarchist theory of education . . . Anarchism considers that the one end and aim of education is to fit children for freedom'.[55] Organizing within the SDF and the Socialist League in addition to the Fabian Society, Wilson defies the usual sectarian categories of social and political history. Hinely states that her 'story also reminds us of what we stand to lose when we impose coherence and typological precision on a historical moment that was neither coherent nor clearly defined for those who experienced it.'[56] The socialist melting pot in late Victorian London was diverse, in terms of ideas, organizations and personalities. And, as Hinely has powerfully argued, in the codification of history according to the political categories of the Left, stories such as Wilson's were lost.

Wilson represents the treatment of anarchism by history, and history by anarchism, on other levels too. Anarchism's own memory as a movement has, as with wider society, been characterized by the persistence of patriarchal attitudes. The pivotal role that women anarchists have played throughout the life of the movement has been obscured by a gendering process which Ruth Kinna describes as 'manarchism'.[57] Even when women anarchists have been recognized, and even celebrated, by the movement and by scholars of anarchism, they have often been relegated to subordinate roles. Possibly the most famous anarchist to a wider audience, Emma Goldman is frequently described as an activist rather than a theorist by scholars, despite her considerable work on a wide range of topics in anarchism, including sex and feminism.[58] Even in attempting to redress the balance in historical accounts, Goldman herself has – as Judy Greenway has argued – become a 'short circuit' for scholars engaged in an 'additive approach', simply seeking to 'add women in' to the pre-existing narrative, rather than offer an authentically inclusive history of anarchism.[59]

Anarchists such as Wilson have also suffered from the prevailing 'anti-anarchist' disposition of the historical discipline itself, which incorporated a patriarchal dynamic but also broader factors leading to the marginalization of anarchism as a whole. Much historical work on anarchism echoed, as Adams has noted, Carlyle's 'Great Men' approach, resulting in a methodologically impoverished approach to historicization.[60] Adams also notes the dominance of political theorists rather than historians in much of this endeavour, constituting in turn an 'anarchist canon' of authoritative figures,[61] albeit one that has (as Kinna notes) evolved over time.[62] For its own part, history in much of the Anglophone world owes its development as a discipline to the rise of the modern nation-state; in 1724 the British Crown endowed Regius chairs in modern history in the ancient universities of England and Scotland (which to this day are still appointed by the state). A contemporary of Wilson's, the Cambridge historian J. R. Seeley (himself Regius Professor) saw the task of the historian as lying in legitimizing the state and state policy. His 1883 book *The Expansion of England*, based on lectures delivered at Cambridge, sought to provide a historical underpinning of the British Empire's claims to global power.[63] History as a discipline, for much of the nineteenth century and into the twentieth, saw its traditional objects of study as states and their leaders, and the key methodological approach deriving from the Rankean tradition, 'the cult of the archive', entrenched a framing of history as 'state history'.

The rise of social history in the course of the twentieth century in the Anglophone world undermined this premise, but whilst Marxism was both a subject of such inquiry and theoretically influential in the field as we have seen, anarchism was, for the most part, ignored. As Chomsky noted in the late 1960s, even when anarchism was emphatically present in the historical record as a mass practice – as in the anarchist revolution in Spain in 1936–7 – it was obscured from the historical record.[64]

History, as history students are well aware, is very much the creature of the time in which it is created. It is not 'the past'. It is a series of narratives and interpretations about the past constructed in the present. So the rise of anarchist studies, and the development of a new anarchist historiography, tells us something about the contemporary moment in which we live as much as it does the time of Charlotte Wilson, the past – which as historians is our subject. The 'anarchist turn' of the twenty-first century may be, at least on some level, more sympathetic to anarchism – and it is possible that in an age of political instability 'visions of a stateless society' (as K. Steven Vincent dubbed them in a nineteenth-century context) are becoming more plausible.[65] It may be that we are once again in a space – as Grubacic and others argue – where political imaginaries are becoming fractured and where anarchism presents new possibilities. But the task of the historian is to historicize and critique; and in this new 'moment' a key task is to distinguish between mythologies and plausible interpretations – a task which had been rendered difficult in terms of anarchism by anarchists as well as their enemies.

'Seeing anarchy' in history and the present

Most studies of anarchism, historical or otherwise, begin with the question of definition. Anarchism can be defined as a school of social and political theories which advocate for society without government, which advance the view that a society without the state – a self-organizing society – is both desirable and possible. It can be defined as a movement (or family of movements) which has its origins in developments in mid-nineteenth-century Europe and the 'socialist schisms' which followed.[66] It has also been seen as a 'sensibility', present throughout history, so Peter Marshall argues, 'wherever people demanded to govern themselves, in the face of power-seeking minorities'.[67]

As these definitions imply, it is a term which poses unique problems for the historian and even for the would-be revolutionary. The crude definitions given earlier are accurate up to a point, within their own frames of reference, but are they useful? Do we know anarchism when we see it, in either the past or the present? Within the historiography of anarchism as it has evolved, possibly the sharpest debate on anarchism is simply whether it is present in a given place and time. Marshall, the author of a widely available and comprehensive history of anarchism, offers a vision of a 'river of anarchy', flowing through the ages and uniting a diverse range of anti-authoritarian ideologies and movements into a 'pre-history' of the modern anarchist movement itself.[68] Patricia Crone has argued for the existence of Muslim anarchists in the Arabian Peninsula in the ninth century, using a narrow definition of anarchism – in her case, simply the rejection of the state – to validate her viewpoint.[69]

The problem of definition is one which has bedevilled historians of anarchism, as George Woodcock, the author of the pioneering *Anarchism: A History of Libertarian Ideas and Movements* (1962), reflected.[70] But as intimated earlier, it has also posed problems for anarchists themselves. At the time of writing, in the midst of the Syrian Civil War, the autonomous region of Rojava at the very least lays claim to an anarchist lineage (and a measure of anarchist participation) but is the subject of immense controversy for anarchists around the world. Whilst the Kurdish and international groups which administer Rojava claim to apply the teachings of Abdullah Ocalan, themselves derived from the anarchist Murray Bookchin's libertarian municipalism, anarchists beyond Syria are divided on the question of whether Rojava is any respect an anarchist – or anarchistic – society. Whilst prominent figures such as Carne Ross and David Graeber have embraced the cause of the autonomous region, other individuals and groups have seen Rojava instead as a state in all but name with only a vestigial commitment to anarchist values.[71]

Meanwhile the protests which rocked the United States and Europe after the 2008 financial crisis have again been claimed by some as anarchist endeavours, with the Occupy movement as we have seen again cited by Graeber as evidence of anarchy in action –

spontaneously organized direct action lacking a central leadership.[72] This echoed earlier anarchist 'revivals'. In 2002 Graeber had famously claimed that the anti-globalization movement of the 1990s heralded the arrival of 'the new anarchists',[73] whilst in the 1960s – in the midst of the student revolt – Colin Ward had detected 'a certain anarchy in the air'.[74] In 1968 Ward could at least claim that anarchists were at the heart of events, even if they didn't dominate them, the May '68 events in France being in part triggered by the activities of anarchists at Nanterre.[75] But in general the picture has been less clear. Spotting anarchism 'in real time' has been tricky, not least because anarchism itself as defined by Bakunin – the 'founder'[76] of the movement as Woodcock notes – is spontaneous, leaderless and needs no overt statement. It is, anarchists hold, a practice first, an ideology second. At other times, the task of the contemporary observer and the historian alike has been easier; during the Spanish Civil War there was, as mentioned earlier, a self-avowed anarchist revolution in 1936–7 in Catalonia and parts of Aragon.[77] A little under twenty years earlier, at the height of the Russian Civil War, there had been another explicitly anarchist uprising in the Ukraine which established the Free Territory before it was ultimately crushed by the Bolsheviks.[78] Unsurprisingly, such large scale, explicit anarchist mobilizations have become the foundational case studies of anarchist historiography, and this is true too of this volume.

But other instances of spontaneous revolt have been less clear-cut, as we have already seen. The 1871 Paris Commune continues to be much debated. The 'socialist schisms' continue, and latterly the term 'anarchism' has been appropriated by right-wing libertarians who seek to espouse their creed of untrammelled property rights as a school of thought known as 'anarcho-capitalism' (heavily critiqued by anarchists such as Iain McKay as 'proprietarianism' – a valorization and reification of property rights rationalized as an anarchism).[79] Few anarchists would agree with such an appropriation, with anarchism commonly accepted to be a form of libertarian socialism and defined in opposition not merely to the state but also to hierarchy, a definition which at face value refutes any 'anarcho-capitalist' attempt to be included in 'the anarchist canon'.[80]

In an attempt to grapple with the problem of spotting 'actually existing anarchism' in the contemporary world, anarchists such as

Graeber and Maia Ramnath have subscribed to a typology of 'capital' or 'big' 'A' and small 'A' anarchism.[81] Here 'capital A' represents movements and ideologies which identify explicitly as Anarchist, with small 'a' representing anarchistic and anti-authoritarian practices present more widely within society which are not necessarily conscious of themselves as anarchisms. As Graeber puts it, the anarchism of the twenty-first century is

> not opposed to organization. It is about creating new forms of organization. It is not lacking in ideology. Those new forms of organization *are* its ideology. . . .. Their ideology, then, is immanent in the anti-authoritarian principles that underlie their practice, and one of their more explicit principles is that things should stay this way.[82]

For Ramnath,

> The big *A* covers a specific part of the Western Left tradition dating from key ideological debates in the mid-nineteenth century and factional rivalries in the International Working Men's Association. It peaked worldwide in the early twentieth century among radical networks that consciously embraced the label while nevertheless encompassing multiple interpretations and emphases within it. Genealogically related to both democratic republicanism and utopian socialism, the big *A* opposed not only capitalism but also the centralized state along with all other systems of concentrated power and hierarchy.[83]

The small *a* meanwhile 'implies a set of assumptions and principles, a recurrent tendency or orientation – with the stress on movement in a direction – toward more dispersed and less concentrated power'.[84]

In these typologies, Graeber and Ramnath's thinking descends from that of the principal nineteenth-century theorist of anarchism, Kropotkin, whose arguments on the 'natural' status of the practice of 'mutual aid' as 'a factor of evolution' laid the groundwork for analyses of anarchism as a practice divorced from an explicit political movement.[85] In Kropotkin's famous *Encyclopaedia Britannica* article on anarchism, he too had argued for anarchism as a 'tendency' which had 'always existed in mankind, in opposition to the governing hierarchic conception and tendency' with 'now the one and now the other taking the upper hand at different periods of history'.[86] This allowed Kropotkin to argue that it 'found its expression in the writings . . . of Laozi' with the 'best exponent of anarchist philosophy in ancient Greece [being] Zeno'.[87] Anarchism was thus scientific, natural and present throughout history.

Yet as Kinna has decisively shown, Kropotkin intended his theory to support and revive the anarchist movement in a period when that movement was in the doldrums (at least in Kropotkin's view); so the 'small a' anarchisms contemporary scholars and anarchist speak of are still framed through lenses developed by, and for, the 'Big A' movement.[88] Though Graeber has written a series of histories (often over the very long term in terms of periodization, in similar style to James C. Scott) outlining anarchistic tendencies in the historical record, it is telling that neither Graeber nor Scott are historians, instead both sharing backgrounds as anthropologists. Big *A* and small *a* isn't a workable typology for historians trying to discern actually existing anarchism in the period before the nineteenth century, whatever usefulness it may have after the emergence of an avowed anarchist movement and school of political theory. The danger is it becomes appropriative, claiming for the 'capital A' movement practices and schools of thought that should never have been identified with anarchism. Equally, ignoring the period before Pierre-Joseph Proudhon famously called himself an anarchist in 1840 misses the fact that 'anarchism did not spring ready made from [his] head' like Minerva from the head of Jupiter and again commits to the classic fallacy that ideas formulated by theorists are the origin of all social and political practice.[89] The mid-nineteenth-century movement had its origins in a diverse range of anti-authoritarian political traditions and vocabularies, and it is the task of the historian to delineate these without teleology – to show what anarchism drew on, rather than to claim these traditions as small *a* anarchist in themselves. This attention allows historians of anarchism to pay better attention to the classic historical conundrums of continuity and change, to trace the evolution of anti-authoritarian practices and languages through the historic anarchist movement and beyond.

Given the difficulties facing scholars attempting to identify anarchism in the present, the challenges facing scholars working on the past then are, in certain respects, still more profound. Yet so too are the possibilities, as Adams notes.[90] Graeber, Ramnath and Scott's work in particular has done much to illustrate the epistemological weakness of traditional historical approaches. This book, as an historical study, adopts 'an anarchist squint' to look for anarchism in the period following the development and emergence of a self-conscious anarchist movement, a movement which sought the destruction of the state and the eradication of hierarchical institutions and social relationships. Its influence outweighed – and continues to outweigh – its numbers of declared adherents.

One key question for the historian of anarchism is 'where did the anarchism go?' in the period after the defeat of the anarchist organizations in Spain in 1939, which Woodcock once believed had meant the death of the movement 'founded by Bakunin'.[91] 'The new anarchists' of the 1990s on heralded by Graeber were clearly in one sense not the children of the same revolution as that movement, operating as they did largely outside its traditional organizations. But in another, they represented a characteristic of anarchism in the post-1840 period that political theorists and historians have missed (which was evident in Wilson's time in the 1880s and 1890s), namely the incorporation of its practices in the pluralistic nature of many forms of socialism. As Dany Cohn-Bendit, a prominent spokesperson for the May 1968 student protestors in France, put it, he was a 'Marxist in the way Bakunin was'.[92] Cohn-Bendit was unusually self-aware in this respect, and unsurprisingly so as a member of the *Federation Anarchiste*, but the practices Graeber ascribes to his contemporary small *a* anarchisms of Occupy and the alter-globalization movement do owe much of their lineage to debates which originally took place in the First International of socialists in the 1860s, which both yielded anarchism and influenced a broader libertarian socialist tradition.[93] The latter tradition has at times both wittingly and unwittingly obscured its links to anarchism, often preferring instead to identify with libertarian forms of Marxism, but all share common roots. For the minority on the left – actual, self-declared anarchists – their activities adjusted in the course of the post-war period and in the wake of the failed revolutions of the interwar era to 'anarchize' society through other means. In Britain, Ward's 'sociological anarchism' as Stuart White has termed it[94] sought to – in Ward's words – 'let' anarchism 'in again by the back window. Not as an aim to be realised, but as a yardstick, a measurement or means of assessing reality'.[95] Society could, for Ward, be more or less anarchist at any given moment. Ward – who identified as 'an anarchist-communist in the Kropotkin tradition' – sought to intervene to 'anarchize' spaces in wider society through his efforts as a propagandist, through his talks on schools and his career as a teacher in further education and through his more substantive contributions to housing and town planning.[96] Though Ward is a celebrated example, numerous other anarchists (not least in an American context the ecologist of freedom, Murray Bookchin) sought to intervene in contemporary society in different ways, creating space for anarchist practices.[97] More recently, Kinna has argued for the 'anarchization' of society, including social relationships, as a meaningful way of assessing anarchism's successes, rather than the destruction of the state.[98]

With this in mind, the resurgence of a self-conscious anarchist movement internationally from the 1980s onwards then does not appear such a radical discontinuity, even if the 'last anarchists' of the post-war era were part of a much broader left milieu in which their own numbers were negligible. This book offers a 'way of seeing' anarchism in the post mid-nineteenth-century period that is both inclusive of the different ways anarchism influenced the broader social and political context but specific too in tracing the 'broad anarchist tradition', as Carissa Honeywell has recently done for Britain.[99]

In doing so reflexivity is a marked feature of this work, which attempts to highlight how anarchism and libertarian socialism interacted with wider political cultures and were changed by them. The viewpoints offered here are global, drawing on the rich vein of work on anarchism around the world which has developed over the course of the last thirty years to show how, and when, anarchism has been influential in the history of the nineteenth and twentieth centuries.

Plan of the book

The book is structured in three parts. Part I, 'Anarchism in an Age of Revolutions, 1840–1939', addresses the development of what has come to be known as 'classical anarchism' and the movement associated with it in the period between the publication of Proudhon's *What Is Property?* and the defeat of the anarchists in Spain in 1939. The first chapter, 'Anarchy Is Order', draws its title from a common paraphrase of Proudhon and highlights how 'the beautiful idea' of a society without government was developed through the interaction of practice and theory in the thirty-two years which followed Proudhon's famous claim to be an anarchist. In the first twenty years, Proudhon's own thought evolved and developed many of the bases for subsequent schools of anarchist thought as both George Woodcock and Proudhon's anthologist Iain McKay have noted.[100] In this section, the historiography of Proudhon's intellectual endeavour is synthesized to show how Proudhon – an influence in mainstream French socialism as well as anarchism – drew on older republican vocabularies and the memory of the Revolution to develop his anarchism. In the next, attention turns to the ways in which Proudhonism influenced the International Workingmen's Association (IWMA), better known to posterity as the First International. Attention then shifts to the well-documented role of Mikhail Bakunin in the International and the ways in which his intellectual formation and Proudhonism collided, fostering 'revolutionary socialism' within the International, which later came to call itself 'anarchism'.[101] Though Proudhon was also an activist and a pluralist in approach – indeed, his support for political abstentionism in part stemmed from his doomed tenure as a member of the French National Assembly in the wake of the 1848 revolution – Bakunin embodied the form as well as the content of 'movement' anarchism and developed an anarchist collectivism distinctive from Proudhon's federalism even as it drew on it.

The chapter also discusses anarchism's relationship with Marx and to demythologize the conflict between Marx and Bakunin within the International which has come to serve as an origin myth of anarchism which recasts Bakunin as prophet and – as Marxist critics have claimed – given anarchism an air of martyrology and religious overtones. Whilst accepting that anarchism's self-mythology does feature religious overtones and draw on religious vocabularies, however, it denies the central Marxist criticism that anarchism is a secular religion, a 'millenarian' belief-system of 'primitive rebels', instead noting the common religious inheritances and vocabularies framing nineteenth-century socialisms. The conflict in the International and the beginnings of socialist mythology are also illustrated through discussion of the events of the Paris Commune, an event which some authorities (wrongly) believed to have been the work of the International. The chapter begins and ends with the split in the socialist movement represented by Marx's orchestrated expulsion of Bakunin and James Guillaume at the Hague Congress in 1872.

The second chapter, 'Words versus deeds', outlines anarchism's development in theory and practice in the period from 1872 up to the outbreak of the First World War. Theorists of anarchism in this period were embedded in the realities of practice. Kropotkin, the greatest of all anarchist theorists, was a dedicated 'revolutionist' whose allegiance to 'the people' stemmed from his sympathies with the serfs his father had mistreated during Kropotkin's childhood as a Russian prince.[102] In his activism – which saw Kropotkin, as with Bakunin before him, jailed – Kropotkin travelled across Europe, thus in his own (heavily mythologized) life story becoming a representative figure of those anarchist revolutionaries – such as his friend Errico Malatesta – who crossed borders to foment revolution and propagandize for 'the beautiful idea' as a 'method of freedom'.[103] As such this chapter covers the emergence of different philosophies of action and practice within anarchism as it faced opportunity and challenge in the four decades to the First World War, not least the contest between anarchist propaganda focused on 'the word' – and the plethora of anarchist newspapers and periodicals that sprang up as a response – and 'the deed', which saw some anarchists embrace the *attentat* – the assassination and the bomb. Syndicalism (revolutionary unionism) rose to prominence from the 1890s, was influenced explicitly by anarchism and was itself the forerunner of anarcho-syndicalism – 'the only mass variant of the anarchist movement in history', according to its historian Vadim Damier.[104] As such, syndicalism stands as a meaningful example of how anarchism as both a theory and a practice interacted with a wider socialist milieu in the pre–First World War era, in a period where – as has been argued earlier – the boundaries between socialisms were much more fluid than later sectarian accounts has allowed for. As Prichard and Kinna note, failure to appreciate the blurred boundaries of socialist traditions has led to a whole series of libertarian socialisms to be seen as 'anomalous',[105] whilst Eurocentricity has also marginalized the importance of contributions to the development of anarchism in its formative phase from the wider world, not least Asia. Alongside the intellectual history there is a social history of the transmission of ideas within Europe and around the world, as anarchism was remade on a global stage. Here an attempt is made to go beyond the 'diffusive' approach, which scholars such as Raymond Craib have rightly criticized as emphasizing the priority of the European movement over the influences of the wider milieux in which anarchist ideas were made and remade.[106]

The third chapter, 'European Anarchisms? Russia and Spain', offers case studies of anarchism in action in Russia and Spain, problematizing the idea of 'European anarchisms' and noting the diversity of influences on anarchism in both countries. An attempt is made to outline the growing secondary material on anarchism in both countries whilst also paying heed to underused primary sources. Here a significant attempt is made to think in terms of political culture. A characteristic of much writing on anarchist history even up the 1990s was racial stereotyping and essentialism, the historian of syndicalism F. F. Ridley notably criticizing discussions of ideologies which conceived of them in terms of racial essentialism, before immediately ascribing (without irony) the purchase of syndicalism in France and Spain to 'the Latin temper'.[107] Though Ridley engaged with political culture in terms of the social construction of political institutions, the nature of the polity and wider society and the evolution of political norms, his perspective was fatally undermined by his ethnocentrism. Even Woodcock in his *Anarchism* is quick to ascribe the vitality of particular anarchist schools in particular places to issues of national character, though his detail on political institutions is arguably greater. The fourth chapter, 'Global Anarchisms: India, Japan and Beyond', focusing on global anarchisms, traces the rise of a broader historiography of anarchism which notes its reflexive nature in theory and practice, and which highlights the ways in which anarchisms around the world influenced the development of anarchism in the fullest sense, and – as is discussed earlier – the ways in which differing conceptions of modernity drawn from global settings played key roles in the development of anarchism as a wider social movement. Finally, there are several issues which for reasons of space have been addressed in specific chapters due to the theme rather than chronology. For example the risings in Spain in the later nineteenth century are discussed in the chapter on European anarchisms where Spain is discussed in detail. The specifically feminist activities of 'first wave' anarcha-feminists are discussed with anarcha-feminism in Part II, whilst individualist anarchism in the United States and egoism are discussed in the context of the rise of 'libertarianism' in the post-war period, where the key points of difference between these anarchist schools of thought and the ideas developed by Murray Rothbard and others are highlighted.

Part II, 'The Seeds beneath the Snow: Anarchism in the Age of the Superpowers', highlights the difficulties anarchism faced as a movement in the post-war period when the ideological contest in political terms was often depicted as between Soviet communism and US capitalism. The sole chapter in this section, Chapter 5, is entitled 'The Last Anarchists? Anarchism, Decolonization and Protest in the Cold War World, 1945–89', and addresses the ways in which declared anarchists and their movements navigated this terrain, and in what ways this had implications for their practice *and* their theory. In terms of social and cultural history anarchism remained a meaningful presence, manifesting itself around the world in given spaces – particularly in the politics of protest from the 1960s on. This reflected both a conscious attempt by anarchists to pursue a strategy of 'permeation' and the fact that the socialist debates of the late nineteenth century and the syndicalist moment of the early twentieth century had left behind a discursive past of libertarian socialism (in a broad sense) which was drawn on by emergent movements in the post-war era and even by some social democratic parliamentarians. Specificity is required here, and the chapter seeks to provide this by differentiating sharply between parliamentarians influenced by libertarian socialist ideas and anti-parliamentary social movement activists drawing on the practices and vocabularies of anarchism, but the explicit identification of at least some influential parliamentarians with the libertarian tradition descended (as they saw it) from Bakunin matters in an era when, George Woodcock once believed, anarchism as a movement was finished. The development of new anarchist critiques which were anchored in ecological and feminist perspectives is also outlined, including the work of Bookchin from the 1960s and the growth of an explicit anarcha-feminism from the 1970s. Thus whilst the 'actually existing anarchism' of the Cold War period was arguably much less prominent than in the interwar era – where anarchist armies fought on the battlefields of the Ukraine and Catalonia in defence of meaningful anarchist revolutions – this chapter sketches critically the emerging debates about the significance of this period to the development of ideology and practice. Critically, it does so from a perspective which includes the relationship of anarchism to decolonization; here, this process of decolonization is considered in anarchism's relationship to not merely national liberation struggles but also transnational ones; the intersection of anarchism and Black Power in the United States is documented to highlight the ways in which Black Power – and the ideologies and practices it drew on – changed anarchism.[108] Finally, the fundamental contention of this chapter is that the period saw the broadening of anarchism's public appeal into an opposition to all hierarchies, most clearly articulated by Bookchin but increasingly a theme present in anarchist practice.

Part III, 'Anarchist Turns': Anarchism in the Age of Postmodernity, addresses the second 'anarchist moment' as outlined by Grubacic and others – the recent past since 2000 and the contemporary era. In the concluding chapter this takes the form of an investigation of developments after 2000 in order to situate them historically, as following the 1990s anarchism became the explicit face of the anti- (or 'alter') globalization movement – with a 'turn' to anarchism manifested in street protests and the form of the critique of capital prevalent through the 1990s on sections of the left. This opened anarchism up to criticisms – made powerfully by Bookchin – that it had essentially become a form of neoliberal performativity – a glorified individualism that was not 'social' but 'lifestyle anarchism'.[109] But a different reading allowed the anarchisms of the 1990s – the beliefs and practices of the 'new anarchists', as Graeber described them – to instead represent pluralisms which had been obscured by the centrality of Marxism on the left and which developed organically from the libertarian socialisms which had developed before 1989. The historical account culminates with the aftermath of the 2008 global financial crisis, assessing how new social movements arose and the ways in which their development structured the 'anarchisms' that would follow.

The book concludes with reflections on the very recent past and contemporary moment, making explicit reference to the crisis of liberal democracy which today's world finds itself in. An age of instability is upon us, which whilst having been the norm in those parts of the world subjected to imperialism over past centuries, is now returning to the centre of the empires themselves, in Europe and the United States. Terrorism, climate change, the failure of supposedly democratic institutions to meet popular needs and the concomitant rise of neonationalism and fascism in many societies are characteristics of formal political spaces which are surrendering their legitimacy. As part of a series of reflections on the treatment of anarchism by history, the book concludes with a consideration of its future. As David Priestland has recently contended, the contemporary age of instability calls for solutions.[110] Through the nearly two centuries since its arrival as a declared political ideology and movement, anarchism – at a local and global scale – has sought to provide them. It is not the task of the historian to predict the future or offer facile parallels with the past, but the anarchism of the early twenty-first century is the product of adaptation and evolution. It may yet evolve again to meet the challenges of the future.

Further reading

General histories

There are a significant number of narrative histories of anarchism in English written by anarchist partisans though these tend to the hagiographic. The classic account by George Woodcock, *Anarchism: A History of Libertarian Ideas and Movements* (1962) is now rather dated and contains a significant number of errors, but nonetheless remains an important book though now out of print. The early historian of anarchism Max Nettlau's work is mostly not translated into English, though his *Short History of Anarchism* which covers anarchism up to the 1930s and is based on a considerable amount of first-hand knowledge is available in a Freedom Press edition, recently reissued by PM Press (2019) – but Nettlau's style is idiosyncratic to say the least and reflects his participation in events. The most substantial general history of anarchism is undoubtedly Peter Marshall's *Demanding the Impossible: A History of Anarchism* (1992), which is widely available in print and due to its sheer breadth is an essential book, though the wide definition of anarchism offered by Marshall poses problems for historians.

Introductions

Ruth Kinna's recent *Government of No-One: The Theory and Practice of Anarchism* (2019) is an excellent thematic introduction to anarchism, but her earlier *Anarchism: A Beginner's Guide* (2009, second edition) should also be consulted and has considerable historical detail. By comparison Colin Ward's *Anarchism: A Very Short Introduction* (2004) is lacking in detail and takes a singular perspective.

Other reference works

The recent *Palgrave Handbook of Anarchism* (2019) edited by Carl Levy and Matthew S. Adams is an indispensable resource for the student of anarchism, containing as it does essays on a wide range of historical topics and essays on anarchist theory and praxis by leading scholars working in anarchist studies across a variety of disciplines. The *Bloomsbury Companion to Anarchism* edited by Kinna (2012) contains a range of excellent essays by leading scholars on specific topics in addition to excellent bibliographies. *An Anarchist FAQ*, edited by the AFAQ collective, is available both online at http://ana rchism.pageabode.com/afaq/index.html and in print from AK Press.

Anarchism in an age of revolutions, 1840–1939

PART I

Anarchism
in an age of
revolutions,
1840–1939

1

Anarchy is order

The origins of 'the beautiful idea', c. 1840–72

> *God gave the earth to the human race; why then
> have I received none?*
>
> –PIERRE-JOSEPH PROUDHON, *What Is Property?* (1840)[1]

Introduction: The making of
'classical anarchism'

In September 1872, Mikhail Bakunin and James Guillaume were expelled from the International Workingmen's Association, known to posterity as 'the First International'.[2] Bakunin was Russian, a member of the minor gentry, son of a diplomat and a legendary revolutionary.[3] Guillaume was a Swiss schoolteacher who later became a printer.[4] The expulsion of these two men from an international socialist organization which in its own time was at best highly marginal to the experience of working-class people whether in Europe or beyond was nonetheless to have profound implications for the development of socialism as both ideology and movement. The expulsion, orchestrated by Karl Marx, represented a fundamental ideological division on the nature of socialism. Was socialism to be achieved through political means and the seizure of the state through the ballot box if necessary? Or was it to be achieved through the destruction of the state itself, with socialism instead realized through a 'social' revolution, creating a non-hierarchical, anti-authoritarian socialist society, decentralized and organized through voluntary federation?

Bakunin and Guillaume, firm friends and political allies, found themselves expelled at the behest of Marx as they represented what would become known later as the 'anarchist wing' of the First International, those members and sections who believed in and argued for non-state socialism organized on cooperative and non-hierarchical lines.[5] Upon their expulsion the majority of the International's 'sections' – those local and regional groups which belonged to the International – defected to form an anti-authoritarian International at St. Imier in Switzerland.[6] As the historian of the International Robert Graham has commented, it was in the anti-authoritarian International that the movement and corresponding ideology today referred to as anarchism was formulated and developed.[7] In the words of another historian of the International, this was 'the first socialist schism', which marked the parting of the ways between Marxism and anarchism.[8]

Anarchism was forged as a coherent school of political ideologies and a movement out of the exchanges in the International, but it did not emerge simply as a reaction to Marx, nor did it have its origins exclusively in Europe. Bakunin may have been the founder of the 'anarchist movement' as Woodcock argued, but he was not the founder of anarchism, and like many early protagonists in the development of anarchism, the influences on him were diverse.[9] Eleven years before the Hague Congress expelled him from the International, he had escaped from exile in Siberia by ship, following which (in the words of Sho Konishi) 'he would spend over a month wandering about revolutionary Japan'.[10] Bakunin's famed revolutionary exploits and escapes took him to France, Germany, England, the United States and Japan amongst other places before he developed his ideas within the First International and the anti-authoritarian International which succeeded it.[11] Originally a revolutionary advocating the cause of pan-Slav nationalism against Russian imperialism, it was comparatively late in life that Bakunin – arguably the most iconic of anarchists – became a declared anarchist.[12]

In Paris he met someone who had claimed the title earlier and who, according to legend, was the first to have done so. In 1840, Pierre-Joseph Proudhon, a former printer from the rural town of Besancon in the French Jura, had written baldly in his book *What Is Property?* the claim 'I am an anarchist'.[13] Proudhon denied that his meaning was to be taken 'satirically'; this was no rhetorical flourish.[14] Proudhon was a decidedly post-Enlightenment thinker, with a typically nineteenth-century belief in societal progress and in science. For him, 'the authority of man over man' was 'inversely proportional to the stage of intellectual development which that society has reached'; 'royalty – the government of man by man' he saw as an 'absurd' order.[15] With the advance of science – and the science of society – it was no longer possible for 'enlightened' society to submit to such an order; 'as society seeks justice in equality, so society seeks order in anarchy'.[16]

Bakunin met Proudhon in Paris in 1844.[17] In the words of his biographer E. H. Carr, 'it was Proudhon more than any other man who was responsible for transforming Bakunin's instinctive revolt against authority into a regular anarchistic creed'.[18] Guillaume, for his part, would later translate much of Bakunin's work after his death and secure his written legacy.[19] In turn, Guillaume in 1872 met another Russian exile, the escaped revolutionist prince Peter Kropotkin in Switzerland. It was during his stay with Guillaume and his comrades in Switzerland that Kropotkin – who would become the most important theorist in the anarchist tradition – experienced his own conversion:

> the equalitarian relations which I found in the Jura Mountains, the independence of thought and expression which I saw developing in the workers, and their unlimited devotion to the cause appealed even more strongly to my feelings; and when I came away from the mountains, after a week's stay with the watchmakers, my views upon socialism were settled. I was an anarchist.[20]

The period between the 1840s and the 1870s was fundamental to the development of what historians and political theorists have typically characterized as 'classical anarchism' and the birth of the anarchist movement itself. But as the earlier stories illustrate, this was no simple translation of ideas into practice, and for all the names cited, it was a process in which thousands were involved across national borders, within and without Europe. To paraphrase the title of a recent book, anarchism *was* movement.[21] This chapter will introduce the key ideas of the period and the ways in which these were embedded in the context of the development of anarchist practices and movements, and their relationship to the broader socialist tradition. It will aim to demythologize the key 'canonical' events which have characterized this period in anarchism's history and link the development of anarchism to broader debates in global history.

The emergence of anarchism in Europe, 1840–64

The publication of Proudhon's *What Is Property?* in 1840 has been taken as a traditional point of departure for historians attempting to chronicle the development of anarchism as an ideology and a political force. Apart from its author's avowal *of* anarchism – which distinguished him sharply from earlier 'philosophical' anarchists such as William Godwin – the book as an intervention was of profound significance for the anarchist movement which would subsequently develop, in part due to the book's central focus on property and the iniquities of capitalism. Proudhon's book did not merely represent an explicit anarchism but also ensured that the anarchist movement which would follow, largely though not solely due to the work of Mikhail Bakunin, would be a socialist one.

As such Proudhon's work existed within and was a product of a European socialist milieu in the nineteenth century which had developed as part of the legacies of the Enlightenment, the French Revolution and the rise of industrial capitalism.[22] In G. D. H. Cole's classic *A History of Socialist Thought*, he argues that the early socialists stood for

> collective regulation of men's affairs on a co-operative basis, with the happiness and welfare of all as the end in view, and with the emphasis not on 'politics' but on the production and distribution of wealth and on the strengthening of 'socialising' influences in

the lifelong education of the citizens in cooperative, as against competitive, patterns of behaviour and social attitudes and beliefs.[23]

As Cole noted, socialism had not yet gained the language and vocabulary of class warfare that would characterize it after Marx, but the questions at the heart of Marxism and anarchism were already present.[24] Though industrial capitalism had brought the transformation of societies across Europe, its benefits had been far from equally shared. Urbanization in Britain – which by 1851 was a predominantly urban society – brought with it poverty, disease and shorter lifespans to workers.[25] In British cities of over 100,000 inhabitants, 'life expectancy at birth dropped from thirty-five years in the 1820s to twenty-nine in the 1830s' with 'life expectancy in the slums the lowest since the Black Death'.[26] Thomas Malthus, an English political economist and ordained vicar, laid the blame for any worsening conditions for the population on that population itself; the issue, for Malthus, lay in overpopulation. His *Essay on the Principle of Population* argued that population would always multiply at a faster rate than the food required for its subsistence and would only be checked by disaster or starvation. One modern scholar sees Malthus's intervention as 'an anti-Jacobin defence of property rights embedded in the religious world-view and theological framework of eighteenth-century Anglican Christianity'.[27]

Seen in this light, Malthus's legitimization of property rights was a response to the events of the French Revolution and ideas which circulated in Britain in the decade following; his *Essay* was first published anonymously in 1798, in response to an article by William Godwin.[28] Godwin for his part is a figure occasionally regarded by historians of anarchism as the first anarchist in all but name; for George Woodcock he was 'the man of reason' who 'stands at the head of the tradition'.[29] By Woodcock's own acknowledgement, Godwin's major work, *An Enquiry Concerning Political Justice*, which sketched out the contours of a possible 'libertarian' society, both 'embraced all the essential features of an anarchistic doctrine' and was the response to the 'immediate impulse' of the French Revolution, though Woodcock is quick to note that Godwin's thinking predated it.[30]

Modern socialism had its origins in the 'radical democratic ambience' of the French Revolution which so terrorized defenders of hierarchy across Europe.[31] Kropotkin – always fascinated by the French Revolution and who wrote a history of it – wrote later that

> the French Revolution, apart from its political significance, was an attempt made by the French people, in 1793 and 1794, in three different directions more or less akin to socialism. It was, first, *the equalization of fortunes*, by means of an income tax and succession duties, both heavily progressive, as also by a direct confiscation of the land in order to subdivide it, and by heavy war taxes levied upon the rich only. The second attempt was a sort of *municipal communism*, as regards the consumption of some objects of first necessity, bought by the municipalities, and sold by them at cost price. And the third attempt was to introduce a *wide national system of rationally established prices of all commodities*.[32]

In the debate that raged between Malthus's successors and socialist evangelists in the course of the nineteenth century, familiar battle lines were drawn. Malthusian arguments typically rested on the idea of politics and economics as arts of the possible – and ensuring that the limits of the possible were narrowly drawn and scientifically delineated. Socialist arguments rested on a number of premises from firstly Malthus being flat wrong to (as in Marx's view) the view that starvation and penury were products of the denial of the means of subsistence and the competitive ethic of capitalism over and above anything else.[33]

For Proudhon, ostensibly the first person to call himself an anarchist, Malthus was wrong inasmuch as he represented a rationalization of the defence of property, rather than a sincere argument about the nature of politics and society, and the implications of this were profound. Proudhon would later write that 'the theory of Malthus is the theory of political murder; of murder from motives of philanthropy and for love of God'.[34] Proudhon's critique of Malthus was acute; Malthus provided what modern political scientists describe as a 'logic of inevitability' – he narrowed the political imagination. In Proudhon's words, this meant that Malthus's followers, the classical political economists, 'establish[ed] as a providential dogma the theory of Malthus'.[35] Proudhon's opposition to Malthus lay at least in part in lived experience. He claimed to be, as Marx later conceded, of humble origins: 'he himself is a proletarian, an *ouvrier*'.[36] But there is division on this amongst historians; his biographer Woodcock argues that the family as a whole 'were peasants gradually becoming absorbed into the urban middle class', with Proudhon belonging to the 'left' branch, less socially mobile, which 'remained for the most part peasants, artisans, and small traders, with a tendency to rebellion'.[37] On this (if little else) Graham sides with Marx, arguing instead that Proudhon 'came from the working class'.[38] What is unequivocal is that Proudhon knew poverty, partly due to his father's profligacy.

A cousin and Proudhon's maternal grandfather had been significant figures locally in the Revolution.[39] His mother Catherine fought hard for her son to gain an education, though the experience of poverty in the local college scarred him, and he was compelled to break off his education to support the family financially through employment.[40] In 1827, he became 'consciously a republican' and two years later made the acquaintance of the socialist theorist Charles Fourier who had a book printed with the firm Proudhon worked for.[41] In the course of the 1830s Proudhon tried his hand at journalism, travelled to Paris and Switzerland, and ultimately received a scholarship from the Academy at Besancon, ensuring his commitment to a life of philosophy.[42] His most famous work, *What Is Property?*, appeared in 1840.

Proudhon sought through an examination of property to call into question its own viability as a concept and to highlight its oppressive character – and the oppressive character of the authorities, chiefly government, which sought to secure the rights of property. At the outset, he situated his 'inquiry into the principle of right and government' in the lineage of the Revolution. This was facilitated by his engagement with 'a tradition of republican ideas that insisted on the interaction of political institutions and social morality'.[43] When Proudhon uttered his famous statement 'Property is theft!', he claimed it as 'the war-cry of '93'.[44] For Proudhon, the state – government – existed to guarantee property and the domination of property by a minority. Focusing on the idea of justice in the republican tradition – a central concern for socialists – Proudhon argued that his critique of property represented an attempt to address the 'last obstacle' in the development of the idea of justice: a recognition that the demands previously uttered – for political liberty – were meaningless and doomed to failure in the absence of a substantive attack on property.[45]

He argued that property itself was a contradiction in terms, defences advocated for it which were based on liberty or natural right taken to their logical conclusion 'always and of necessity [lead] to equality; that is the negation of property'.[46] This was because, in practice, property frustrated liberty – for most people 'it exists only potentially'.[47] Liberty by contrast

> is an absolute right, because it is to man what impenetrability is to matter – a sine qua non of existence; equality is an absolute right, because without equality there is no society; security is an absolute right, because in the eyes of every man his own liberty and life are as precious as another's.[48]

Proudhon anticipated and denied the later libertarian and anarcho-capitalist argument of 'original appropriation'. Rights have to be reciprocal in order to be just and valid, but by the definition commonly understood, property was exclusive. Proudhon was quick to nuance this between domination and possession. It was right and proper for people to possess the means for survival, but the reciprocal (and logical) perspective was that it was fundamentally immoral to deny them these rights. That in practice meant that *possession* of necessities was foundationally distinct from *private* property, which claimed exclusive rights based on no more a claim than appropriation legitimized by legislation and the state. This meant in turn that – based on reciprocity – all had the 'right of occupancy':

> If the right of life is equal, the right of labour is equal . . . so is the right of occupancy. Would it be not be criminal, were some islanders to repulse, in the name of property, the unfortunate victims of a shipwreck struggling to reach the shore?[49]

As K. Steven Vincent shows, property in the pejorative sense was for Proudhon 'the type of ownership that was characteristic of the unproductive idle class which lived on interest and rents'.[50] In similar vein to Rousseau's allusions, he looked to an imagined past to illustrate his thinking. He emphasized 'the right of possession' over the 'right of property' arguing that – in the past – 'men lived in a state of communism'.[51] This had been displaced, though Proudhon was no apologist either for communism or for an idealized past (unlike some anarchists who would follow, such as Kropotkin).

Instead Proudhon's mode of argument rested on Enlightenment premises of progress and the uncovering of truth through science; for Proudhon, he was inferring from the 'natural' development of society. As Vincent notes, he 'disapproved of revolutionary upheavals'[52] – Proudhon opposed both violence and strike action - and Proudhon himself was careful to stress that he was 'no agent of discord, no firebrand of sedition. I anticipate history only by a few days'.[53] History was still progress; and whilst Proudhon didn't espouse a law of history in the fashion of Marx, he nonetheless saw social and political organization approximating to the age:

> Thus, in a given society, the authority of man over man is inversely proportional to the stage of intellectual development which that society has reached; and the probable duration of that authority can be calculated from the more or less general desire for a true government – that is, for a scientific government. And just as the right of force and the right of artifice retreat before the steady advance of justice, and must finally be extinguished in equality, so the sovereignty of the will yields to the sovereignty of the reason, and must at last be lost in scientific socialism. Property and royalty have been crumbling to pieces ever since the world began. As man seeks justice in equality, so society seeks order in anarchy.[54]

For all the emphasis on science, the centrality of property to Proudhon's critique was emphasized in quasi-religious tones; for Proudhon, 'the right of property was the origin of evil on earth, the first link in the long chain of crimes and misfortunes which the human race has endured since its birth'.[55] The fundamental anarchist objection to the state had its origins in the state's role guaranteeing this 'evil'; Proudhon's critique of 'proprietors', who excluded others from occupancy of property – or granted the right only on the basis of rent – rested on the premise that the proprietor's claim to the land was de facto illegitimate. If liberty was taken as an intrinsic human right and property was necessary for freedom – but in practice was only a potential for most – then, as Proudhon famously stated, property was not only 'theft' but it was also 'impossible', as the proprietor's right of exclusion negated any reciprocity which would in turn guarantee the plausibility of a right. Proudhon dismissed arguments that a right to property could be gained by original appropriation, but he also dismissed arguments that a right to property could be derived from labour. In a savage critique of classical political economy, Proudhon argued that for the 'collective force' of labour, which meant that 'all property becomes, by the same reason, collective and undivided . . . labour destroys property'.[56]

Ultimately, property represented authoritarianism – the authority of proprietor over tenant, owner over worker. It rendered liberty impossible. As such, it was itself impossible – at least beyond the sense of basic possession, which was not what Proudhon had in mind. The modern nation-state, in turn, guaranteed the rights of the proprietor and existed for that purpose, rendering liberty a farce. Proudhon's apparent faith in science equated to the statement that 'politics is the science of liberty. The government of man by man . . . is oppression. Society finds its highest perfection in the union of order with anarchy'.[57]

It is common in treatments of Proudhon's thought for him to be regarded as an 'unsystematic thinker'. For Woodcock, who was also his biographer, he was a 'man of paradox'.[58] On the same theme Peter Marshall argues that he 'gloried in paradox . . . he is one of the most contradictory thinkers in the history of political thought . . . he made no attempt to be systematic or consistent'.[59] More recently, assessments of Proudhon have altered somewhat. Greater attention has been paid to his republican heritage, and greater appreciation offered for the impact of Proudhon's life experience upon his changing views. In 1848 Proudhon – well known by now in France for his ideas, not least for his propagandizing through various newspapers he was involved with (including *Le Representant du Peuple, Le Peuple* and the later *La Voix du Peuple*, which he founded with money from the Russian revolutionary Alexander Herzen[60]) – was belatedly elected to the National Assembly following the Revolution which established the Second Republic. Until this point, despite Proudhon's declared anarchism, there had been some ambiguity as to the continuing role of the state in the society he envisaged of egalitarian exchange between workers' associations. The 1848 experience was pivotal for him. His experience of the National Assembly rendered him unequivocal about political abstentionism; famously, he characterized his tenure in the Assembly as his exile to a 'parliamentary Sinai'.[61] He was removed from the people who had sent him there; and in holding his office his interests were divergent from theirs, something he recognized in his book *The General Idea of the Revolution in the Nineteenth Century*, published in 1851. His critique of representation thus became profound and visceral. To be elected, to engage in electoral politics, was now, for Proudhon, to consent to 'wash one's hands in shit'.[62]

Proudhon's life experience in part lends system to thought sometimes decried as unsystematic when it would be better to characterize it perhaps as consistently evolving. Moreover, though he befriended Karl Marx, his socialism was not – ultimately – to Marx's taste and at least in part this was due to what Proudhon saw as Marx's penchant for system-building. Proudhon was, as Robert Graham notes, against communism; though a socialist, he did not subscribe to the distributive principle of from each according to their ability, to each according to their need, because he feared the only way such a principle could be enacted would be through the development of a state apparatus. This distinguished him sharply from those in the social anarchist tradition who would come later, notably Kropotkin, who did not believe that a state was necessary to operate society on communist principles.

Proudhon's objections to Marx were stated (politely) in a letter he wrote to him in 1846. Turning to 'ideas of organization and achievement', Proudhon argued that it was 'the duty of all socialists to keep a critical and sceptical frame of mind':

Let us seek together, if you will, for the laws of society, the manner in which these laws are manifested, the progress of our efforts to discover them. But for God's sake, after having demolished all a priori dogmatisms, let us not in turn dream of making our own, of indoctrinating the people. . ... since we are in the lead, let us not set ourselves up as leaders of a new intolerance; let us not be the apostles of a new religion, one that makes itself a religion of reason, a religion of logic.[63]

Proudhon's most profound rejection of the state is offered in *General Idea of the Revolution*, after the failure of his attempt to intervene via electoral politics. It was here he offered his famous excoriation of government. A fundamental value of government was the denial of liberty. Government arrogated to itself rights and powers that vitiated any conception of liberty which Proudhon could countenance. The condemnation of government ran thus:

> To be GOVERNED is to be kept in sight, inspected, spied upon, directed, law-driven, numbered, enrolled, indoctrinated, preached at, controlled, estimated, valued, censured, commanded, by creatures who have neither the right, nor the wisdom, nor the virtue to do so . . . To be GOVERNED is to be at every operation, at every transaction, noted, registered, enrolled, taxed, stamped, measured, numbered, assessed, licensed, licensed, authorised, admonished, forbidden, reformed, corrected, punished. It is, under the pretext of public utility, and in the name of the general interest, to be placed under contribution, trained, ransomed, exploited, monopolised, extorted, squeezed, mystified, robbed; then, at the slightest resistance, the first word of complaint, to be repressed, fined, despised, harassed, tracked, abused, clubbed, disarmed, choked, imprisoned, judged, condemned, shot, deported, sacrificed, sold, betrayed, and to crown all, mocked, ridiculed, outraged, dishonoured. That is government; that is its justice; that is its morality.[64]

Proudhon's views on government were born from bitter experience. In the wake of the arrival of the Second Empire and the collapse of the Republic he had found himself in jail, not to mention the lifelong bitterness he felt following his brother's death in military service.[65] It was the death of his brother which, in Proudhon's words, 'finally made me an irreconcilable enemy of the existing order'.[66]

In terms of his positive contribution, the social anarchism Proudhon is associated with is today known as mutualism, though the term 'mutualism' has broader applications and Proudhon did not invent it. This too was born out of a measure of practical experience. 'MUTALITY', as Proudhon termed it, was a 'system of guarantees which determines the old forms of our civil and commercial society . . . the natural form of exchange . . . the synthesis of the two ideas of property and communism'.[67]

For Proudhon, mutualism was a system of organizing society and the economy based on reciprocity and cooperation. At its core were principles of voluntary association, federation and free credit. In the wake of the 1848 revolution he attempted a Bank of the People – supported by subscription – which would enable a 'right' to credit for the masses.[68] This was cooperation and federation in action. It is well known that the bank failed, but this was an early attempt at a cooperative commercial venture that would – in Proudhon's view – diminish and ultimately destroy the capitalist system, based as it was on exclusivity of property and credit. As Shawn Wilbur notes, Proudhon analyses the '"right to credit"' and the duty to extend it, concluding that if they exist they must be equal'.[69] The greater availability of credit would make Proudhon's workers' associations viable, enabling them to take over the administration of society. Peter Marshall's assessment of Proudhon's ambitions is succinct: 'as mutualism developed economic organisation would eventually replace the political one and the State would eventually wither away'.[70] Proudhon's thought was not merely that of a philosopher. He was an activist and a propagandist, a known quantity in French politics. His advocacy of federalism – that the free associations of producers should federate with one another to ensure local control of production and reciprocity of exchange – became a defining point of departure for the anarchists that would follow, as would his severe critique of Jacobinism and state power.

The First International and the impact of Bakunin

Proudhon's influence, as is well recounted in both historiography and mythology, was felt within the First International of the 1860s, though not in the straightforward way sometimes assumed. In 1864, at St Martin's Hall in central London, the International Workingmen's Association (IWMA) – the International – was founded. The First International was the result of an initiative by French and British workers the previous year to foster international solidarity and strengthen their hand in industrial disputes.[71] The IWMA was a federal organization;

though the headquarters for much of its life were in London, it was an organization comprised of national and sub-national 'sections'. Karl Marx, who had been sceptical of organizations generally up to this point, joined the International due to what he saw as its possibilities for effecting change. He became its secretary. The International operated via correspondence between its member sections and through Congresses which adopted positions and platforms.

Numerous figures who were to become iconic in the history of anarchism were members of the International, including most importantly Bakunin, but also Kropotkin and the young Errico Malatesta. The French sections in particular were heavily engaged with the legacy of Proudhon, though Proudhon himself died shortly after the International was established. There were divergent Proudhonian factions, however, and this was to be of significance; in fact Samuel Hayat has argued that the International helped construct 'Proudhonism' as a school of thought and lend it coherence.[72] Hayat's work shows the relationship between practice and thought in the genealogy of anarchism as thought and movement; the 'Proudhonists' of the French section of the First International were, Hayat argued, drawing on Proudhon's work (particularly the *General Idea of the Revolution* and the *Political Capacity of the Working Classes*) to 'legitimise their position by actively resorting to Proudhon and his vocabulary'.[73] It was not as straightforward, as the political theory approach to anarchist studies would often have it, of ideas being constitutive of subsequent political realities and interventions, but instead serving as a toolkit, providing materials for workers to use to support broader political ambitions.

The French Proudhonists were not, as Hayat notes, reflective of the broad mass of French workers, but they did represent a series of skilled trades whose experience was reflected in Proudhon's ideas. Eugene Varlin, who would later be an influential figure in the Paris Commune, was one of them.[74] Their use of Proudhon was fundamentally grounded, so Hayat argues, in a defence of the 'cooperative socialism' with which they were familiar and which drew on the 'distinctly anarchistic' *General Idea of the Revolution* in order to do so, including its savage critique of the state.[75] They regarded the state – as Proudhon had – as the guarantor of property rights and the agent of a capitalist class, inimical to the interests of the workers.

This led to several premises which became major points of fracture within the International:

[They emphasised] the necessity of working class autonomy and the primacy of social struggle. They argued that although the International was open to everyone, delegates must come from the ranks of the manual workers only, and the economy must be the IMWA's sole terrain of intervention. This was a major object of controversy within the IWMA.[76]

As Hayat argues, Proudhon's thought (as Proudhon had argued himself) was as much a product of his political and social environment as an agent of changing it. The French Proudhonists averred his views, but in doing so they also averred a broader socialist critique of capitalism that was not reducible to Proudhon alone but which was developed in the 'lived experience' of French political and economic life, as Proudhon's ideas themselves had been.[77]

For the International, this meant from early in its life anti-statist, and in Marxist eyes, anti-political views were present in it before the arrival of Mikhail Bakunin, despite the posthumous mythologization of the International as an epic battle between the followers of Bakunin and the followers of Marx. Bakunin himself was not a member at the International's foundation but joined in 1868 through the Geneva section. Prior to this he had been working through an organization called the League of Peace and Freedom and established an Alliance for Socialist Democracy to act as an implementation organization for which he also sought membership of the International, which was ultimately rejected, with the Alliance subsequently disbanded. Historians disagree on how substantively 'real' the Alliance ever was.[78] Bakunin only became a declared anarchist relatively late in his life, but he had been a socialist and a revolutionary much earlier. It is regularly remarked in the historiography that Bakunin is significant for the history of anarchism at least as much in terms of form as well as content, being the archetype from which the image of the anarchist revolutionary has followed. Paul Avrich described Bakunin as 'an activist rather than . . . a theorist of rebellion', and this assessment was in line with how Bakunin has been seen throughout the near-century-and-a-half since his death.[79] Like Proudhon, he was averse to dogmatic systems: 'No theory, no ready-made system, no book that has ever been written will ever save the world . . . I cleave to no system, I am a true seeker.'[80] For Kropotkin, he was a 'moral personality'.[81] In Woodcock's assessment, 'of all anarchists, Bakunin most consistently lived and looked the part':

> Bakunin . . . was monumentally eccentric, a rebel who in almost every act seemed to express the most forceful aspects of anarchy . . . he was gigantic, and the massive unkemptness of his appearance would impress an audience even before he began to win its sympathies with his persuasive oratory . . . But Bakunin remains too solid a figure to be dismissed as a mere eccentric. If he was a fool, he was one of Blake's fools who attain wisdom by persisting in folly, and there was enough greatness in him . . . to make him one of the most influential men in the general revolutionary tradition as well as in the particular history of anarchism.[82]

It is worth bearing in mind these assessments even as Bakunin's recent biographer Mark Leier argues they often mask a tendency in the literature to caricature – and Leier is right.[83] Nonetheless both for anarchist partisans – who elevate Bakunin mythologically into a supernatural embodiment of class-struggle anarchism and direct action ('the most notorious radical of the nineteenth century' as Leier argues[84]) – and for detractors in the Marxist tradition and beyond, the mythological construction of Bakunin matters and has significance for both the nature of anarchist practice which followed (in part through the selective reconstruction and mobilization of his memory). As Colin Ward has shown, Bakunin's origins as an enlightened aristocrat placed him alongside Alexander Herzen, Peter Kropotkin and Leo Tolstoy as an elite rebel.[85] But he was not in a meaningful sense an 'anarchist' until the mid-1860s and even then preferred the term 'revolutionary socialist' to refer to his comrades and supporters who sought (as Proudhon had done) a *social*, rather than merely *political* revolution. Prior to the 1860s he had been a socialist but in the context of Slav nationalism, regarding pan-Slavic liberation struggles against the Russian Empire as an opportunity to build free societies.[86] As a young man raised in 'idyllic' Pryamukhino as the son of a diplomat, he had received an education in Enlightenment values consonant with the

Russian nobility of that time.[87] He followed his father into state service as an artillery officer, but after a few years abandoned his post.[88] His ambitions lay in an academic career and to that end Bakunin studied first in Moscow, and later in Berlin and Paris. He became interested in Hegelian ideas, but his increasing turn towards political radicalism and his failure to return home when ordered ensured that he was stripped of his lands and exiled *in absentia* by the Tsar.[89]

Bakunin was not Proudhon, however derivative of Proudhon's thought he was in certain respects.[90] Whatever the jibes Marx levelled at Proudhon – with Marx decrying Proudhon as the 'philosopher of the lower middle class' – Proudhon had known poverty and Marx in any event at other times conceded Proudhon's status as an *ouvrier*. Bakunin was no *ouvrier*. But what he shared with Proudhon was an 'instinctive' socialism, at least in the 1840s when he met him.[91] Bakunin's ideas would develop further and diverge significantly from Proudhon's. As Leier notes, Bakunin even in the mid-1840s was briefly prepared to call himself a communist, though he would cease using that label later and cede it to Marx.[92] Proudhon was firmly anti-communist throughout, never believing that Louis Blanc's formulation – 'from each according to their ability, to each according to their needs' – was possible or even necessarily desirable. Bakunin's collectivism – the economic underpinning of his mature anarchism from the later 1860s – was not Proudhon's mutualism, either. But the experience of friendship with Proudhon was substantive for Bakunin and continued despite their differences until Proudhon's death (Bakunin saw Proudhon again shortly before he died).[93] When Bakunin eventually joined the First International in 1868, there was already a significant divergence of view between non-state socialists and state socialists over questions such as the state itself and participations in elections. Bakunin did not simply 'create' these, nor were the debates that would ultimately rupture the International simply the result of a personality clash between Bakunin and Marx (however real that was).

Debates in the International, 1864–72

As Graham notes, the 1866 Geneva Congress 'was the first at which policy issues were the subject of debate by delegates from the

International's various sections'.[94] The French Proudhonists, though
split into two camps, argued for a 'worker-controlled education
system . . . [and] reject[ed] the state being given the role of a "superior
authority"'.[95] Varlin, who was in the minority Proudhonist faction,
went further, arguing for what 'he described as "non-authoritarian
communism"'.[96] Varlin's faction argued against Proudhon's own
patriarchal vision of society, instead arguing for 'equal rights for
women in opposition to [Henri] Tolain and his group, who agreed with
Proudhon that a woman's place was in the home'.[97] Tolain's group, in
classic Proudhonist fashion, argued that 'the self-emancipation of the
working class' could only be effected by the working class itself and
thus sought (unsuccessfully) to proscribe membership to workers
only.[98]

In Lausanne in 1867 property became a subject of serious
discussion, with a divergence between the Proudhonists over the
question of land but an acceptance of the collective ownership of
'larger enterprises'.[99] By this point, serious tensions were emerging
between the General Council, based in London, and the International's
national and sub-national sections. Dominated by Marx, the General
Council sought to act as an executive whereas many of the
International's sections envisaged it as a 'correspondence bureau'. In
1868, in Brussels, Bakunin was by now a member, in time to witness
a Belgian delegate (Cesar De Paepe) offer an 'essentially anarcho-
syndicalist conception' of the International's future, arguing for it
as – in itself – a mechanism for workers' control of society beyond
borders.[100] This 'programme' was approved in Basel the following
year:

> Cooperatives, credit unions and trade union organisations would
> become responsible for coordinating production and distribution
> between self-managed enterprises, while the workers' mutual aid
> societies would provide sickness, disability and pension benefits.
> Federal councils of recallable delegates would coordinate the
> activities of the federated groups, at the local, regional, national
> and, ultimately, international levels.[101]

In September 1871, Marx persuaded a London conference to
repudiate some of this vision, specifically in offering a reorientation

of the International's objects towards the formation of political parties to engage in electoral contests.[102] At the Hague Congress in 1872, Marx orchestrated the expulsion of Bakunin – who wasn't present – and Guillaume, who was. The International split, and the majority of the sections formed the anti-authoritarian International, which met at St. Imier in Switzerland shortly thereafter.

As we have seen, tensions existed within the International prior to Bakunin's arrival in it, however strongly he is identified with the split. For one, Guillaume – the other man expelled in 1872, dismissively referred to by Marx as Bakunin's 'valet' – had developed anarchistic ideas and positions years prior to meeting Bakunin and had been a member of the International, and a delegate to its Congresses for several years by that point.[103] When Guillaume met Bakunin in January 1869, as Wolfgang Eckhardt shows, much of his political thinking had already been shaped by his experiences in political activism in Switzerland.[104] The Jura sections which had developed in Switzerland associated strongly with craft industries such as watchmaking and of which Guillaume was a part derived its anarchistic sensibility from political contest before Bakunin's arrival:

> On 20th February 1869 Bakunin made his first visit to Le Locle in the Jura Mountains and found a sophisticated movement, which was drawn to and propagated revolutionary socialism because of its own experiences. Guillaume summed up the self-assertive mood in Jura as follows: Bakunin 'was an invaluable assistant in this propaganda'.[105]

Guillaume, like the other workers of the Jura who so impressed Kropotkin that he became an anarchist on his 1872 visit, was his own person. As Marianne Enckell puts it, '[b]etween the Swiss Jura watchmakers and Bakunin, there was therefore an encounter, and complementary experiences'.[106] Bakunin subsequently published in Guillaume's newspaper and the Jura sections renamed themselves the Jura Federation – adopting an abstentionist political position in opposition to other Swiss sections – but the groundwork had been laid before.[107]

The supposed Proudhonist influence in the International – though real – was nonetheless itself reflective of the fact that libertarian socialist tendencies were diverse and hardly homogenous. The French delegates did not share the same views, and other sections (including those of the Jura) drew on Proudhon in different ways to articulate their arguments. For his part, Bakunin's ideas went through significant evolution in the period after his first meeting with Proudhon in 1844. He finally renounced his pan-Slavism and commitment to nationalist movements following the failure of the Polish uprising of 1863.[108] By 1864, based primarily in Italy, Bakunin had commenced his 'anarchist turn', looking towards the development of a form of socialism that would guarantee both liberty and equality.[109] In 1867 in his 'Federalism, Socialism and Anti-Theologism', he had established a series of interconnected ideas that formed the basis of his anarchist collectivism. Though his initial plea for a 'United States of Europe' was, at first glance, redolent with the language of states, a closer inspection showed how Bakunin sought to destroy state power. He drew explicitly on Proudhon:

> The son of a peasant, and thus instinctively a hundred times more revolutionary than all the doctrinaire and bourgeois socialists, Proudhon armed himself with a critique as profound and penetrating as it was merciless, in order to destroy their systems. Resisting authority with liberty, against those state socialists, he boldly proclaimed himself an anarchist; defying their deism or their pantheism, he had the courage to call himself simply an atheist or rather, with Auguste Comte, a *positivist.*

The 1848 revolution in France had failed because, in establishing a republic, it had recreated the same structures it should – in Bakunin's mind – have sought to destroy, creating a class of politicians whose interests diverged fundamentally from those of the masses. The socialism of 'regimentation' was, in Bakunin's view, no socialism at all. This rendered arguments against socialism grounded in the experience of 1848 fallacious:

> What succumbed in June 1848 was not socialism in general. It was only state socialism, authoritarian and regimented socialism, the kind that had believed and hoped that the State would fully satisfy the needs and the legitimate aspirations of the working

classes, and that the State, armed with its omnipotence, would and could inaugurate a new social order. Hence it was not socialism that died in June; it was rather the State which declared its bankruptcy toward socialism and, proclaiming itself incapable of paying its debt to socialism, sought the quickest way out by killing its creditor.[110]

Bakunin synthesized key elements of Proudhon's thought with aspects of Marx; Bakunin adopted a federalist perspective against Marx's centralized state, emphasizing the significance of 'individual and collective freedom' as Proudhon had done. 'Liberty' was, for Bakunin, incompatible with a statist approach:

Liberty, to the political republican, is an empty word; it is the liberty of a willing slave, a devoted victim of the State. Being always ready to sacrifice his own liberty, he will willingly sacrifice the liberty of others. Political republicanism, therefore, necessarily leads to despotism. For the socialist republican, liberty linked with the general welfare, producing a humanity of all through the humanity of each, is everything, while the State, in his eyes, is a mere instrument, a servant of his well-being and of everyone's liberty.[111]

It was in this essay – delivered as a speech – that Bakunin offered his equal prioritization of freedom and socialism which has since been regarded by many anarchists as definitional for the movement and its aims – 'liberty without socialism is privilege, injustice . . . socialism without liberty is slavery and brutality'.[112]

The Marx-Bakunin conflict as it is narrativized owes much to the elision of more profound debates about the nature of socialism with the personalities of the respective individuals. Marx was an academic thinker, a system-builder par excellence and a theorist far more widely read than Bakunin, though it was a measure of his grudging respect for his adversary that on their reunion in 1864 after sixteen years apart Marx was prepared to credit Bakunin as 'one of the few' who had 'moved forwards' rather than 'backwards' in terms of his socialism.[113] Bakunin's initial friendly relations with Marx in Paris in the 1840s soured quickly, as Proudhon's had, though their relationships with

Marx were different. With Proudhon – notwithstanding his election in 1848 – more marginal in activist terms than Bakunin, who despite incarceration would remain a powerful force in the activist milieu in the decades which followed, Proudhon could be dismissed (and was) by Marx in intellectual terms. Bakunin's presence on the activist stage and consistent commitment to action, from an ill-fated uprising in Dresden in 1849 to a rebellion in Lyon in 1870, meant he was harder to dismiss. He had followers and adherents in many countries, having travelled and corresponded widely. Famously his supporter Giuseppe Fanelli's mission to Spain in 1868 helped promote the cause of what would become anarchist collectivism, which retained purchase in Spain long after anarchist communism had become the dominant social anarchist school elsewhere.[114]

Bakunin represented, as Joaquin Pedroso has insightfully claimed, an 'anti-intellectual' socialism, not because he was against ideas, theories or 'science' – his body of work and his original academic aspirations indicate otherwise – but because he feared the potential power of elites within a 'scientific' socialist society:

> While celebrating reason and scientific method Bakunin diagnosed a kind of intellectual monomania exhibited primarily by Marxists . . . that relied exclusively on Reason and science . . . to bring about revolution. Moreover, he was also wary of hierarchically institutionalised forms of scientific discovery and the dogmatic insistence on the univocity of rational thought incited by such monomania . . . He consistently questions the uncritical deployment of Reason and science in political philosophy.[115]

Pedroso shows how Bakunin anticipated the later problems of state socialism through a critique of the scientistic dogmatism of the Marxists' approach. Though he accepted in some part Marx's analysis of society and economics, he was more scathing about his positive proposals: '[w]hile the Marxists may have discovered the laws of political economy, their scientific pretensions in translating those laws into revolutionary action seemed elitist and totalitarian to him'.[116] Historians have often been critical of Bakunin's own fondness for secret societies and argued for a measure of dishonesty in his publicly articulated view of the role of the intellectual in revolution, with Marshall going so far as to claim that his 'invisible dictatorship' of secret societies 'would be even more tyrannical than a Blanquist or a Marxist one'.[117] But Pedroso contends that Bakunin's vision restricted the revolutionary's role to 'channelling the popular instincts of the people but never denying the peoples' central role in making revolution'.[118]

The war of manoeuvre within the International was real, however. But the anarchists were not merely the victims of a Marxist campaign, as Errico Malatesta later recollected. They, like the state socialists, sought to advocate for their view and gain adherence to it on the part of the organization:

> we did just what they did; we sought to make use of the International for our own party aims. The difference lay in the fact that we, as anarchists, relied chiefly on propaganda, and since we wanted to gain converts for the anarchist cause, emphasised decentralisation, the autonomy of groups, free initiative . . . while the Marxists, being authoritarians as they were, wanted to impose their ideas by majority strength – which was more or less fictitious – by centralisation and by discipline. But all of us, Bakuninists and Marxists alike, tried to force events rather than relying upon the force of events.[119]

Marx was also the victim of Bakunin's anti-Semitism, which – for all Bakunin's pledges of racial and gender equality – never left him.[120] Yet for all the antipathies, Marx and Bakunin at least purported to be friends for much of the three decades in which they knew each other. As late as 1864–5 Marx saw Bakunin as a potential ally, not an enemy, in an attempt to enlist supporters in Italy for his efforts in the International.[121] Towards the end of his life, Bakunin admitted that their personalities were too dissimilar for them to have been real friends, but it is clear from their interactions up to 1872 that reducing the debate between state socialists and those who stood for the social revolution to a simple personality clash is a vast oversimplification. Marx and Bakunin represented two tendencies as much as they constructed them. The anarchists did not just object to Marx's schema; in Proudhon's hands they had declared their opposition to 'Jacobinism' *tout court*, which meant state socialism as a whole.

In 1871 Jura was to be the springboard for an attempt to contest the future direction of the International which staked out the conflict between state socialists and anarchists in blunt terms. The London Conference held in September 1871 – not a full Congress – was responded to by a document, drafted by Guillaume, which would become known to posterity as the Sonvillier Circular.[122] It was sent to sections throughout the International. Decisions taken by the General Council at the London Conference, which had altered the ambitions of the International to pursuing electoral success, were repudiated in the strongest terms. The premises under which the meeting had been held in the first place were questioned. And yet the Circular did not accuse the Council of bad faith; quite the contrary. It argued instead that the moves the Council had made were consonant with its beliefs:

> We do not cast aspersions on the intentions of the General Council. The personalities that it comprises have been the victims of a fatal necessity: they wanted, in good faith and for the triumph of their particular doctrine, to introduce the principle of authority into the International: the circumstances seemed to encourage this tendency, and it seems natural that this school, whose ideal is the conquest of political power by the working class, believed that the International, as a result of recent events, had to leave behind its original organisation and transform itself into a hierarchical organisation, directed and governed by a Committee.
>
> But while these tendencies and events are explainable, we feel no less obliged to fight against them in the name of the Social Revolution that we pursue, of which the program is 'the emancipation of the working classes by the working classes themselves', without the direction of any authority, even an authority elected by and consented to by the workers.[123]

At the Hague Congress in 1872 these divisions bore legendary fruit with the expulsions of Guillaume and Bakunin. However, the subsequent defection of sections and the foundation of the anti-authoritarian International at St. Imier spoke to the fact that they were neither alone nor 'leaders' of a movement in any straightforward sense. The anti-authoritarian International met for the first time at St. Imier less than a fortnight of the conclusion of the Hague Congress, with the opening statement featuring a clear statement of an anarchist position: 'that the destruction of any political power is the proletariat's first duty'.[124] The direction of travel was by now clear.

The International existed within an age of revolutions, and during its life Bakunin for his part remained actively involved in insurrectionary activity. This led to an ill-fated affiliation with the nihilist Sergei Nechaev which has dogged Bakunin ever since, but it also led to his participation to the failed uprising in Lyon in 1870 which prefigured another, more significant, revolutionary moment, the Paris Commune of 1871.

Action and memory: The Paris Commune

The Commune was a pivotal 'site of memory' for the development of anarchist thought and practice. The First International was still, for the moment, intact – though as we have seen wracked in increasingly acrimonious internal strife. But both main strands in its socialist debates were to take Paris as a critical reference point. For Bakunin, writing shortly after the Commune's defeat, it was a vindication of 'revolutionary socialism', which was, in the early 1870s, how those who would later announce themselves as anarchists described themselves:

> Revolutionary socialism has just attempted a first demonstration, one both practical and stunning, in the Paris Commune. I am a supporter of the Paris Commune. It became all the more evocative and powerful in the heart and mind of the European proletariat, precisely because it was massacred and drowned in blood by the thugs of clerical and monarchic reaction. Above all I support it because it was a clearly expressed, bold negation of the state.[125]

Louise Michel, later an iconic figure in the anarchist movement, participated in and fought for the Commune. For her, the Commune's failures held lessons as much as its successes. It had been, she remembered, 'an immense abbatoir', when the slaughter of Bloody

Week – when the French government forces retook the city – meant the 'numbers of dead [couldn't] be calculated'. Michel claimed the slaughter only ceased because the authorities 'feared the plague'.[126] But like Bakunin she saw in the Commune a vindication of anti-parliamentary socialism and claimed that it showed the way to the future, for though the Commune was defeated, 'unvanquished under the avenging flames of the fire, it will be reborn even stronger, for it understood how useless political changes are that put one set of men in place of another set of men'. She continued that 'every revolution will now be social and not political; this was the final breath, the supreme aspiration of the Commune in the ferocious grandeur of its marriage with death'.[127]

As John Merriman shows, the Paris Commune sprang into life on 18 March 1871, after workers prevented government forces seizing cannons on the Montmartre. Just over a week later, the Commune was formally established in the form of a 'municipal council'. For ten weeks, Paris became a socialist society, organized in opposition to the national government and drawing on the tradition of the Commune of the 1790s, invoking the spirit of the Revolution. It did not appear out of nowhere – as Merriman argues, from the defeat of the Second Empire by German forces the preceding autumn, cries for a Commune had been heard in Paris.[128] In September posters had appeared calling for a Commune, and members of the First International were key to the development of revolutionary agitation. Critically, Proudhon's ideas were at the heart of it; Eugene Varlin, a prominent figure in the Commune responsible for finance and who established cooperative workshops (including one in which Michel worked), was, as we have seen, a Proudhonist and a member of the International.[129] As Robert Tombs writes, 'Proudhon's influence saturated Communard socialism'.[130] In a sense, as we have seen in the International, this should be unsurprising – as Proudhonism was a fundamental organizing paradigm for many French labour activists in the period.

In Merriman's account the Commune was a genuine popular uprising. Under the Empire, Paris had been remade according to Imperial design, with new boulevards laid out and medieval Paris destroyed, with the consequence of families and workers displaced into slum conditions which would provide the tinder for the Commune's fire. For Marx, the Commune caused him to elaborate on his thinking on revolution; notwithstanding some anarchist caricature, Marx was far from sanguine that seizure of state power alone would be enough to enable the proletariat to begin the transition to communism. As he famously put it in his *Civil War in France*, 'the working class cannot simply lay hold of the ready-made state machinery, and wield it for its own purposes'. This was because 'the centralised state power with its ubiquitous organs of standing army, police, bureaucracy, clergy, and judicature – organs wrought after the plan of a systematic and hierarchic division of labor – originates from the days of absolute monarchy'.[131] Though the Revolution had 'swept away' the 'relics' of its monarchical heritage, it had come in turn 'under the direct control of the propertied classes' with the result that 'the state power assumed more and more the character of the national power of capital over labor, of a public force organized for social enslavement, of an engine of class despotism'. This could not be eliminated simply at a stroke, as the 1848 revolution had learned. The Commune, though ultimately defeated, represented 'the glorious harbinger of a new society'.[132]

On this the socialist movement – not yet ruptured – was united. But the ultimate defeat of the Commune and the massacre of the Communards launched by President Adolphe Thiers's forces in the 'Bloody Week' that Michel remembered so well would also convince many who would follow of the necessity of an anarchist approach and even – for some – of the necessity of violence against a seemingly merciless state which sought their destruction and gave no quarter. Estimates of the Communard dead vary widely, with Merriman arguing for as many as 17,000 deaths, noting that 'some estimates have reached as high as 35,000'.[133] Eugene Varlin, the Proudhonist and 'non-authoritarian communist' who George Woodcock would later claim as an anarchist, was murdered in the streets of the Montmartre the day after the fighting was over, denounced, savagely beaten by a crowd, then shot.[134] Many Communards fled into exile. Some went to Switzerland, including the anarchist geographer Élisée Reclus, who was under sentence of deportation. There they would play a part in the split in the International.[135] Others went to England, where they would foreshadow the community of 'companions' in London which would develop in the 1880s.[136] Some fled to Spain, where one would have a son, Emile, who would become a propagandist of the deed and a protagonist in the anarchist violence of the 1890s.[137]

The Commune was a powerful memory for the socialist movement as a whole and remains a crucial landmark in the development of revolutionary socialism. For anarchists, it was of pivotal importance in exhibiting unequivocally the irredeemable nature of state power. The exile which followed helped foster the anarchist diaspora, and the violence inflicted on the Communards justified in the eyes of many a change of direction from words to deeds, which will be discussed in the next chapter.

Conclusion: 'Classical anarchism'?

There has been much debate in recent historiography over the term 'classical anarchism'. Whilst much of this chapter has focused on the development of ideas by those retrospectively termed 'classical anarchists' and how those intersected with wider movements in the mid-late nineteenth century, it has argued against seeing anarchism as a singular, coherent, body of thought in this period in the fashion which political theorists have been wont to. As Robert Graham has persuasively argued, anarchism in the age of revolutions – whether 1848 or the Commune – was a movement, or series of movements, in evolution. In point of fact, as he shows, whilst there were anarchists prior to 1864 it was only the debates within the First International which hardened them into a movement and allowed the development of particular schools of anarchist thought and practice.

What is clear is that the anarchism which existed in Europe in 1872 was still 'embryonic', though it was increasingly conscious of itself as an anarchist endeavour. The language of revolutionary socialism would, in the course of the anti-authoritarian International, give way definitively to the language of anarchism. Though the split in the socialist movement which this represented has been historicized – rightly – as of profound significance for the development of socialism, later sectarianism has been too easily imposed on the socialisms of the 1860s and 1870s. Bakunin was keenly aware of the many nuanced positions held within the First International; in a letter to Guillaume in 1869 he chided his friend for being 'amazed' at the behaviour of some of the Proudhonists led by Tolain. They were, for Bakunin, the 'second, and bad sort'.[138] The others – represented by Varlin, who became increasingly radical in the course of the International and who died in the Commune – were Bakunin's 'sort'.

The years 1848 and 1871 represented important sites of memory for anarchists and for their self-understanding. For both Proudhon and those who followed him, 1848 proved the failure of political revolutions, definitively, though he had already had his suspicions. The National Assembly had become divorced from the interests of the people it represented. It was also responsible for the dispersal of people and ideas. Joseph Dejacque, a declared anarchist, found himself exiled in New York (by way of London, Jersey and New Orleans) where he published his paper *La Libertaire* in the late 1850s, which foreshadowed the exile and dispersal of French anarchists which would follow the Communard experience in 1871.[139] The Commune was read in different ways; for Michel, looking back, it was showed that a popular revolution – meaning a social revolution – was the only viable revolution. For Peter Kropotkin who would follow, the Commune actually represented failure as much as success; however popular, it was still too political. The turn to provide public workshops was tardy; people needed food else reaction would take root. It was no coincidence then that food was a critical aspect of Kropotkin's thinking as he sketched it two decades later in *The Conquest of Bread*.

The codification of the anarchisms – movements, actions and thought – into 'classical anarchism' has both engendered misunderstanding and been the creature of wilful misrepresentation. For Marxists writing in the tradition of Engels's division of 'utopian' and 'scientific' socialisms, anarchism would as a result be easy to dismiss on the grounds of its supposed rejection of dialectics and its anti-scientific pretensions. Yet anarchism's relationship with science was hardly 'anti-scientific'. Bakunin – often characterized as unsystematic and chaotic in his thought – in fact offered, as we have seen through Pedroso's account, a significant critique of the misuse of the language of 'science' in the construction of socialist proposals and ideas. He was critical too of what he saw as Proudhon's lack of awareness of the full implications of scientific developments and in this came close to Marx. The third key thinker of classical anarchism – Kropotkin –

is discussed in the next chapter as the conscious movement came to grapple with the question of how to promote and implement an anarchist society in an era where it was commonly felt revolution was imminent. Kropotkin's relationship with science differed again from both Proudhon and Bakunin, problematizing still further any uniform reading of a 'classical anarchism' founded on the supposed correspondences between the thought of three men. Moreover, as the accounts of the International offered by historians have shown, there was no straightforward translation between ideas and realities. In fact, ideas – as we have seen with the 'Proudhonists' – were often useful toolboxes and resources to legitimize activism on the ground. In this, one consistent feature of supposed 'classical anarchism' may be deserving of the 'charitable approach' Davide Turcato commends: the argument, made by anarchists from Proudhon on, that they sought to interpret and explain changes in society, rather than provide blueprints for systems.[140]

Further reading

Classical anarchist thought

The key texts of the classical anarchist thinkers have been anthologized in recent times by a number of editors, but in particular Proudhon and Kropotkin's works have been addressed by Iain McKay. His *Property Is Theft!* (2011) is the definitive Proudhon anthology, including excellent essays on Proudhon's life and thought. The anthology includes key sections of *What Is Property?*, *General Idea of the Revolution in the Nineteenth Century* and the *System of Economic Contradictions* amongst many other works including Proudhon's famous letter to Marx. McKay has anthologized Kropotkin in two volumes, *Direct Struggle Against Capital* (2014) and *Modern Science and Anarchy* (2018). Again, excellent introductions are present in both. Kropotkin's *Conquest of Bread* has recently been reissued as a Penguin Classic with an introduction by David Priestland (2014), whilst *Mutual Aid* is available in an edition from Freedom Press (2009) with an essay by McKay. The most frequently cited anthology of Bakunin's writing remains the edition by Sam Dolgoff, *Bakunin on Anarchy* (1971), though there has been a recent Anarres edition of writings from his anarchist period, *Bakunin: Selected Texts, 1868-1875* (2016). Historical assessments of classical anarchist thought are available in George Crowder, *Classical Anarchism* (1991), though this is out of print. William Godwin has recently been the subject of an excellent biography by Richard Gough Thomas, *William Godwin: A Political Life* (2019). The standard biography of Proudhon in English is still that of George Woodcock, *Proudhon* (1987), whilst Mark Leier's *Bakunin: The Creative Passion* appeared in 2006. K. Steven Vincent's 'Visions of a Stateless Society' essay in volume II of the *Cambridge History of Nineteenth-Century Political Thought* (edited by Gareth Stedman Jones and Gregory Claeys, 2011) does a good job of linking together anarchist and libertarian thinkers with the wider intellectual milieu.

The early anarchist movement

The development of the anarchist movement from the debates within the First International has been well served by recent scholarship, including Robert Graham's accessible history *We Do Not Fear Anarchy, We Invoke It!* (2015), which charts the arrival of the First International and the Marx-Bakunin conflict with verve and great erudition. Wolfgang Eckhardt's *First Socialist Schism*, translated into English in 2016, is a major work of scholarship which draws heavily on correspondence which will be of interest to serious students of the subject. Fabrice Bensimon, Quentin Deluermoz and Jeanne Moisand (eds), *'Arise Ye Wretched of the Earth': The First International in a Global Perspective* (2018) contains a number of essays which are of interest, not least Hayat's essay drawn on here which offers a good critique of the Proudhonist factions in the International. Enckell's essay on Bakunin and the Jura Federation is also vital. Finally, the events of the Paris Commune and their significance are well interrogated in John Merriman's *Massacre: The Life and Death of the Paris Commune* (2014).

2

Words versus deeds

Anarchism and syndicalism before the First World War, 1872–1914

Introduction: Kropotkin, Malatesta, Michel and Goldman

In 1886 Peter Kropotkin arrived in London. By now, Kropotkin was an exile; having escaped imprisonment in Russia, he would not return until 1917 in the wake of the February Revolution. In the period between the 1880s and his return home, Kropotkin would author most of his important works. His three main books – *The Conquest of Bread*, *Mutual Aid* and *Fields, Factories, and Workshops* – along with numerous other writings, were all composed in London. London was, in the late nineteenth century, 'the crossroads of cosmopolitan anarchism', as Davide Turcato has put it.[1] In 1889, the Italian anarchist Errico Malatesta came to the city. He had visited before, but during this stay he would be a witness to the Great Dock Strike of 1889 and be involved in the organization of his newspaper *L'Associazione*, translated to London from Nice part-way through its short-lived run. He would meet William Morris at a Socialist League meeting, Morris having previously been an ally of Charlotte Wilson within the Fabian Society.[2]

Kropotkin was by the time of Malatesta's arrival involved with Wilson's anarchist newspaper *Freedom*, for which he wrote regularly. Another counterpart of Wilson's was Louise Michel, who arrived in London in 1890 and was involved in Wilson's International School project, part of the wave of anarchist education initiatives that took hold in Britain and beyond in the period up to the First World War.[3] Five years earlier on the other side of the Atlantic, Emma Goldman had arrived in the United States from the Russian Empire and by her own admission was swayed to anarchist socialism in the wake of the execution of the 'Haymarket martyrs', a group of anarchists executed in the United States in 1887.[4]

These names are famous examples of the reality of the anarchist diaspora before the First World War, the constant movement of revolutionaries across borders and the fundamentally transnational and international nature of anarchism during 'the first globalization'.[5] For Bantman,

> The anarchists' transnational endeavours, between France and Britain, and in many other areas across the globe, were manifestations of a reactive working-class globalisation which was very much prompted by resistance to the elite globalisation.[6]

Malatesta had organized in Argentina before arriving in London; Kropotkin had travelled widely and in the early 1870s had experienced his anarchist 'conversion' during a visit to the Jura Federation in Switzerland. Goldman's journeys were just beginning; she would be deported from the United States to Russia after the Bolshevik Revolution, and Michel was in exile, having been deported to New Caledonia following the defeat of the Commune, amnestied and subsequently later imprisoned on her return to France. The experience of movement disseminated anarchist ideas, but also changed the relationship of revolutionaries to place, as Turcato has noted. The privileging of the European over the global south has militated against an understanding of the consistency of anarchism's evolution; having organized in Egypt, Malatesta would go on to organize in Argentina.[7] Whilst the quartet documented here are well known, they are also representative of the many nameless anarchists who crossed borders and lived on their wits in the period – because they were also all involved in, and represented, the essential question of how to pursue the anarchist revolution in the period when anarchism had come to understand itself as both an *idea* and a *movement*.

This question was the question of words versus deeds. Was anarchism to be promoted by 'propaganda of the word' – which is to say the dissemination of ideas through texts and oratory, through speeches and newspapers – or was it to be advanced by the 'deed', the militant action, often violent, which would inspire the masses to revolt. For Johann Most, 'the most vocal advocate of propaganda by deed in the United States near the end of the nineteenth century'[8] the 'deed' or 'attentat' (attack) was a message:

> So our question is this: what is the purpose of the anarchists' threats – an eye for an eye, a tooth for a tooth – if they are not followed up by action? ... The great thing about anarchist vengeance is that it proclaims loud and clear for everyone to hear, that: this man or that man must die for this and this reason; and that at the first opportunity which presents itself for the realization of such a threat, the rascal in question is really and truly dispatched to the other world.[9]

Most's views led a series of exiles first to London, later to the United States, where he would have a significant influence, including on Emma Goldman.[10]

Of the four famous names cited earlier, Kropotkin's involvement in deeds was the most marginal, although in 1881 at the Social Revolutionary Congress he had extremely reluctantly concurred with the adoption of 'deeds' as a stratagem. Indeed he did so only nominally, in his endorsement of the draft declaration; he had inveighed against 'deeds' in much of the debate.[11] The others for their parts were all involved in, or supported, specific actions. Malatesta made his name as a revolutionary, participating in the Benevento rising of 1877, where as part of a group of armed anarchists who seized the village of Lentino he 'carried out the anarchist ritual of burning the archives which contained the record of property holdings, debts and taxes'.[12] Goldman in her American years was involved in an attempt to assassinate the industrialist Henry Clay Frick, along with her long-time counterpart Alexander Berkman, who was ultimately jailed; Dan Colson goes so far as to say that 'from her beginnings in the movement, Goldman was associated with the violent wing of anarchism', citing her relationship with Most.[13] Michel fought on the barricades of the Commune itself, the event often taken – as John Merriman has powerfully argued – as the point of departure amongst anarchists for the debate about deeds versus words.

It was a period of movement and changes in theory and praxis. In the period up to the 1870s, anarchist collectivism was the most current strand in terms of the movement's ideology. It synthesized Proudhon's ideas with Bakunin's, but it fell short of communism. After the 1880s, increasingly two new currents – communism and syndicalism – would become more prevalent. Although syndicalism – revolutionary unionism – was not openly recognized as such until the early 1890s, it had its origins in both Proudhon's thinking on workers' associations and the experiences of union activism in the United States, including the development of the 'Chicago idea' as Kenyon Zimmer has shown.[14] Anarchist communism had, in some forms, existed prior to the 1870s but had been a marginal current.[15] The work of Kropotkin would do much to advance its cause and ensure that it became the dominant mode of socialist anarchism outside of Spain. It was Kropotkin's anarchist communism which was later to prove influential in the Ukraine during the years of the Free Territory during the First World War, and it was Kropotkin's anarchist communism that was to be remade by Hatta Shuzo in the 'pure anarchism' of early twentieth-century Japan.[16]

But as we saw earlier with Wilson, it is dangerous to impose conformity where there is none. The anarchist currents of the 'first globalization' were in dialogue with each other, and the attempt to codify some as schools of thought with doctrinal purchase was actively resisted by some, with Malatesta, an anarchist communist suspicious of syndicalism – supporting the position of an 'anarchism without adjectives'.[17] Though Malatesta had himself in his most popular pamphlet argued that it was not the task of the anarchist to simply answer bad faith questions about how a potential anarchist society might perform certain functions, it was nonetheless the case that the period before the First World War saw increasing attempts to provide such answers.[18] A key area was education; the 'modern school' discussed by Francisco Ferrer sought to provide the opportunity for revolutionary consciousness at the level of pedagogy.[19]

This was also the era when, in the 1890s in particular, anarchism became most strongly associated with violence. The arguments over deeds were seemingly answered firmly in the affirmative in France in particular, where a series of high-profile 'attentats' (the anarchist Johann Most's term for actions such as assassinations) were undertaken by a series of anarchist assassins who were later to be regarded as martyrs. Ravachol, Vaillant, Henry – all were names which were to become symbolic in the transition of anarchism in the popular mind to a movement associated with violence and assassination. Taken by both many contemporaries and later scholars as irrational and self-defeating in their actions, they seemed to illustrate the classic misreading of Bakunin's famous aphorism that 'the passion for destruction is a creative passion' too.[20]

These names listed earlier highlight the purchase that mythology still has on anarchist historiography. Whilst they are important and whilst in the case of the four prominent names given first they are representative in their own way of broader currents (and we will return to them), they are far from the totality of the story. They do not of themselves explain the nature (for example) of Andalusian anarchism in the period, dismissed by Marxists as the work of 'primitive rebels'.[21] They also represent an individualization and mythologization of anarchist 'heroes' or 'exemplary' lives which, in the twentieth century, would come to constitute part of an anarchist liturgy.[22] But the anarchist diaspora of the forty years prior to the First World War was made of diverse communities, from the French 'companions' in London to the Japanese anarchists involved in the High Treason Incident of 1910.[23] They included at least some of the syndicalists involved in the Liverpool Transport Strike of 1911 and at least some of the syndicalists active in the Durham coalfield before 1914, just as they included more famously members of the Industrial Workers of the World (IWW) in the United States.[24]

Charlotte Wilson's experience illustrates the ways in which anarchism was a current in the broader socialist movement in the period at the end of the nineteenth century and influential beyond those who would formally declare themselves anarchists. The Fabian

Society's formal statement of the nature of socialism which Wilson penned delineated a libertarian socialism which would still be cited by Labour politicians a century or more later. Meanwhile, in Britain, the Whiteway anarchists, inspired by Tolstoy, formed their own community in 1898, drawing on the historical tradition of Gerrard Winstanley and the Diggers from the seventeenth century.[25] The period after the split in the First International up to the outbreak of the First World War was a moment of anarchist and socialist possibilities; during those decades, networks and movement, space and place, helped shaped anarchist attempts to respond to the questions their (differing) situations asked of them, from the local, to the national, to the transnational. The persistent question as we have seen was how to progress the social revolution, a question that often been framed in terms of an opposition of 'deeds' versus words', and it is to 'deeds' we turn first.

Propaganda of the deed

In January 1894, Auguste Vaillant stood trial for his life for the bombing of the French Chamber of Deputies which had taken place the month before in Paris. Vaillant stood accused of throwing a bomb from the gallery which had inflicted shrapnel wounds on a number of observers. His act followed the death of Ravachol, an anarchist executed earlier that year for a previous *attentat*. It would in turn be followed, also in 1894, by the bombing of a cafe at a railway station – the Cafe Terminus – by the young anarchist Emile Henry. Henry was the son of a Communard, in exile in Barcelona, where Henry was born before he came to France, growing up in Catalonia as Bakunin's message of anarchist collectivism took root after the mission of his emissary Giuseppe Fanelli.[26]

Vaillant's trial was of significance for the extent to which it was documented by the bourgeois press. It was an instruction in the use of the 'weapons of the weak' by anarchists; given a platform – the courtroom – anarchists used these stages to articulate their beliefs and legitimize their cause.[27] As Elun Gabriel has argued, anarchists used the courtroom in a practice of 'performing persecution':

The rituals of the legal system provided anarchists the opportunity to speak during their trials, and, for those condemned to death, before their executions as well. Anarchists embraced these moments of speech as chances to witness to their faith. They could also demonstrate the power of a faith that gave them the courage to face death and the confidence that their suffering would contribute to the world's redemption.[28]

For Gabriel, anarchists 'operating from a position of relative institutional powerlessness... adopted another vocabulary of persecuted evangelizers, that of Christianity'.[29] This attempt to use the courtroom and the scaffold as a vehicle to promote anarchist ideas refutes the oft-made claim that propagandists of the deed were purely irrational. It also highlights the way deeds and words intersected; the reportage was relatively more important than the act itself. In terms of Vaillant, his trial was not the first time he had appeared in the press – even the foreign press. In 1885, *The Times* – under the headline 'The Paris Socialists' – reported on an appearance by Vaillant at a meeting of the Paris municipal council where he protested against police brutality in their actions against a demonstration where they seized a red flag.[30] Vaillant was, a later story revealed, 'a municipal councillor'.[31] Two months earlier, described as 'M. Vaillant, the Anarchist', the paper reported his successful moving of a resolution 'condemning the expulsion of foreign Revolutionists'.[32] In July 1887 he was reported to have participated in a riot at a meeting of a rival political group which was 'broken up' by anarchists. Vaillant 'took the chair . . . inveighed against the chamber, advocated an insurrection . . . The meeting ended with cheers for the Commune and for Anarchy'.[33]

Charles Malato, a French anarchist in exile in Britain, wrote a sympathetic account of Vaillant's life in the *Fortnightly Review* in 1894.[34] Malato stated that he 'love[d] and admire[d] Vaillant, as just as some English republicans love and admire Cromwell, who was also a regicide'.[35] Vaillant's anarchism, according to Malato, had waxed and waned, though the English press had consistently identified him as an anarchist. Malato told a story of a 'future anarchist' who 'grew up in misery': a man with a 'gentle, even somewhat timid, look'.[36] Vaillant, the son of a gendarme, had been abandoned to poverty by his father and had tried other political avenues, including – as Malato noted – the municipal council. Malato and Vaillant had been part of the same small group of anarchists in the late 1880s, and Malato was at pains to trace the 'humane' nature of the man who would bomb the Chamber of Deputies in December 1893.[37]

The Times' correspondent was present on the day of the bombing, the ninth of December. Having arrived shortly after 3 p.m., the correspondent described the afternoon's business as having 'gone on interminably' until Vaillant's attack rendered the day – in the correspondent's opinion – 'uniquely memorable' a little after 4 p.m.[38]

> of a sudden, mingling itself with the diffused glow that falls from the ceiling where the electric light burns behind glass, there shot a sort of dull red gleam just above the heads of the Conservatives, and immediately following this, like the report of two or three duelling pistols, the sound of an explosion was heard . . . It was a bomb. A bomb had been thrown from the second or upper gallery. Dynamite had invaded the Chamber of Deputies.[39]

The Times' coverage of Vaillant's subsequent trial highlights key issues around how propagandists of the deed were understood at the time, how they understood themselves and how we have understood them since. Though The Times' correspondent was laconic and dismissive of Vaillant's motives, they reproduced in full his courtroom speech. In the time between the attack and his appearance in court – just under a month – the French legislature has passed two of the *lois scelerates* ('villainous laws'), repressive laws that criminalized anarchism and anarchist propaganda.[40] This formed part of a broader moral panic about anarchism and ensuing wave of repression on the part of the French authorities which Richard Bach Jensen has argued 'perpetuated the very problem of violent anarchism it was supposed to be resolving'.[41] Vaillant's statement in court exists in the context of his recognition of both his imminent death and the prevailing atmosphere towards anarchism in France.

Vaillant began by stating that he wished to 'expound his theoretical ideas' and was 'not an orator', so begged permission to read aloud his 'declaration'. Permission given, Vaillant launched into a justification of his action which was, in truth, an exposition of anarchist ideas and a broader critique of bourgeois society. He noted that 'among the exploited, there are two classes of individuals', the first of which corresponded to the group 'born to be slaves and content with the little which is given it'.[42] The second group, amongst whom Vaillant numbered himself,

> thinks and studies, and, casting a glance around, perceives the social injustices. Is it their fault if they see clearly, and suffer at the sight of others suffering? Then they throw themselves into the fray and become the exponents of the claims of the people.[43]

Though Vaillant did not cite Bakunin in his declaration, such a self-conception fitted closely to Bakunin's sense of the role of the intellectual in revolution.[44] He moved to the international dimension of anarchist critique, noting from his own bitter experience in Argentina that 'everywhere I have come I have seen the unfortunate bowing under the yoke of capital . . . there more than anywhere also I saw capital like a vampire come to suck up to the last drop the blood of the unfortunate pariahs'.[45] This last sentence clearly mirrors a famous one from Marx: 'Capital is dead labour, that, vampire-like, only lives by sucking living labour, and lives the more, the more labour it sucks.'[46] More than two decades after the split in the International, avowed anarchists were emphatically indebted to Marx's thought and ideas. Vaillant referred to history to justify his decision for violence; referring back to the French Revolution, Vaillant was quick to note that the current political settlement in France rested on a bedrock of violence: 'permit me to say that if the *bourgeois* had not committed massacres during the Revolution, they would most likely still be under the yoke of the *noblesse*'.[47] He condemned the role of the deputies he had attacked in sanctioning the violence of the French state against workers at home and oppressed colonial populations abroad. He charged them with hypocrisy: 'by the side of all this, how insignificant is the weight of that for which I am blamed to-day!'[48]

Vaillant then turned to the justification for propaganda of the deed, which he began with a succinct aphorism: 'I might have continued only to state our claims, but the deafer a person is the louder one has to speak to make himself heard.' He emphasized his view that the act of bombing was a form of communication: 'the explosion of my bomb is not only the cry of the revolted Vaillant, but that of an entire class demanding its rights, and soon destined to join deeds to words'.[49] For Vaillant, history – in true Enlightenment style – *was* progress. Ideas would have their time, 'for you may be sure that it will be all in vain [that] you make your laws. The ideas of those who think will not be stopped'.[50] He made the comparison with the Enlightenment and the ideas of the Revolution explicit:

> Just as in the last century all the forces of Government could not prevent the Diderots and the Voltaires from disseminating emancipating ideas among the people, so all the forces of Government today will not prevent the Reclus, the Darwins, the Spencers, the Ibsens, the Mirbeaus, and others from disseminating those ideas of justice and liberty which will break down the prejudices which keep the masses in ignorance, and these ideas, once received by the unfortunate, will ripen into acts of revolt, as they have done in me.[51]

'In this way', Vaillant continued,

> the process will continue until the disappearance of authority enables all men to organise themselves freely according to their affinities, so that each may enjoy the product of his labour. Then will disappear those moral maladies known as prejudices, and human beings will finally live in harmony, their only aspiration being the study of the sciences and the love of their fellows.[52]

When Vaillant was condemned, he was reported to have shouted 'Vive l'anarchie!'.[53] Vaillant's statement of his endeavours was in many ways unremarkable of anarchist testimonies, but as an historical source it is worth interrogating to elicit the complexities of anarchism in the age of propaganda of the deed. Vaillant drew on diverse intellectual influences and was compelled to cite them. The relationship between idea and action was important to him, and he conceived himself of being part of a broader transnational movement engaged in an international struggle against capital. Science also played a fundamental role in Vaillant's thinking; anarchism in his view was the triumph of the advance of reason – and the ultimate utopia that anarchism would inaugurate would leave humanity the time to 'study the sciences', a sentiment characteristic of Kropotkin's anarchist communism. More than that, Vaillant explicitly cited Darwin. Kropotkin had not yet published *Mutual Aid* – which would not appear until the next decade in book form – but the idea of scientific progress which Darwin represented was here invoked in the cause of anarchism.[54] Kropotkin had published his article 'The Scientific Bases of Anarchy' in the journal *Nineteenth Century* in 1887.[55]

Vaillant was deprecated as a serial failure in court, but he received a more sympathetic hearing from anarchists such as Malato abroad. This fitted with contemporary scholars who have examined the anarchist *attentats* of the 1890s as a precursor to modern terrorism, who have regarded the anarchist propagandists of the deed as 'radicalized' through poverty and marginalization.[56] These teleological and ahistorical readings obscure as much as they reveal; though anarchist propagandists of the deed did – as Merriman has argued – play a role in inaugurating 'the age of modern terror', they were not – as Merriman has also clarified – simply interchangeable with later terrorists.[57] Their actions were located in a specific context. One aspect of how is reflected in Vaillant's speech. Vaillant had said in the courtroom shortly before his declaration that he had evolved from propaganda of the word to propaganda of the deed: 'On returning from America I thought that I could be satisfied with the establishment of libraries to prepare brains for the revolution.' When he had ultimately decided 'not to delay to make my revolution myself', he conceived of it as part of a 'class soon destined to join deeds to words'.[58]

Vaillant's speech showed how the boundaries between 'deed' and 'word' as later understood could shift and be blurred. It emphasized the rootedness of the act in a broader ideological framing. But even in its own terms, it highlighted itself as an exceptional act, which while part of a broader movement raised the issue of the tensions at the heart of it. As John Merriman and Constance Bantman have shown, the impact of the memory and legacy of the Commune in terms of both the dispersal of individual Communards and the transformation of practice within the socialist, and specifically anarchist, movement was of real significance. The areas of Paris that fought hardest for the Commune were, according to Merriman, likely to foster and promote committed anarchist groups later – as he puts it representing 'continuities in space'.[59] The roots of propaganda of the deed have often been traced to Bakunin and his emphasis on immediate revolution – a stance in keeping with Vaillant's decision 'make [the] revolution' himself. Bakunin's relationship with Sergei Nechaev and his oft-alleged (and now highly debated) co-authorship of Nechaev's *Catechism of a Revolutionary*, which drew on Russian Nihilism to offer an amoral revolutionary doctrine, is customarily adduced as evidence (it is worth noting that the author of the standard history of anarchist terrorism, Bach Jensen, is unequivocal on Bakunin's rejection of Nechaev and repudiation of violence[60]). The debates in the anti-authoritarian International – which survived until the late 1870s – emphasized the task of the anarchist as propagandist, but the emphasis here was on the word, despite an increasing awareness of 'deeds'. And for most anarchists that was the propaganda they engaged in – that, and the propaganda of workplace organization. Newspapers and oratory, pamphlets and education (in the workplace and out of it) were to play critical roles for anarchist activity both up to the First World War and beyond.

Kropotkin, the principal anarchist thinker after Bakunin and the most significant anarchist thinker of all, was at best equivocal about propaganda of the deed and for his whole career emphasized the priority of the word. Bach Jensen notes Kropotkin's presence at the 1881 Social Revolutionary Congress which endorsed propaganda of the deed as a strategy, but also reminds us that 'in the debates [Kropotkin] voiced his preference for nonviolent propaganda'.[61] Indeed, Bach Jensen shows that the Congress' resolution in favour of developing bombs was encouraged by an *agent provocateur* of the French police.[62] Kropotkin, as with the majority of anarchists, envisaged violence within a particular context only: 'in the service of mass revolution, rather than . . . random acts of terror'.[63] In Bach Jensen's authoritative account, propaganda of the deed was a phenomenon which meant different things to different anarchists, and terrorism was but one, highly marginal, aspect of it. For the anarchist who originally coined the phrase, Paul Brousse, it could even mean illustrative acts such as the demonstration in Berne in 1877 where a red flag was brought out, intended 'simply to show the workers that they had no right to demonstrate in ostensibly free Switzerland'.[64] Indeed, for Caroline Cahm, the originator of the term 'propaganda of the deed' had in mind 'a token resistance', for all his articles celebrating violence which offended Kropotkin's sensibilities.[65]

Nonetheless, attacks attributed to anarchists grew in number from the late 1870s, hitting a peak in the 1890s, until they began to wane in the early twentieth century.[66] The 1881 assassination of Tsar Alexander II – to whom Kropotkin had once been a military page (aide) – at the hands of the Russian revolutionary group Narodnaya Volya ('People's Will') focused further attention on deeds, and in the course of the 1890s high-profile attacks became a regular occurrence.[67] In France, Vaillant's attack was followed by Emile Henry's bombing of a cafe at a railway station – the Cafe Terminus bombing. This shocked the public for its indiscriminate nature and has been represented as an evolution of terrorism from attacks on heads of state and officials to attacks on civilians, though Vaillant had said in his earlier courtroom speech that 'a sword of Damocles hangs over the bourgeois'.[68] Vaillant, facing death at the guillotine, uttered his last words in a shout: 'Vive l'anarchie! My death will be avenged!' (as Joll translates them).[69] It duly was; the president of the Republic, Sadi Carnot, was killed that December, stabbed in the heart with a dagger by an Italian anarchist named Santo Casiero. As Mitchell Abidor recounts, 'legend has it that the name "Vaillant" was inscribed upon it'.[70] In December 1901, another president would die – this time the US president William McKinley was assassinated by Leon Czolgosz. Emma Goldman found herself under arrest as a suspected accomplice.[71]

But anarchist opinions on propaganda of the deed-as-*attentat* varied both at the time and *with* time. Whilst Goldman in her 1931 memoir *Living My Life* was notably circumspect about the McKinley assassination, in her contemporary article written for the journal *Free Society* she was noticeably less ambiguous in her assessment. But even in 1931, Goldman recollected that in her thoughts whilst incarcerated on suspicion of involvement in the assassination she had regarded Czolgosz as a martyr:

> What was his life, I wondered; what the forces that drove him to this doom? 'I did it for the working people,' he was reported to have said. The people! Sasha also had done something for the people; and our brave Chicago martyrs, and the others in every

land and time. But the people are asleep; they remain indifferent. They forge their own chains and do the bidding of their masters to crucify their Christs.[72]

The Christian overtones, as Gabriel argues, are impossible to miss. Her defence of Czolgosz, published a month after the assassination, echoed Vaillant's own justifications from 1893. For Goldman, 'McKinley, more than any other President, had betrayed the trust of the people', presiding over the violence of capital and empire manifested at home and abroad in 'the blood of massacred Filipinos' who had died at the hands of American imperialism. As such, Czolgosz acted because of a 'strong social instinct, because of an abundance of love and an overflow of sympathy with the pain and sorrow around us'. She further argued – again in the spirit of Vaillant – for anarchism as the inexorable path of progress:

Some people have hastily said that Czolgosz's act was foolish and will check the growth of progress. Those worthy people are wrong in forming hasty conclusions. What results the act of September 6 will have no one can say; one thing, however, is certain: he has wounded government in its most vital spot. As to stopping the wheel of progress, that is absurd. Ideas cannot be retarded by restraint.[73]

Such defences of propaganda of the deed found detailed expression in Malatesta's earlier arguments on the subject. As with both Vaillant and Goldman, Malatesta was sanguine about the reality of the world in which the anarchists were making their arguments; most people he knew were unwilling to listen. Malatesta endorsed direct action as a means of fostering greater consciousness; Proudhon had made the intellectual argument about the injustices of property and capital, but that injustice had to be demonstrated and exemplified, he argued in the pages of the short-lived *L'Associazione*. Responding to a suggestion from a correspondent that anarchists should commemorate their anniversaries with public acts of theft and expropriation which would illustrate the reality of oppression and create the conditions for propaganda of the word, Malatesta 'whole-heartedly endorse[d]' it.[74] 'Action of this sort', he continued, offers the double advantage of a direct assault on property and of being feasible for all . . . private ownership is the foundation upon which the entire edifice of exploitation, oppression, infamy, corruption, hate, vice, criminality and warfare making up much vaunted modern civilisation rests.[75]

'The great revolution', Malatesta reminded his readers, 'the mass uprising will come as a result of relentless propaganda and an exceptional number of individual and collective revolts'.[76] But by 1894 and the wake of the Cafe Terminus bombing, Malatesta was more wary of *attentats*: 'We cannot, and we ought not to be either avengers, nor dispensers of justice. Our task, our ambitions, our ideal is to be deliverers.'[77]

Though the popular image of anarchism became indelibly associated with propaganda by the deed, it is true to say that it was never more than a marginal current within anarchist practice. In the context of France, it also had a very specific location in the wake of the repression of the Commune and as part of the French 'illegalist' tradition.[78] 'Deed' also meant different things to different anarchists, and the boundaries between 'deeds' and 'words' were considerably more ambiguous than much subsequent commentary has rendered them. As Bach Jensen succinctly puts it, 'the equivocation over the exact meaning of "propaganda by the deed," and whether it justified individual terrorism or not, was never to be decisively resolved or clarified by the anarchists.'[79]

Propaganda of the word: Publishing, journalism, translation

Journalism is perhaps the most immediately recognizable form of 'propaganda of the word' which anarchists engaged in in the period up to the First World War. The extent of the anarchist press and its distribution also keenly emphasizes the significance of transnationalism and networks in the 'age of globalisation'.[80] Such connections and transitions were critical not merely to didactic propaganda but, as Constance Bantman and David Berry have argued, to the reformulation and remaking of anarchism:

physical journeys should also be read as journeys of the mind: the atypical trajectories depicted here are both physical and figurative, the crossing of borders – physical and ideological – often go together.[81]

The establishment of the *Freedom* newspaper in London in the course of 1886 – a newspaper that was to survive in print until 2014 – was but one example of a global trend of anarchist propaganda of the word.[82] *Freedom* made regular use of international correspondents and reprints of articles from foreign publications to build a sense of an anarchist community that spanned the globe. Benedict Anderson claims that 'anarchists were the most productive translators of the era – out of need'.[83] *Freedom* republished speeches given by anarchists and extracts of books, with Kropotkin's work central to its project.

Proudhon as we have seen advanced his ideas effectively through the radical French press from the 1840s, and as a conscious anarchist movement began to develop from the 1860s and then more substantively following the split in the International, so did a plethora of anarchist papers. Kropotkin alone was involved in numerous ventures. In 1879 he founded *Le Revolte* with money from Élisée Reclus; it ran until 1914, changing its name in 1895 to *Les Temps Nouveaux*.[84] Jean Grave took over as editor after Kropotkin's expulsion from Switzerland in 1883.[85] In the United States, one of the longest-running anarchist newspapers in the world, *Fraye Arbeter Shtime* – 'the Free Voice of Labor' – was founded in New York in 1890.[86] It finally ceased publication in 1977. *Fraye Arbeter Shtime* was part of a flourishing Jewish anarchist community in New York in the period before the First World War, where the shared experience of immigration and marginalization played a key role in fostering an anarchist consciousness.[87] Mollie Steimer immigrated to the United States from the Russian Empire at the age of fifteen, subsequently working in the garment trade. By nineteen she was a friend of Emma Goldman's and had founded an anarchist group which was committed to propaganda by the deed. During the First World War, she was involved in the publication of a newspaper – *Frayhayt* – which was an underground publication due to its opposition to the war. She was ultimately arrested and deported from the United States.[88] As Carl Levy notes, there were 'Yiddish-speaking communities of Jewish anarchists who thrived in the "Yiddishland" of East-Central Europe and the Czarist Empire, as well as in the cosmopolitan world cities of London, Paris, New York and Buenos Aires'.[89]

Malatesta's L'Associazone began its life in Nice so it could be smuggled into Italy, before it was necessary to relocate it to London where it concluded its short run. Newspapers were regularly smuggled across frontiers, Most's Die Freiheit being smuggled into Germany.[90] Rudolf Rocker, later to become the major theorist of anarcho-syndicalism, was involved in a number of anarchist periodicals during his exile in Britain, including the short-lived paper Dos Fraye Vort ('The Free Word') based in Liverpool and subsequently Arbeter Freint and Germinal, both based in London.[91]

In engaging in prolific journalistic activity, anarchists were building a 'counterpublic', a space where their own ideas and activism could flourish against the hegemonic social and political ideas of their time.[92] They were both building their own community and engaging in internal dialogue, and propagandizing to the broader public. It ensured the development of different strands of anarchist theory and practice. In Buenos Aires, the newspaper La Voz de la Mujer articulated an anarchist feminist critique at the end of the nineteenth century, as Maxine Molyneux has shown.[93] In Japan, the anarcha-feminist Kanno Suga had been 'one of Japan's first female journalists' before the First World War.[94] Kanno was executed in 1911 after being convicted alongside other anarchists in what was known as the 'High Treason Incident', a plot to kill the Japanese emperor (though as Bowen Raddeker notes, 'most of the defendants sentenced had been entirely ignorant of the conspirators' plans').[95] Bowen Raddeker also notes the 'political career' of Suga's fellow anarchist, Itô Noe, which

> was similar to Suga's in that she, too, became a commentator on women's issues, in increasingly radical magazines. The first of these was the journal Bluestocking (Seitô) from 1911, in which Noe's contributions included translations of a few essays by Emma Goldman.[96]

As Laursen has shown, in Britain the anarchist Guy Aldred became involved with the Indian independence movement through his support for the nationalist activist Shyamaji Krishnavarma and Krishnavarma's publication the *Indian Sociologist*.[97] Even where anarchists were supporting a wider milieu of revolutionary publications and interventions in the written space, they conceived of themselves as doing so in the service of the anarchist cause – though Laursen is critical of Aldred's self-delusions.[98] Nonetheless, at least two of the friends Aldred made through his enterprise became anarchists – Har Dayal and M. P. T. Acharya – and they would remake anarchism in an Indian context as a consequence.[99] The printed word was one network; education was another.

Words or deeds? Education

One means by which propaganda of the word could be effectively carried out beyond the level of journalism and oratory was through the provision of education. In the nineteenth century the extension of state educational provision globally was itself an intrinsic part of state formation for the modern nation-state.[100] As such, for anarchists, it was a key site of contestation. Propaganda of the word was itself education, with Haia Shpayer-Makov noting that 'throughout this most active period in its history, the movement placed primary emphasis on the education of the masses through reason'.[101] As Matthew Thomas has argued, the question of education animated the wider socialist movement beyond the anarchists, 'since socialists of all persuasions saw children as the harbingers of the future, a social force that could transform society'.[102] The anarchist school movement became closely associated with the influence of Francisco Ferrer, whose *Escuela Moderna* (Modern School) was founded in Barcelona in 1901.[103] Anarchist, or at least libertarian, interest in education long predated Ferrer, however. William Godwin, often incorporated within the 'anarchist canon' as the first major thinker to develop a substantively 'anarchistic' critique in his 1793 volume *An Enquiry Concerning Political Justice*, had also been involved in developing a proposal for a libertarian school in 1783.[104] For Godwin, the legitimacy of the state and the extent to which it could depend on citizens for its support rested on the principles inculcated through education. To change that, education had to be contested. As he put it in his prospectus for the seminary at Epsom, 'Let the most oppressed people under heaven change their mode of thinking and they are free . . . our moral dispositions and character depend very much, perhaps entirely, on education.'[105]

Ferrer for his part had been a Republican radical involved in an unsuccessful 1885 rising which had resulted in his exile to France. In Paris, he was involved in education and acted as a language tutor to a wealthy Parisian – Mlle. Meunier – whom he eventually won over to the cause of libertarian education and whose legacy funded the foundation of the modern school. In Paris and London Ferrer mixed with the radical diaspora and amongst others met Michel and Malato.[106] Ferrer's own reflections offer some insight into the lack of a firm binary between words and deeds in the debate over anarchist propaganda:

> After a while, it seemed to me that we were wasting time if we were not prepared to go on from words to deeds. To be in possession of an important privilege through the imperfect organisation of society and by the accident of birth, to conceive ideas of reform, and to remain inactive or indifferent amid a life of pleasure, seemed to me to incur a responsibility similar to that of a man who refused to lend a hand to a person whom he could save from danger.[107]

For Ferrer it was clear that deeds were a higher order of activity, and for him education constituted propaganda of the deed, rather than merely the word. In Ferrer's schema, education was to be non-hierarchical, to celebrate the individuality of the pupil, to be led by the pupil's interests and to avoid the conformity imposed by standardization so beloved of the state. Ferrer believed in educating without segregation of gender, as he also believed in educating social classes together. There was to be 'no reward or punishment'. In his book, published posthumously in English, he reflected with some measure of satisfaction on the success of his endeavour, noting the numbers on roll.[108] Ferrer was also interested in developing the possibility of a 'modern university' and also based a printing house within the school, which published texts by anarchists such as Malato and Élisée Reclus.[109]

Ferrer was shot in Montjuich prison in 1909 after being held on charges of involvement in organizing a rebellion in Barcelona.[110] As Avrich notes, his 'martyrdom' caused an international outcry and also ensured that his educational legacy was more closely examined outside of Spain, with the modern school movement in the United States and elsewhere drawing on Ferrer's example.[111] In Britain, as Thomas has shown, anarchist schools had existed for some time before Ferrer, Wilson and Michel's International School in Fitzroy Square in London having been founded in 1890.[112] Thomas shows that Michel's school – like Ferrer's later effort – was organized around a concept of integral education – *education integrale* – which sought to end the divide between 'brain work' and manual work.[113] This was an important precursor for an anarchist society where the community as a whole would have the opportunity to participate in all kinds of work and where its egalitarianism rested on the premise that this would ensure an equitable division of tasks, as Kropotkin would later discuss in *The Conquest of Bread* and *Fields, Factories and Workshops*. The wider anarchist milieu in London was involved in the administration and work of the school, as Thomas shows, with Kropotkin, Morris and Malatesta all serving on the committee and Charlotte Wilson teaching alongside Michel.[114] One observer visiting a history class noted that they were teaching anarchist history; the lesson was on the subject of the Haymarket martyrs.[115] The school lasted until 1893 when it closed; it transpired that one of the teachers had been an agent of the French police.[116]

In Whitechapel, a libertarian school was again founded in 1906, whilst in Liverpool an anarchist communist Sunday School was established in 1908 which subsequently 'affiliated to Ferrer's League for the Rational Education of Children'.[117] In John Shotton's account, the Liverpool school was in part the product of a meeting between its founder, Jimmy Dick, and Ferrer himself, who visited Liverpool in 1907.[118] The lectures offered by speakers at the school featured a familiar range of topics, including the Commune.[119] After Ferrer's execution the school renamed itself 'the International Modern School' in honour of Ferrer's vision and published a pamphlet, 'The Martyrdom of Francisco Ferrer'.[120] The anarchist school movement spread to the United States and beyond, but as

David Gribble argues anarchist influences in education went further and were more abiding.[121] In Judith Suissa's assessment, Ferrer saw his school as the 'embryo of the future, anarchist society; as proof that, even within the authoritarian society surrounding it, an alternative was possible'.[122] This echoed Bakunin's views on the First International itself – further developed in the anti-authoritarian International – of the organization acting as an anarchist society *within* wider society.[123] This symbolized the anarchist principle of prefiguration, as it came to be known later in the twentieth century: the unity of means and ends. Effecting the social revolution might be done through propaganda, but particular kinds of activism could be the revolution themselves. One such was syndicalism.

Syndicalism: 'Building a new world in the shell of the old'

What was syndicalism? At its simplest, syndicalism was revolutionary unionism. As two recent historians of syndicalism, Hirsch and van der Walt put it:

> Syndicalism . . . refers to a form of revolutionary trade unionism, centred on the view that revolutionary union action can establish a collectivised, worker-managed social order resting on union structures.[124]

For the political scientist F. F. Ridley, syndicalism was 'the direct action of its time', 'a movement rather than a theory'.[125] As it developed in the late nineteenth and early twentieth centuries, it evolved as a school of practice rather than ideology which conceived of industrial action in holistic and militant terms. Unlike 'craft unionism', which sought to organize workers discretely and hierarchically by craft and skill, in American parlance syndicalism was a form – at least – of revolutionary industrial unionism, which sought to organize workers across labour divides. In the European model which linked the Spanish and French experiences, it was based on local organization, federated to form a larger whole, drawing distinct emphases from Proudhon's thinking on workers' associations and Bakunin's emphasis on direct action and immediate revolution.[126] The term 'anarcho-syndicalism', representing a distinctively anarchist orientation within syndicalism (or a syndicalist orientation within anarchism), took longer to emerge, and despite the definite anarchist influences within syndicalism up to 1914 it remained the case that there were significant numbers of syndicalists who identified as Marxists as well as anarchists, in addition to many syndicalists who identified as neither.[127] But fundamentally syndicalism was a mass practice that was not satisfied with winning industrial disputes; it sought to destroy capitalism.

As Kenyon Zimmer, Steven Hirsch and Lucien van der Walt have noted, the rise of syndicalism has often erroneously been attributed – in classic political theory fashion – to the work of George Sorel.[128] But Sorel's writings and activity were marginal to the lived experience of syndicalism, which was a movement influenced by anarchist ideas and one which would increasingly be associated with anarchism explicitly.[129] In the Chicago of the 1880s, the 'Chicago Idea' of democratic, revolutionary unionism coupled with insurrectionary activity represented the beginning of a syndicalist trend in the United States.[130] In France, the Charter of Amiens codified by the Confédération générale du travail (CGT) in 1906 is a canonical point of reference for the significance of syndicalism within the French trade union movement. The Charter spelled out the political significance of militant activity within the economic sphere:

> In daily protest work the union pursues the coordination of working class efforts, and the growth of the well being of workers, through the carrying out of immediate improvements, such as the diminution in work hours, the increase in salaries, etc. But this task is only one side of the work of syndicalism: it prepares complete emancipation, which can only be fulfilled by expropriation of the capitalists; it advocates as a method of action the general strike; and it considers that the union, today a resistance group will be, in the future, a group for production and redistribution, the basis of social reorganization.[131]

In this passage, concerns for the material improvement of the workers' present conditions are united with a political programme to be pursued through the use of economic power. This framing defined syndicalist unions as 'not reformist, as [they do] not confine itself to reforms . . . fighting for reforms is a means of systematically accumulating power and capacity for a class war'.[132]

Despite Malatesta's misgivings, syndicalism became increasingly influential in countries where he had organized (though he remained impressed by the power of strike action). Malatesta for his part worried that syndicalists, despite their good intentions, by confining themselves to union activism might find themselves being co-opted by the capitalist system in the same way the craft unions had been. In Britain, a syndicalist 'moment' took place in the period from 1910 to 1914, when during the 'Great Unrest' organized labour posed a serious and credible political challenge.[133] In South America, syndicalist organizations dominated several labour movements. In Argentina, the Federación Obrera Regional Argentina (FORA) was founded in 1901, and though it later split into rival organizations, it ensured the Argentinian labour struggle had at its heart 'an anarchist "mass movement"' with 250,000 members in the two syndicalist FORAs by the 1920s.[134] This was paralleled in Cuba, whilst in South Africa as van der Walt has shown syndicalist unions offered an opportunity for Black workers denied membership of craft unions to engage in industrial conflict and political conflict across racial lines.[135]

The North American experience of industrial unionism and the experience of syndicalism in Europe and the global South are, strictly speaking, related but distinct, though – as above – they are often discussed together due to their common features. Pivotal to the memory of industrial unionism and syndicalism in the United States (and around the world) is the Haymarket affair of 1886–7. On 4 May 1886, following the shooting of strikers by police the previous day, a demonstration was held in Haymarket Square in Chicago, organized by a number of prominent anarchist union leaders. As the meeting was drawing to a close, an unknown assailant threw a bomb at police; eight were killed. At least four demonstrators were shot by police. Eight prominent anarchists – only some of whom had been involved in the demonstration – were subsequently arrested: August Spies, Adolph Fischer, Albert Parsons, Samuel Fielden, Louis Lingg, Michael Schwab, George Engel and Oscar Neebe. Seven were sentenced to death; Neebe was ultimately sentenced to fifteen years in jail,

Schwab was belatedly pardoned, as was Neebe. Lingg committed suicide in prison. Four were executed on 11 November 1887. Spies – at the gallows – famously uttered the last words 'the day will come when our silence will be more powerful than the voices you strangle here today'.[136] The Haymarket affair sparked an international outcry due to the weakness of the case against the anarchists, who became known as the Haymarket martyrs. As Zimmer has noted, the case identified the anarchists strongly with the campaign for the eight-hour day which had sparked the initial strikes and demonstrations, even though they themselves were sceptical of it as potentially leading to accommodation with the capitalist system.[137] Haymarket became an immortal memory in the anarchist and syndicalist traditions, and gave rise to International Workers Day on the 1st of May. Haymarket stood as an iconic moment when the state stood against the workers and murdered them. As we have seen, it was a story told in anarchist schools in the decades which followed.

Lucy Parsons, anarchist communist and anarcha-feminist, was one of the founders of the IWW in 1905, again in Chicago. Albert Parsons's widow, she was a pivotal figure in American social anarchism and labour organizing in the decades before the First World War. The IWW was founded a year before the CGT formalized the Charter of Amiens, and it sought workplace democracy and workers' control of industry, key syndicalist emphases. In the Preamble to the IWW's Constitution, a class analysis was offered which emphasized the reality of a 'dichotomous' class system[138]:

> The working class and the employing class have nothing in common . . . Between these two classes a struggle must go on until the workers of the world organise as a class, take possession of the means of production, abolish the wage system, and live in harmony with the Earth.[139]

In the *Syndicalist* newspaper which was published in Britain in 1912, similar sentiments were expressed as follows:

> CLASS WAR against capitalism, such war having for its object the CAPTURE OF THE INDUSTRIAL SYSTEM and its management by the workers themselves for the benefit of the whole community.[140]

For Benedict Anderson, anarchism – with syndicalism at its heart – was the 'dominant element in the self-consciously internationalist radical Left' in the period up to the outbreak of the First World War.[141] This was explicable in a number of ways. The theoretical analysis at the heart of the Marxist project and the emphasis by socialist parties on inroads within existing political systems after the split in the First International did not cohere with the lived experience of the bulk of workers globally. The dismissive attitude Marxism maintained towards peasants and rural workers in favour of its idealized industrial proletariat was not shared by anarchism, and syndicalism as a mass practice of workers' control and democratic unionism was able to transcend different workplace experiences.[142] Syndicalism, as noted earlier, represented a synthesis between means and ends – the unity articulated in anarchist positions in the debates during the 'socialist schism' of 1872. Syndicalism was a 'method' embraced by anarchists as it represented an expression of anarchist values. It represented conflict in the economic, not the political, sphere. It represented a radically democratic form of action, which rejected the bureaucracies of 'traditional' unions. In its aspirations for workers' control of industry – where workers could self-manage industry through their revolutionary unions – it echoed Proudhon's thinking on the priority of workers' associations. Where it differed was in its embrace of the revolutionary general strike – encapsulated by the IWW leader 'Big' Bill Haywood's memorable phrase of the workforce successfully destroying capitalism having 'folded [their] arms'.[143]

Within the historical literature one consistent emphasis is on syndicalism as a method of anarchist practice which 'succeeded' propaganda of the deed, with the *attentat* having demonstrated its ultimate ineffectiveness, not least through damaging the 'image' of anarchism as a movement and industrial conflict representing a more consistent and effective anarchist 'means' to effect revolutionary change. Marshall's assessment of the Spanish situation is representative: 'the anarchists soon recognized the inability of terrorism to overthrow the State and turned to propaganda among the workers and peasants'.[144] Yet as Zimmer shows, syndicalism did not in truth represent an 'either/or' with violence. The 'Chicago Idea' of the 1880s – of mass union activity coupled with a determination to build paramilitary force for ultimate revolt, spearheaded in the case of the Independent Working People's Association (IWPA) by a number of anarchists including some of the Haymarket martyrs – was not syndicalism, though it was a precursor.

Syndicalism relied on the embrace of the revolutionary general strike as a tactic to force the capitalist class to its knees and inaugurate the transformation of society through the practice of workers' control. But equally, syndicalism did not preclude violence, either. The most famous anarcho-syndicalist union was the Confederación Nacional del Trabajo (CNT), founded in 1910.[145] By the 1930s it would number around 1.5 million members, and it would play a key role in the Spanish Civil War and the anarchist revolution which took place during it (see Chapter 3). In its campaigns in the 1920s, it would frequently use violence, not least in self-defence due to the practice of employers hiring gunmen to target trade unionists.[146] The CNT unlike other syndicalist unions was explicitly an anarchist-led organization (as Woodcock notes) from the start.[147] Writing in 1938, the chief theorist of anarcho-syndicalism, Rudolf Rocker – who himself had been involved in labour organizing in London's East End before 1914 – argued that syndicalism and anarcho-syndicalism were possible through 'the development of solidarity' engendered through the lived experience of class struggle:

> It grows into the vital consciousness of a community of fate, and this gradually develops into a new sense of right and becomes the preliminary ethical assumption of every effort at the liberation of an oppressed class . . . To cherish and strengthen this natural solidarity of the workers and to give to every strike movement a more profoundly social character, is one of the most important tasks which the Anarcho-Syndicalists have set themselves.[148]

For Rocker, syndicalism and anarcho-syndicalism represented, as in the IWW's preamble, the opportunity to build the new world in the shell of the old, based on anti-hierarchical premises and enunciating anarchist values of direct action and mutual aid. This last principle was developed most profoundly by Peter Kropotkin, who sought to contest the bounded rationalities of nineteenth-century science in a way Rocker's syndicalists put into practice, and it is to his thought we turn now.

'Modern science and anarchy': Kropotkin, mutual aid and anarchist communism

Rocker prefaced his book with some reflections on the ambitions of anarchism. To state these, he drew on the greatest of anarchist theoreticians, Kropotkin. Kropotkin's contribution to the development of anarchist theory and practice is hard to overstate. His contribution to the movement over decades was vast. During his London period after 1886 he composed most of his major works, which customarily began as articles in periodicals before subsequently appearing as books. This mode of composition, taken together with Kropotkin's avowed goals as an anarchist propagandist, explains the readability and enduring nature of his texts – particularly *The Conquest of Bread*, first published in 1892, which offered a comprehensive if succinct introduction to a potential anarchist communist society.

In Rocker's assessment, the theory of mutual aid had been Kropotkin's most vital contribution:

> Anarchism found a valuable advocate in Peter Kropotkin, who set himself the task of making the achievements of modern natural science available for the development of the sociological concepts of Anarchism. In his ingenious book, *Mutual Aid – a Factor of Evolution*, he entered the lists against so-called *Social Darwinism*, whose exponents tried to prove the inevitability of the existing social conditions from the Darwinian theory of the struggle for existence by raising the struggle of the strong against the weak to the status of an iron law for all natural processes, to which even man is subject. In reality this conception was strongly influenced by the Malthusian doctrine that life's table is not spread for all, and that the unneeded will just have to reconcile themselves to this fact.[149]

The magnitude of the challenge Kropotkin embraced accounts in part for why he has been subsequently discredited as a thinker by those hostile to his views, including critics on the left. Kropotkin, like Proudhon and Bakunin before him, styled himself as an interpreter of change rather than a 'system-builder'. Where he differed, however, is that whilst he did not conceive of himself as a theoretician in the way often criticized by anarchists who sought to ground their movement in practice, he recognized the significance of defending and promoting anarchism as a scientific endeavour. This was in sharp contrast to Bakunin, who had seen attempts to treat politics as science as 'political theology'.[150] Kropotkin sought to contest the ground with Marxism, but in part because he felt that arguing for anarchism's practicality relied on doing so. Proudhon had been compelled to contest Malthus's legacy; Kropotkin, a self-trained geographer who during his brief military career had sought postings in Siberia and Manchuria to avoid more distasteful service and who had conducted surveys in the field, knew that anarchism had to confront social Darwinism, as Rocker remembered.

By the 1880s vernacularized Darwinian ideas had been introduced into popular discussion of social policy.[151] In Britain, the debate between T. H. Huxley and Matthew Arnold on the nature of education reflected this, as did the developing body of eugenicist and 'racial science', which sought to attribute to innate characteristics 'degenerate traits' such as criminality and intellectual inferiority. Though the purchase of eugenics on policy in Nazi Germany in the 1930s and its horrific consequences is well known, the pervasiveness of eugenics in social policy regimes around the world and its persistence to the present day is less commented on. Cesare Lombroso, a phrenologist who advocated for the supposedly 'scientific' study of race through the examination of individuals' heads and features, published a number of works outlining his theories of criminality and racial degeneration in the course of the 1890s. Several focused on anarchists.[152] Eugenics, as Daniel J. Kevles has shown, was far more pervasive, however; it – and social Darwinist discourses – influenced a wide range of social policies including education policy; in Britain, intelligence testing for secondary school entry would become widespread as late as 1944.[153] Social Darwinism rested on what Kropotkin saw as a corruption of Darwinist thought. Social Darwinism argued that a logic of competition was intrinsic to the natural world; it could not be escaped; as Rocker put it, it was an 'iron law'. Social policies had to be developed in light of that, and economics through markets was most successful when it emphasized *competition* over *cooperation*. Though the star of Malthus had fallen somewhat in the course of the nineteenth century, social Darwinism based on a vernacularized understanding of natural selection threatened to give 'a pseudo-scientific gloss' to policies which entrenched the interests of the rich at the expense of the poor, positing hierarchy as inevitable and life in the state of nature, as Hobbes long before had put it, as 'nasty, brutish, and short'.[154] This 'scientization' of inequality provided additional legitimacy for the state and its coercive apparatus, and legitimized nationalism and militarism in turn. As Iain McKay puts it, Kropotkin was the 'first post-Darwinian socialist'.[155]

In response, Kropotkin developed the theory of mutual aid, which was central to his thought, and it is the mischaracterization of this theory by his opponents and by subsequent writers that has led to the contention, made frequently in the political theory literature, influenced by both classical contractarian political theory and Marxism, that anarchists have an overly optimistic view of human nature.[156] Benedict Anderson summed up the Marxist view of anarchism succinctly, noting that 'orthodox Marxist politicians and intellectuals . . . long cast anarchism, "utopian" rather than "scientific", into the dustbin of history, and created a good deal of falsified historiography to ensure that it stayed there'.[157] Even in his own time Kropotkin was aware of the dismissive air of those who characterized anarchism as 'utopian'; in the chapter on food in *The Conquest of Bread* he met that challenge head-on with the lines

> That we are utopians is well known. So utopian are we that we go to the length of believing that the revolution can and ought to assure shelter, food and clothes to all – an idea extremely displeasing to middle-class citizens, whatever their party colour, for they are quite alive to the fact it is not easy to keep the upper hand of people whose hunger is satisfied.[158]

In *Mutual Aid*, arguably his most significant yet controversial book, Kropotkin argued that he was correcting a common misperception of Darwin. He stated that during his travels in Siberia and Manchuria, what he had seen with his own eyes had been 'the extreme severity of the struggle for existence which most species of animals have to carry on against an inclement nature'.[159] He had not, on the other hand, seen – though he was 'eagerly looking for it' that bitter struggle for the means of existence, among animals belonging to the same species, which was considered by most Darwinists (though not always by Darwin himself) as the dominant characteristic of the struggle for life, and the main factor of evolution.[160]

Kropotkin saw something else. What he found was that within species cooperation against a hostile environment was paramount in determining survival. He argued purposefully that this went beyond 'love'; that instead there was

> the conscience – be it only at the state of an instinct – of human solidarity. It is the unconscious recognition of the force that is borrowed from each man from the practice of mutual aid; of the close dependency of every one's happiness and on the happiness of all; and of the sense of justice, or equity, which brings the individual to consider the rights of every other individual as equal to their own.[161]

Kropotkin believed that the bastardization of Darwin's ideas on natural selection – trivialized as the 'survival of the fittest' – had been misinterpreted out of context to legitimate the existing social order. This 'one single generalisation . . . soon became the very basis of our philosophical, biological, and sociological speculations'.[162] Kropotkin then turned to sketch mutual aid amongst animals, showing how species did practice mutual aid beyond the level of kin. He then turned – as he was wont – to an assessment of the historical record, arguing for the principle of cooperation as evidenced in guilds and medieval city-states, before turning in the recent past and the present to labour unions and a famous favourite of Kropotkin's – the lifeboat association. For him, this last encapsulated the reality of mutual aid and was a convincing rebuttal to the economics of the dismal science: human beings risking and sacrificing their lives for the benefit of people they did not know and for no material gain.[163]

As Kinna has argued, Kropotkin's theory served a specific political purpose, but in this he was – as Rocker put it – 'entering the lists' against those invoking the 'science' of Darwinism to legitimate inequality and capitalism. By contrast, Kropotkin's theory of mutual aid legitimized his anarchist communism, a society which synthesized liberty without government with the distributive principle of 'from each according to their ability, to each according to their need'. This was the vision hinted at in Vaillant's courtroom speech at his trial. Though *Mutual Aid* had not been published at the time of Vaillant's trial, the articles which made up its chapters had been (in *Nineteenth Century*). Vaillant invoked science in his defence and argument for anarchism. Kropotkin had made that possible.

Kropotkin's social anarchism was a marked evolution on Bakunin's thought. Whereas Proudhon had not rejected competition and whereas Bakunin had still felt differentials might be necessary in relation to rewarding contribution, Kropotkin rejected both premises. He couched his advocacy of anarchist communism in scientific, 'sociological' terms:

> We are beginning to think of society as a whole, each part of which is so intimately bound up with the others that a service rendered to one is a service rendered to all. When you go into a public library . . . the librarian does not ask what services you have rendered to society before giving you the book, or the fifty books, which you require . . . By means of uniform credentials . . .. the scientific society opens its museums, its gardens, its library, its laboratories, and its annual conversaziones to each of its members, whether he be a Darwin or a simple amateur. . . In the same way, those who man the lifeboat to not ask credentials from the crew of a sinking ship . . . Thus we find a tendency, eminently communistic, springing up on all sides, and in various guises, in the very heart of theoretically individualist societies.[164]

Kropotkin's ideas reached a wide audience not merely through his books but, as McKay has argued, through his journalism.[165] He was a prolific writer, who was accessible and who took his mission as a propagandist seriously. His propaganda helped secure the status of anarchist communism as the prevailing school of anarchist ideology outside of syndicalism, though many anarcho-syndicalists conceived of the post-revolutionary society as a communist one. At the outbreak of the First World War, anarchism developed both theories – despite the claims of Marxists then and since – and a mass movement in a number of countries. Despite the characteristic historiographical view of the First World War and the rise of the Soviet Union as twin nails in the anarchist coffin, the greatest experiments were yet to come.

Conclusion: A 'first anarchist moment'?

The writing of anarchism back into global history in the several decades prior to the outbreak of the First World War is a project now well advanced. As Anderson has argued, the privileging of Marxism in accounts of global socialist movements is ill-founded and represents an older historiography mired in partisan accounts. The anarchist turn in contemporary historiography emphasizes the significance of anarchism globally in the period up to 1914, examining the emergence of an anarchist diaspora through the age of the 'first globalization', one which in its activists and encounters changed and reframed its own praxis. With syndicalism as a mass practice of revolutionary activity in many countries in the years prior to the outbreak of war, and a widespread dissemination of anarchist ideas through publishing, translation and the anarchist press, anarchism offered a coherent and pliable framework for the ambitions of workers and the oppressed around the globe. Anarchist uprisings took place in Spain and Italy, titanic industrial action was waged by syndicalist unions and propaganda of the deed ensured that anarchism – however 'grievously misconstrued' as Charlotte Wilson would have it – played an integral role in the constitution of the modern 'political subject', to borrow Claudia Verhoeven's phrase.[166]

As David Goodway and his colleagues argued in 1989, the historiography – such as it was – to that point had argued teleologically that anarchism had been predoomed to fail.[167] It ran counter, so it was argued, to the nature of modernity itself. It was backward-looking, embraced fantastical views of history and utopian ideas of society, and relied on deeply flawed assumptions regarding human nature. It was, as Lenin would later put it in relation to left communism and anarchism, 'an infantile disorder'.[168] But as this chapter has shown, the evolution of the historiography in the course of the past several decades has illustrated the fundamental inaccuracy of this assessment, at least in terms of anarchism's historical impact and relevance. Though never a dominant political current, anarchism was hugely influential on the left globally up to the outbreak of the First World War and even where it did not take substantive root as a mass movement (as in Britain) it was influential on the wider socialist milieu in ways that have been too easily dismissed. As Anderson has argued, anarchism's intrinsic internationalism ensured that it was able to offer a fundamental critique of the state and colonialism at the height of nationalism, and it benefited from an analysis which allowed adaptation to local circumstances. Anarchism's prospects – if not bright, then certainly through the medium of syndicalism, alive and well – at the outset of the First World War, suffered severe challenges in the wake of it. The arrival of the Soviet Union as a countervailing, and antithetical, force on the international left after the Bolshevik Revolution of 1917 would pose severe problems. So too would the split in the movement itself occasioned by the Manifesto of the Sixteen, where a number of prominent anarchists, including Kropotkin, took the side of the allies in what other anarchists (such as Malatesta) regarded straightforwardly as an imperialist war. But for all the oft-cited caveats about the impact of the First World War upon anarchism, it remains the case that the greatest examples of all of 'anarchy in action' – the anarchist revolutions in Russia and Spain – were yet to come, and it is these we consider next.

Further reading

Anarchism in the 'first globalization'

Constance Bantman's *French Anarchists in London, 1880-1914: Exile and Transnationalism in the First Globalisation* (2013) is a superb study of the anarchist diaspora and the dissemination of anarchist ideas and praxis in the late nineteenth century. Benedict Anderson's *The Age of Globalization: Anarchists and the Anticolonial Imagination* (2013) is also vital. Alex Prichard, Ruth Kinna, Saku Pinta and David Berry's edited collection *Libertarian Socialism: Politics in Black and Red* (2012) also has a wide range of essays highlighting the ways in which libertarian socialisms crossed borders in the period (not least the introduction).

Propaganda of the deed

The standard history of anarchist terrorism is Richard Bach Jensen, *The Battle Against Anarchist Terrorism* (2014), though its perspective is largely – as the title implies – focused on the efforts against it rather than propaganda of the deed in itself. Constance Bantman's essay 'The Era of Propaganda of the Deed' in the *Palgrave Handbook of Anarchism* (2019) should be a vital starting point for any student wishing to gain an understanding of the historical context of propaganda of the deed and its ultimate implications. Mitchell Abidor's collection of primary sources *Death to Bourgeois Society* (2016) is extremely useful, and John Merriman's scholarly assessment of propaganda of the deed in France, *The Dynamite Club* (2009), is essential.

Syndicalism

The edited collection by Steven Hirsch and Lucien van der Walt, *Anarchism and Syndicalism in the Colonial and Postcolonial World, 1870-1940: The Praxis of National Liberation, Internationalism, and Social Revolution* (2010), is vital to understand syndicalism in historical perspective, not least in terms of its relationship with anarchism globally. Constance Bantman and Bert Altena's edited collection *Reassessing the Transnational Turn: Scales of Analysis in Anarchist and Syndicalist Studies* (2014) is a key text, as is David Berry and Constance Bantman (eds.), *New Perspectives on Anarchism, Labour and Syndicalism* (2010). Rudolf Rocker's *Anarcho-Syndicalism: Theory and Practice* (1938) remains an essential text.

3

European anarchisms?

Russia and Spain

*I owe it to you to say frankly that, according to my view,
this effort to build a communist republic on the basis
of a strongly centralized state communism under the
iron law of party dictatorship is bound to end in failure.
We are learning to know in Russia how not to introduce
communism, even with a people tired of the old regime
and opposing no active resistance to the experiments of
the new rulers.*

–PETER KROPOTKIN, 'Message to the Workers of the Western World' (1920)[1]

[T]he state is a virus that can take hold in each of us.

–JOSÉ PEIRATS, *Anarchists in the Spanish Revolution* (1974)[2]

Introduction: Anarchism, Marxism and the politics of memory

The Russian Revolution of 1917 and the Spanish Civil War are key
reference points for the contemporary anarchist movement. Over
time, the memory of both has been incorporated into an anarchist
liturgy, through which the anarchist 'past' is framed. Central to this

has been the issue of anarchism's relationship to Marxism.[3] For anarchists – including anarchist historians such as Robert Graham and Iain McKay – the lived experience of the Russian Revolution and the development of the Soviet Union which followed was vindication of Bakunin's critique of Marx in the First International. In Spain, so anarchist memory runs, an anarchist revolution was defeated as much by the efforts of Stalin and state socialism as it was by Franco. Taken together, as the two events often are by anarchists, they are the empirical case studies that prove the validity of the anarchist critique of state socialism and its condemnation of the Marxist idea of the dictatorship of the proletariat.

Understanding why they have been historicized in this way is pivotal to understanding contemporary anarchism and its place on the broader left, but the Russian Revolution and the Spanish Civil War are also of central importance for their contributions in terms of 'actually existing anarchism'. While anarchism may ultimately have been defeated in both cases, it nonetheless remains true that anarchism was a significant force in both and that both featured examples of anarchism in action as a mass practice. The story of anarchism in Russia (and the wider Russian Empire) is complex and will be outlined in what follows, but anarchism was central to events in St Petersburg (known as Petrograd from 1914) and beyond. In the Ukraine, an anarchist movement emerged which for a period attempted a major social revolution, strongly associated with the military leadership of the anarchist communist Nestor Makhno, described by his biographer Alexandre Skirda as 'anarchy's cossack'.[4] In Spain, the military coup against the republic met fierce anarchist resistance and was followed by an anarchist revolution in Catalonia and Aragon, immortalized for English-language speakers in George Orwell's account of Barcelona in 1936, 'a town where the working class was in the saddle'.[5] In both Spain and the Ukraine within two decades of each other, anarchist collectives and communes were a reality. Both existed amidst the realities of war. As with other topics of anarchist history, both have come under greater historical scrutiny in recent times, though in both cases it is also true that Anglophone commentators have mistaken the lack of English-language works for a lack of scholarly discussion.

To return to the issue of anarchism versus Marxism, this issue was pivotal in the thinking of anarchist protagonists in both events *at the time*, though in different ways. As Kropotkin – by now returned to Russia – reflected in the quotation which opened this chapter, the experience of the Bolshevik Revolution had been (in his view) an example of 'how communism cannot be introduced'. This was consistent with his long-expressed views on the nature of an anarchist society and an anarchist revolution, of a piece with the 'social revolution' anarchists from Proudhon onwards had argued for. But for Kropotkin, and for other anarchists such as Voline, whilst the Russian Revolution of 1917 may ultimately have been captured by the Bolsheviks, in itself it represented a *social* revolution. The Bolsheviks had not initiated it; they had merely appropriated it. This was the 'unknown revolution' Voline wrote of, the 'spontaneous revolution' which Bakunin had argued would usher in an anarchist society.[6] It was a revolution not of a proletariat but of urban workers and peasantry alike. This claim is open to debate but it merits examination, as does the experience of collectivization and workers' control in revolutionary Spain. This chapter attempts to draw together this historiography, beginning in Russia.

Anarchism and revolution in Russia

In the decades prior to the revolutions of 1905 and 1917, Russia represented the most autocratic regime in the European 'sphere' (characterized as such here due to Russia's geographic and cultural status as both a European and Asian country). For Richard Pipes, the empire was 'a country of contradictions':

There was the discrepancy between the dynamism of Russia's cultural and economic life and the immobility of her political system. Incompatible was the monarchy's insistence that it control all branches of the administration and its willingness, in 1864, to give the country an independent judiciary. There was a marked divergence between Russia's 'high' culture, fully abreast of Western Europe's, and the culture of the peasantry, four-fifths of her population, who lived in a world of their own, resentful of everything derived from and associated with the non-Orthodox west. These contradictions produced in Russia a permanent state of tension in which mingled fear and hope and no one could feel confident where the country was heading.[7]

As we have seen, both Bakunin and Kropotkin themselves were products of an aristocratic culture that embraced Enlightenment values but in the context of a political settlement which repudiated change. As Pipes notes, 'Russia was the last European country to deny its citizens any voice in government'.[8] The supposed liberalization of the 1860s under Alexander II was a forlorn one, with constitutional changes not reflecting a substantively changed attitude to the dispersal of power on the part of the Tsar. In Paul Avrich's view, it had been the 'arrival of the industrial revolution and the social dislocation it produced that called a militant anarchist movement into being'.[9] The dynamics of Russian society – which diverged sharply from those European societies which had developed an industrial base and urban proletariat which at least at some level resembled that described by Marx – would play the formative role in how that movement would develop.

As George Woodcock argued in the 1960s, the lineage of Russian anarchism was considerably longer than the life span of any organized group, characterizing as he does the Russian populist movement which emerged from the 1860s as reflecting 'an anarchistic tradition native to Russian society'.[10] As Anthony d'Agostino has argued more recently, the 'revolutionary events' of 1917 'had already been germinating in the minds of several generations of Russian intellectuals'.[11] Anarchism, however diffuse, was a part of that: 'a lively intellectual force among Russian revolutionaries, as it was in the West'.[12] In Woodcock's account, anarchist theory and the Russian political imagination had a reflexive relationship in the period when anarchism itself developed as coherent body of thought and practice in the second half of the nineteenth century. Both anarchism in general and Russian manifestations in particular had a focus on the agrarian; Bakunin and Kropotkin were powerfully influenced by the agrarian society they had known in Russia, by the plight of the peasants and the serfs, and drew from Russian populism an idealization of small village communities – the famous *mir* – which could self-organize and provide an embryonic anarchist society in the absence of the state. The privileging of the small village community was something they held in common with other Russian 'native movements of rebellion' which all expressed 'a hatred of distant power':

> All these movements stressed the autonomy of the *mir* or *obschina*, the natural peasant community, and the idealized image of this institution became a kind of Platonic myth that united a wide variety of Russian thinkers during the nineteenth century.[13]

Avrich recounts the 'traditional folk myth . . . [of the] . . . boyars and officials of old Muscovy' which was mobilized repeatedly by Russian radicals (including, later, by opponents of the Bolsheviks).[14] This myth ran that the Tsar – seen by the peasantry as a benevolent figure, as opposed to the nobility and the officials – was, as Woodcock puts it, 'unaware of the atrocities committed in his name'.[15] As Avrich puts it, this was the formulation of the 'traitorous boyars and the tsar from whom they concealed the people's suffering'.[16] This was at times constructed in anti-Semitic terms, often during nationalist uprisings and peasant revolts, where Jewish communities found themselves persecuted and subjected to pogroms.[17]

But the fascination with the *mir* on the part of Russian radicals, separated from nationalist myths and stereotyping, stemmed from the emphasis on 'autonomy' which the *mir* offered. Alexander Herzen, revolutionary and writer-in-exile who had been deeply impressed as a teenager by the Decembrist uprising of 1825, was a friend of Bakunin's and influential on Proudhon, whose journalism at one point he supported financially.[18] In Isaiah Berlin's account, Herzen 'feared mobs, he disliked bureaucracy and organisation . . . idealised Russian peasants, the village communes, the *artels*'.[19] A 'socialist in the Proudhonian sense'[20] according to Woodcock, Herzen in his own words argued that

> the communal system, thought it has suffered violent shocks, has stood firm against the interference of the authorities; it . . . successfully survived up to the development of socialism in Europe. This circumstance is of infinite consequence for Russia.[21]

Woodcock for his part was careful to argue that later Russian anarchism was effectively indigenous, developing without reference to 'respected expatriate leaders like Kropotkin' and referring to events in the Ukraine as 'a fruit of prodigious Russianness'.[22] Woodcock's account has been influential, but these assertions are open to question. Aside from the straightforward conflation of the Ukraine and Russia, there are other issues with Woodcock's account which in many respects replicates a traditional Western perspective on Russia as disconnected and cut off from the wider world in the period before the rise of the Bolsheviks and which takes as normative the Enlightenment experience and the state formations which followed it in Western Europe. By contrast, Sho Konishi has persuasively argued in his recent study of Japanese-Russian cultural and intellectual transfers that Western modernity was only one conception of political and cultural modernity, with alternative modernities, including the construction of an anarchist modernity through intellectual and cultural exchange between Japan and Russia. The privileging of Western modernity within historiography (with history as a discipline as conceived of in the West itself a creation of Western modernity) ensured that anarchists such as Woodcock ultimately reproduced the boundaries of nation-state within the histories of anarchism they attempted to write. The more networked historiographies outlined in Chapter 2 offer an opportunity for a more authentically anarchist historiography and also a more critical exploration of anarchism. As we have already seen, anarchism may have originated as a political movement in Europe, specifically in the wake of the split in the First International, but it developed as a global movement. As Konishi has argued, the intellectual and cultural exchange which took place between Russia and Japan in the period after the 1850s (and which will be discussed in greater depth in the next chapter) at times had direct influence on anarchist practice in Japan, Russia and beyond. Konishi specifically states that Kropotkin's thought on evolution and mutual aid owes a good deal to Lev Mechnikov's reflections on the nature of cooperation and revolution, which developed in turn through Mechnikov's engagement with Japanese society during his tenure as a language teacher in Tokyo in the 1870s.[23]

Contra Woodcock, anarchism in Russia as it developed in the decades before the 1917 revolutions was a transnational phenomenon, as with anarchism elsewhere in the world. What is true is that in the writings of Bakunin and Kropotkin, the experience of Russian society – a largely peasant society, rather than a proletarian one – did much to shape anarchism's vocabulary *beyond* Russia. Bakunin's ideas of 'spontaneous' revolution derived in no small measure from his historical understanding of peasant revolt as it had taken place throughout Russian history. More specifically, in 1861 the Russian Tsar Alexander II – whom Kropotkin briefly served as a page due to his aristocratic heritage – emancipated the serfs, which in theory represented a move away from feudalism and opened up the possibility of Russia moving decisively towards a more liberal society. This did not subsequently take place – with the peasants 'strugg[ling] under the crushing burden of taxes . . . [and] paralyzed by the restrictions of communal tenure'.[24] The continued oppression of the peasantry persisted in the second half of the nineteenth century played a key role in the development of Kropotkin's anarchism, but it also sparked unrest within Russia itself. In the course of the 1870s the *narodnik* (populist) movement – a movement which attracted disaffected intellectuals – conducted a 'go to the people' campaign where the peasantry were valorized as agents of revolutionary change and which sought an alliance between intellectuals and peasants in a fashion which mirrored Bakunin's thought.[25] As Pedroso argues:

> At most, intellectuals (in Bakunin's mind the committed revolutionaries who entered into secret societies) were to act as 'midwives' for the revolution. They were seen as effectively channelling the popular instincts of the people but never denying the peoples' central role in making revolution.[26]

In this fashion, 'thousands of young people' – Fedotov claims 'chiefly undergraduates of universities' – engaged in a mission to the people in the course of the 1870s, seeking to 'prepare the social revolution'.[27] This was only a beginning; the clash between autocracy and radicalism in Russia from the 1870s became increasingly characterized by violence. In 1878 *Narodnaya Volya* – the People's Will – attempted (and failed) to assassinate the Governor of St Petersburg, when Vera Zasulich shot General F. F. Trepov as she infiltrated his office 'ostensibly to obtain a permit authorizing her to seek employment as a governess'.[28] Zasulich was subsequently acquitted and fled the country, with Trepov wounded rather than killed. This foreshadowed the more spectacular act of propaganda of the deed conducted by the group in 1881, the assassination of Alexander II himself.[29] The death of the Tsar and the arrival of his heir Alexander III on the throne ushered in a period of 'relentless persecution of all revolutionaries' as Woodcock puts it.[30] For Avrich, 'the dark clouds of reaction enshrouded the country once more'.[31] Economic problems fostered the development of the *déclassé* intelligentsia Bakunin had yearned for, sparking 'student unrest on an unprecedented scale in Russia's history'.[32] In 1884 legislation had been passed which had 'banished liberal professors to obscure locations in the provinces, and destroyed all semblance of university authority and academic freedom'.[33] This was followed by a long period of unrest which culminated in the assassination of the imperial Minister of Education by an expelled university student in 1901.[34] In 1905, Russia had its first revolution, and the first establishment of a St Petersburg Soviet. Anarchists found themselves in the thick of it – not least through engaging in propaganda of the deed, which resulted in severe repression. But 1905 was, in Avrich's words, a 'prelude' to what was to follow.[35]

1917 *and after*

The outbreak of the February Revolution in 1917 represented the confluence of the 'long-term political, social and economic problems and discontents' documented earlier and the 'disasters of the Great War', which destroyed what remained of the legitimacy of the Tsarist regime.[36] For Rex Wade, it was initially

> primarily a popular revolt, with what little leadership it had coming from factory-level activists and isolated individuals who emerged as leaders of demonstrations and attacks on police stations . . . Neither the revolutionary parties, whose main leaders were in exile, nor the social-political elite provided effective leadership before 27 February.[37]

Sparked by industrial action, the February Revolution was 'incomplete' in light of what was to follow, with a new Provisional Government under the aristocratic leadership of Prince Lvov constituted in the State Duma (parliament). But the fact that the revolution had its origins in workers' activism had an abiding significance, for the formation of the Provisional Government was accompanied by the parallel formation of the Petrograd Soviet, a workers' council, which 'had the actual power and popular authority, but not the responsibility for governing'.[38] As Sheila Fitzpatrick puts it, 'the new Provisional Government would represent the elite revolution, while the newly-revived Petrograd Soviet would speak for the revolution of the people'. This was the basis of 'dual power' which would subsist until a Constituent Assembly elected by the people as a whole could be established.[39]

The aftermath of the February Revolution brought revolutionaries in exile back to Russia; in April, the exiled leader of the Bolshevik faction of the Russian Social Democratic Labour Party (RSDLP), Vladimir Lenin, arrived in a sealed train, famously given passage through German territory to foment revolution in an enemy state.[40] Lenin – through his April Theses – positioned the Bolsheviks as the most radical party faction, critiquing the other parties in the Petrograd Soviet and the Provisional Government alike for what he saw as their conservatism.[41] Contrary to the prevailing interpretation of the ultimate success of the Bolsheviks being attributable to superior 'organization and discipline', Fitzpatrick argues that it was their political positioning that was their 'greatest strength . . . the party's stance on the extreme left of the political spectrum'.[42] Fitzpatrick states that 'among the socialist parties . . . only the Bolsheviks had overcome Marxist scruples . . . [and] caught the mood of the crowd'.[43]

A central question for anarchists and scholars of anarchism alike has been was that 'mood' anarchist? Sometimes teleologically, anarchist partisans have elided the 'anarchistic' character of nineteenth-century Russian populist movements with the events of 1917, but more sober assessments of Lenin and the Bolsheviks' activities between February and October have seemed to reinforce the idea that, in Fitzpatrick's words, Lenin did – for the moment – deviate from 'Marxist scruples' as commonly understood. This has helped explain why, at the outset of the October events and for some time thereafter, anarchists were 'enthusiastic' participants, prepared to work alongside the Bolsheviks towards what – fleetingly – appeared to be a common end.[44] 'The rhetoric of 1917', as Iain McKay has termed it, was Lenin at his most 'libertarian', offering a critique of the state itself which used a vocabulary familiar in part to anarchists (even as it formally dismissed anarchism).[45] In the April Theses Lenin called for the 'abolition of the army, police and the bureaucracy' and argued for the transfer of power to 'the hands of the proletariat and the poorest section of peasants'.[46] In *State and Revolution*, written in late summer, Lenin appeared to recognize at least some anarchist critiques of the state, even as the work in general stood as a rejoinder – for Lenin, the bourgeois state had to be destroyed through 'violent revolution'. What differentiated his position from the anarchists (presented as an elaboration of Engels's views) was that he believed the *subsequent* 'proletarian' state would be the form which would ultimately 'wither away'.[47] When Lenin embraced the slogan 'all power to the Soviets', this appeared to anarchists to be an endorsement of the dissolution of centralized authority. As Grigori Maximov later argued:

> Moreover, the Bolsheviks in their drive towards seizure of power and dictatorship, were forced to cast away (for the time being only, as subsequent events proved), their orthodox Marxism and to accept Anarchist slogans and methods. Alas, this was but a tactical move on their part, not a genuine change of programme. The slogans formulated by the Bolsheviks . . . coincid[ed] with the slogans of the Anarchists . . . 'Abolition of the army,' 'Arming of the workers,' 'Immediate seizure of land by the peasants,' 'Seizure of factories by the workers,' 'A Federation of Soviets,' Wouldn't the realisation of these great slogans lead to the full triumph of Anarchist ideology, to the sweeping away of the basis and foundations of Marxism?[48]

D'Agostino's recent reassessment stresses the commonalities between anarchism and Bolshevism in 1917, and the extent to which anarchists too were prepared to depart from doctrinal purity to ensure the success of the revolutionary enterprise; it also calls into question the extent to which the evolution of anarchism and Marxism should be seen as separate stories or regarded 'historically as one'.[49] In the case of the October events and for some time thereafter, anarchists and Bolsheviks did – at face value – work in harmony. The Military

Revolutionary Committee (Milrevcom) of the Petrograd Soviet, which 'engineered the Bolshevik *coup d'etat*' featured 'at least four anarchist members'.[50] The long-awaited Constituent Assembly finally met in January 1918, only to be dispersed by forces led by an anarchist sailor, Anatoli Zhelezniakov, acting under Bolshevik orders.[51]

But Zhelezniakov's tale is illustrative of the fate of Russian anarchism, and anarchists, following the October Revolution. He had done more than merely dismiss the Constituent Assembly with the phrase 'the guard is tired' on 5 January 1918; on the night of the storming of the Winter Palace (25 October) itself which inaugurated the October Revolution, he personally led 'a contingent of sailors' in the attack.[52] And yet he would subsequently find himself 'outlawed' by the Bolsheviks, only to be pardoned, then to die in the Red Army's fight against White Russian forces in 1919.[53] Zhelezniakov was more fortunate in terms of his historical legacy than most; his memory, erased of its anarchism, was reappropriated by the Soviet state as one of the formative heroes of the Soviet Union.[54] Yet as both an anarchist and a sailor, he was an important precursor of the most significant left-wing rebellion against Bolshevism which would take place at the Kronstadt naval base in 1921.

But in 1917, the Russian anarchists had seized the opportunity of the collapse of the Tsarist regime to emerge from the political underground and engage in propaganda of deed and word. That summer, Kropotkin returned to Russia.[55] His was the most high-profile of a series of anarchist 'returns'; Emma Goldman and Alexander Berkman would return to Russia less voluntarily as deportees in January 1920.[56] Goldman and Berkman missed the high-water mark of anarchist participation in the revolution, though Kropotkin didn't. The anarchist movement that had gone underground after 1905 resurfaced, representing different schools of anarchist thought and practice (Avrich enumerates anarcho-syndicalists, anarchist communists and individualists – as well as small 'groups of Tolstoyans'[57]). The 'factory committees' established in industry became key sites of agitation for anarchists, as documented by Maximov. Indeed, in his view

the revolutionary bodies pushed to the front by the course of revolution were anarcho-syndicalist in their general character. These were of the kind which lend themselves as adequate instruments for the quickest realisation of the Anarchist ideal – Soviets, Factory Committees, peasant land committees and house committees, etc.[58]

Maximov also noted the widespread dissemination of anarchist periodicals, he himself having been involved with *Golos Trouda*, the *Voice of Labour*.[59] But the major anarchist contribution of the revolutionary period came in the Ukraine.

Makhno, the Free Territory and Kronstadt

In anarchist legend, Nestor Makhno is an iconic figure and one who has come under increasing historiographical scrutiny, with recent studies by Colin Darch and Sean Patterson developing the scholarly literature from earlier work by Alexandre Skirda and Michael Malet.[60] Peter Marshall's assessment of Makhno as responsible for 'organizing an area of four hundred square miles with a rough population of seven million . . . one of the few examples of anarchy in action on a large scale in modern history' is a representative one as far as anarchist interpretations go.[61] For Avrich, Makhno was a 'born military leader', 'among the most colourful and heroic figures of the Russian Revolution and civil war'.[62] In the historiography, anarchists and their opponents alike have often elided Makhno with the anarchist experiment he 'inspired'.[63] The mythic persona of Makhno has in turn led to the construction of 'Makhnovism' and 'Makhnovshchina', but it remains the case that Nestor Makhno was a declared anarchist who sought to promote anarchist communism.

He is also a divisive figure with a mixed historical reputation beyond the anarchist fraternity. His biographer Skirda claims that Makhno has been wrongly condemned by his opponents, demonized by his Bolshevik adversaries as an anti-Semite and a pogromist, a nationalist rather than a socialist revolutionary.[64] It is significant to note that Makhno strenuously denied these charges, but it is important to state unequivocally that the charge of anti-Semitism is not simply reducible to Bolshevik demonization as Skirda implies.[65] Brendan McGeever, author of the most significant recent study of anti-Semitism in the Russian Revolution, cites a letter from an historian of pogroms, Elias

Tcherkower, which attributes responsibility for anti-Semitic pogroms to Makhno. Tcherkower acknowledges that 'in some cases' Makhno 'sternly punished' those of his followers responsible but ultimately holds Makhno culpable. Makhno admitted that there had been at least two occasions when elements of the Insurrectionary Army had committed atrocities against Jews but stated that on each occasion he had executed the perpetrators, claiming that 'throughout its entire existence, the Makhnovshchina took an uncompromising line on the anti-Semitism of pogromists'. He further cited the participation of Jewish units within his army and individual Jews within the movement more widely as evidence against the charges. His account does not, however, invalidate Tcherkower's claim that sections of his forces did engage in pogromist activity, though it does dispute the responsibility for this.[66] McGeever states correctly that the issue is 'deeply contested'. The anarchist tendency to mythologize the Makhnovshchina and the opposite Bolshevik commitment to demonize do not change the fact that by Makhno's own admission, troops belonging to his forces committed atrocities against Jews.

Makhno turned twenty-eight two days after the storming of the Winter Palace and the beginning of the October Revolution.[67] He had only been out of prison since the aftermath of the February Revolution, when he had been released from a jail term handed down ostensibly for his supposed role in an act of propaganda of the deed which 'claimed the life of a district police officer'.[68] He was a convinced anarchist, having joined a group in his hometown of Gulyai-Polye in the wake of the 1905 Revolution. Alexander Shubin argues that Makhno's group had engaged in 'four bloodless robberies' before infiltration by *agents provocateurs* was followed by at least two murders, one of an infiltrator and another of the 'police constable'.[69] Shubin claims that 'Makhno had not committed any murder', but that the authorities sought to make an example of him. A death sentence was commuted to hard labour on the basis of his (supposed) age: 'his parents had at some point falsified his date of birth – he was still considered a minor'.[70] Jail was to prove educational as 'for a time . . . he shared a cell with an older, more experienced anarchist named Peter Arshinov, who taught him the elements of libertarian doctrine and confirmed him in the faith of Bakunin and Kropotkin'.[71] Later, he would include in his speeches 'scientific terms that he had picked up in prison'.[72] Arshinov would later participate with Makhno in the anarchist movement as it developed in revolutionary Ukraine after 1917. This account of Makhno's intellectual development contradicts a popular perception that he lacked a theoretical understanding of anarchism. Woodcock's account – though at times reproducing the 'naive' and 'primitive' characterization of rural anarchism given by Hobsbawm of Andalusian peasant anarchism – offers an appreciation that Makhno sought in the years 1917 to 1921 to promote 'free communism' in the Ukraine.[73]

Makhno, head of the Gulyai-Polye Soviet by August 1917, was not alone in his project. Anarchist intellectuals fled Petrograd and Moscow, increasingly persecuted as they were by the Cheka, and he was ultimately joined by a series of figures including Voline and Arshinov. Voline would act as propagandist at the time and since; his *Unknown Revolution* would offer a detailed account of the anarchist experience in the Ukraine, setting it in the context of the broader anarchist participation in the Russian Revolution and Civil War. The *Nabat* ('Alarm') – a confederation of anarchist organizations – came into being in late 1918 and Makhno's movement formally established relations with it in January 1919, though these relations were more ambiguous than some historians have supposed.[74] In the course of 1917 Makhno had re-established the anarchist communist group of which he had once been a part, with Shubin noting 'the group was influenced by the ideas of Piotr Kropotkin, albeit in an extremely abstract and simplified form'.[75] In Shubin's account, the Soviet became a nexus for 'a network of mass organisations that supported Makhno's policies: unions, factory committees, farm labourers' committees, and popular gatherings (*skhody-sobraniya*)'.[76] Critical amongst these policies was the question of land reform; by September 1917 'a congress of soviets' in Gulyai-Polye had opted for the seizure and redistribution of 'gentry-owned lands'.[77] Shubin sums up the scale of Makhno's achievement in a sentence: 'Makhno had established soviet power in his territory earlier than Lenin, and was ahead of him in building a new society.'[78] This was possible according to Makhno because the

> instinctive anarchism clearly illumined all the plans of the Ukraine's toiling peasantry, which gave vent to an undisguised hatred of

all State authority, a feeling accompanied by a plain ambition to liberate themselves. The latter, indeed, is very strong in the peasants: in essence it boils down to, first, getting rid of the bourgeois authorities like the gendarmerie, the magistrates sent out by the central authorities, etc.[79]

These efforts were to be severely disrupted by conflict, including the occupation of Ukrainian territory after the Bolshevik government signed the Treaty of Brest-Litovsk ending the war and ceding effective influence in the Ukraine to the Central Powers (eventually through a proxy regime of the 'hetman' Skoropadsky, which Makhno would, in due course, wage war upon).[80] In the short term, he fled. A visit to Moscow recounted in his memoirs included meetings with both Lenin and Kropotkin, before he returned to Ukraine to lead partisan activity against occupying German and Austrian forces. In September 1918 Makhno, leading a group of 'partisans' and having returned to Ukraine with the support of the Bolsheviks, engaged Austrian forces acting in support of the Hetmanate and defeated them at the Battle of Dibrivki, which began the Makhno military legend and led to his christening as *Batko* – 'little father'.[81] After the withdrawal of German and Austrian forces two months later, Makhno and his supporters were able to implement a serious attempt at a libertarian communist society:

> With his active support, anarchistic communes were organized in Ekaterinoslav province, each with about a dozen households totalling one hundred to three hundred members. There were four such communes in the vicinity of Gulyai-Polye, and a number of others were formed in the surrounding districts . . . Though only a few members actually considered themselves anarchists, the peasants operated the communes of full equality. . . and accepted Kropotkin's principle of mutual aid as their fundamental tenet . . . the first such commune . . . was named in honor of Rosa Luxemburg, not an anarchist but a Marxist . . . a reflection of Makhno's undoctrinaire approach.[82]

Various names have been ascribed to the territory in question, the 'Free Territory', 'Makhnovia', and the army which fought for it – the

Black Army, the Revolutionary Insurrectionary Army, the Insurgent Army. Its fortunes waxed and waned; in the course of 1919 Makhno's army was called upon to fight a series of White Armies – anti-Bolshevik forces including former Tsarist officers – and on two occasions Makhno made tactical alliances with the Bolsheviks in this fight. But the Bolshevik authorities ultimately would not tolerate the survival of an anarchist society in their midst, and in November 1920 the Red Army captured and executed a number of Makhno's commanders.[83] Makhno had earlier (in 1919) been the subject of an assassination attempt by the Cheka.[84] In 1921 Makhno fled into exile in Paris.[85]

The repression of the Free Territory by the Bolsheviks was mirrored in their actions elsewhere from 1918 onwards. The Cheka – the Bolshevik secret police – were founded in December 1917 and early in 1918 began to target anarchists. Anarchist newspapers were shut down, and anarchist activists (along with members of left parties which opposed the Bolshevik regime) were arrested. When Zhelezniakov and his comrades shut down the Constituent Assembly, ostensibly due to a shared antipathy with the Bolsheviks to representative government, they were acting in support of a regime that sought ultimately to destroy them and their movement. The year Makhno fled to Paris this reached its most profound and iconic illustration with the suppression of the rebellion at Kronstadt.

Kronstadt was a naval fortress on Kotlin Island in the Gulf of Finland which guarded the approach to Petrograd. Home of the Russian Baltic Sea Fleet, it was a hotbed of radicalism during the Revolution; in 1917 its sailors had risen in support of the Revolution and had supported the Bolsheviks in the seizure of power in October. That year, Trotsky had famously referred to them as 'the pride and glory of the revolution'.[86] When they rose in revolt in 1921, the uprising briefly threatened the survival of the Bolshevik regime, at least in Lenin's eyes. The proximate cause for the rising was the perilous economic situation. As Russia had collapsed into civil war following the Treaty of Brest-Litovsk in 1918, conflict with White Armies with foreign support and even direct foreign military interventions had thrown society into chaos. Famously, Trotsky's reorganization of the Red Army is credited with the ultimate victory over anti-Bolshevik forces, but Russia went through years of economic turmoil and increasing shortages. The Bolshevik policy – war communism – sought to guarantee the survival of the regime through often brutal means and set the needs of the towns and cities against those of the country. Russian agriculture and industry were both in decline with output below 1914 levels, but the need to provide food for the cities and the war effort saw the Bolshevik – now Communist Party – apparatus implement policies of seizure – *prodrazverstka* – which alienated much of the peasantry.[87] This was exacerbated in the wake of victory in the Civil War by the demobilization of Red Army troops, many of whom returned to the villages and gained first-hand insight into the oppression of family members, not to mention those who returned to the cities and saw the below-subsistence-level rationing faced by many industrial workers.[88]

Strikes broke out in Petrograd in later February 1921, following earlier strikes in Moscow (which since 1918 had once again been the capital). The authorities responded with lockouts, aiming to 'starve the strikers into submission'.[89] The strikes escalated and began to incorporate 'pleas for the restoration of political and civil rights . . . which . . . became insistent and widespread'.[90] A manifesto circulated in Petrograd attributed by Avrich to the Mensheviks 'amounted to nothing less than the accusation that the Bolsheviks had betrayed the fundamental principles of the revolution'.[91] It was in this context that the Kronstadt Commune went into open revolt. As Avrich puts it:

> The Kronstadters had long been regarded as the torch bearers of revolutionary militancy, a reputation which remained largely untarnished throughout the Civil War, despite their volatility and lack of discipline.[92]

The Kronstadt rebellion has often been elided in popular mythology with anarchism; in truth, the political basis of the revolt was much broader. Though there was a not insignificant number of anarchists amongst the sailors, only one of the 'Provisional Revolutionary Committee' elected by the Commune during the outbreak of the rebellion was, in any sense, an anarchist.[93] Avrich claims that no contemporary 'anarchist source' indicates any 'outstanding role' for the anarchists in the events at Kronstadt.[94] However, the political demands of the Kronstadt Commune amounted to the critique of the betrayal of the revolution put forward by the Mensheviks in Petrograd, with one specific addition: 'freedom of speech and press for workers and peasants, anarchists and left-wing socialist parties'.[95]

The rebellion was crushed savagely by the Red Army under Trotsky's orders, who assaulted the fortress across the ice. Though many of the economic demands of the revolt were acceded to, for anarchists it became an iconic moment when Bakunin's prophecies as to the nature of Marxian revolution were fulfilled. As Kathy Ferguson argues, Kronstadt was a 'turning point in anarchist participation in the Russian Revolution'.[96] It would scar anarchist memory and form a critical element in the 'anarchist imaginaries'[97] which would follow, taken as representative of the broader Bolshevik persecution of anarchists, but also a foundational element of the anarchist diagnosis that the Bolsheviks had ultimately sabotaged the 'social revolution'. Kronstadt was the point of no return. Emma Goldman encapsulated this view succinctly:

> in spite of their bitter experiences and martyrdom under the Bolshevik regime, most of the Anarchists clung tenaciously to the hand that smote them. It needed the outrage upon Kronstadt to rouse them from the hypnotic spell of the Bolshevik superstition.[98]

This shared anarchist view of the Russian experience would be influential in terms of subsequent events in Spain.

Anarchism and revolution in Spain

A 'millenarian' movement?

During the middle years of the Vietnam War, Noam Chomsky famously wrote:

> If it is plausible that ideology will in general serve as a mask for self-interest, then it is a natural presumption that intellectuals, in interpreting history . . . will tend to adopt an elitist position, condemning popular movements and mass participation in decision making, and emphasizing rather the necessity for supervision

by those who possess the knowledge and understanding that is required (so they claim) to manage society and control social change.[99]

Chomsky subsequently turned his attention to an acclaimed study of the Spanish Civil War by Gabriel Jackson which had received the American Historical Association's biennial award several years earlier.[100] In what was effectively a forensic review of Jackson's text, Chomsky highlighted the selectivity of Jackson's reading of events. According to Chomsky's critique, Jackson's own political views ensured an inexorable causal logic to his conclusions; the anarchist revolution in Catalonia and beyond was doomed to fail, as it was 'a kind of aberration, a nuisance which stood in the way of the successful prosecution of the war to save the bourgeois regime from the Franco rebellion'.[101] In a passing comment on the views of the Marxist historian Eric Hobsbawm, Chomsky noted that Hobsbawm's interpretation was still more negative, with the anarchists being characterized as culpable in the 'failure of social revolution in Spain'.[102] Even worse than damnation was silence; due to the strictures of the liberal historical imagination, 'this astonishing social upheaval seems to have passed largely from memory'.[103]

The new historiography of the Spanish Civil War which has developed in Spain and beyond since the end of the Franco dictatorship has fundamentally broadened the historical interpretations available in the Anglophone literature, along with the translation of Spanish language works into English.[104] Chomsky's account – while having some purchase – nonetheless also mistook the lack of English-language works for the lack of a historiography; the first edition of Jose Peirats's *Anarchists in the Spanish Revolution* was available from 1964.[105] But the Spanish Civil War experience was a cornerstone of anarchist self-mythology prior to that. This reflected the status events had been accorded at the time and the 'lessons from history' anarchist movements around the world had inferred from the experience. In these eyes, anarchism was never a marginal or invisible presence in Spain – what was at issue instead was how anarchist movements had responded to the challenges of war and revolution. The reality of an anarchist revolution in Spain was never in doubt. When, on 19 July 1936, the army rebellion against the left-wing government of the Second Republic (a rebellion which began two days earlier in Morocco) reached the cities of Spain, the revolt was met on the streets by Republican – and anarchist – forces. In a story well known to anarchists, in Barcelona and Catalonia anarchist forces defeated the revolt and were offered political authority by the *Generalitat*, the local government, which they refused on principle, though they accepted collaboration with the local government through a Central Committee of Antifascist Militias (CCMA).[106] Thus began the anarchist revolution, when collectivization of agriculture and industry took place on a large scale.

Anarchists around the world greeted developments in Spain with genuine excitement. In London, *Freedom* gave over its August issue – the last before a name change to *Spain and the World* – to an 'information bulletin of the C.N.T. and F.A.I'.[107] Its front page, under the banner headline 'THE TRUTH ABOUT SPAIN', offered a potted history of Spanish anarchism and the background to the anarchist revolution by the 'veteran revolutionary historian' Max Nettlau.[108] What it made clear – and what was pivotal in the anarchist revolution in Spain – was that anarchism had a long history there. Nettlau chronicled the influence of Bakunin's emissary Fanelli, noting the formation of a Spanish 'branch' of the First International in his wake.[109] Nettlau cited 'generations of struggle for autonomy and federalism, association and solidarity, and for the highest cultural aims: free thought; a free social life; for what is now called in Spain, Libertarian Communism'.[110] Observers on the ground agreed. Gaston Leval (real name Pedro Piller), the son of a Communard exile who was an anarcho-syndicalist militant in the CNT, recollected in his later history of the collectives an encounter with a militant in Levante:

> 'Now I can I die, I have seen my ideal realised.' This was said to me in one of the Levante Collectives . . . by one of the men who had struggled throughout their lives for the triumph of social justice, economic equality, and for human liberty and brotherhood . . . His ideal was libertarian communism, or anarchy.[111]

The heritage Nettlau alluded to was real. Proudhonism had had a significant impact in Spain, though Proudhonist federalism as manifested in Spain was separate from 'Bakuninst' anarchism. As

such, participants in the revolution would accordingly find tracing a
direct line to Proudhonism contentious – of which more later– though
Woodcock cited the example of Pi y Margall, a translator of Proudhon,
who went on to be the short-lived president of the first Spanish
Republic in 1873 as testament to the purchase of 'federalism' within
Spain in the later nineteenth century.[112]

The 'mission' of Fanelli to Spain is seldom underplayed in histories
of Spanish anarchism. In Julian Casanova's words, the 'anarchist
seed' was 'sow[n]' by 'Giuseppe Fanelli, sent by Michael Bakunin'
who 'arrived in Spain in November 1868'.[113] The Spanish Federation of
the International, the Federación Regional Española (FRE), founded
in Barcelona in 1870, was 'dominated by supporters of . . . Bakunin,
committed to principles of revolutionary, bottom-up unionism which
would later define anarchist organisational practice'.[114] When in
1872 the International split, so too did the FRE (although, as George
Esenwein shows, the divisions in the FRE predated the Hague
Congress), with the majority siding with Bakunin.[115] The FRE adopted
an anarcho-collectivist position in line with Bakunin's ideas. Margall's
presidency ended in civil strife, the cantonalist movement which
promoted regional autonomy clashing with the forces of the central
government.[116] In this, the revolt at Alcoy – where workers, encouraged
by anarchists, had engaged in a general strike and subsequently seized
the town – was the anarchists' most significant action in a drama in
which they played only a 'minor part'.[117]

A central historiographical debate on anarchism in Spain at
least since the publication of Hobsbawm's *Primitive Rebels* in
1959 has focused on the question of 'millenarianism'. Elements of
this thesis – that Spanish anarchism held a religious impulse, was
'irrational' and even owed something to national 'character' – were
shared by Hobsbawm (a Marxist critic of anarchism) and Woodcock
(an anarchist propagandist). They both drew on Gerald Brenan's
1943 work *The Spanish Labyrinth*, which for its part argued strongly
for 'millenarianism'. Brenan traced the roots of Spanish anarchism as
a movement (correctly) to Bakunin but contextualized it by Bakunin's
'instinctive understanding of certain primitive classes of people' and
consequent promotion of a 'gospel . . . [a] his vision of the future,
which was to lead them, after many vicissitudes, to a heaven upon
earth'.[118] He was, then, 'the creator of the peasant Anarchism of

Southern and Eastern Europe . . . everything of importance in Spanish Anarchism goes back to him'.[119] In Brenan's depiction of Fanelli's effect on his audiences, religious language is to the fore: 'conversion', 'sacred texts', 'initiates', 'Pentecostal scenes'.[120] It was, for Brenan, an 'atmosphere of intense emotionalism, half denunciation of the evils of the capitalist world and half messianic expectation of immediate bliss to come'.[121] For Hobsbawm, this appealed to 'primitive rebels' in societies which had not yet attained a mature, class-conscious proletariat.[122] James Joll later contended that 'perhaps it was . . . because a population accustomed to centuries of religious fanaticism responded readily to a fanaticism of another kind'.[123] Ruth Kinna has recently traced how Joll was also indebted to Norman Cohn's work in addition to Brenan in making this assessment.[124]

The historiography of Spanish anarchism over the past several decades has, in large part, rejected the premises of the 'millenarian' thesis. Temma Kaplan's work on the anarchists of Andalusia – the same anarchists of whom Hobsbawm had written in *Primitive Rebels* – offered an explicit rejoinder to the 'millenarian' account. For Kaplan

Andalusian anarchism was a rational, not a millenarian response to a specific social configuration . . . even exploited people have political options from among which they choose . . . Much of what was creative in Andalusian anarchism has been overlooked because historians' emphasis on national leadership has left open the issue of popular political consciousness and action.[125]

Kaplan's work was a key moment in the transition of the historiography to a more nuanced reading of Spanish anarchism, though it remains the case that what Danny Evans and James Michael Yeoman have identified as the 'Spanish exceptionalism' argument did not disappear immediately – indeed has not fully disappeared – from scholarly literature.[126] Kaplan argued that anarchism in Andalusia represented a rational response to prevailing political and economic conditions; according to this account, it was the polarization of classes in Andalusia which made the anarchist diagnosis (and solution) plausible.[127] As Kaplan puts it, the question was not the poverty of the Andalusian peasantry, which was present elsewhere in Spain, but the contrast with 'wealth'; in the area of Northern Cadiz Province which she studied lay the 'oldest and richest sherry vineyards in the world':

In Almeria, where almost everyone is poor, the idea of revolutionary social changes might seem Utopian, for if everything were equally divided, everyone would be equally poor. But in Sanlucar, where productivity and wealth were obvious even to the hill people who came down to plow and harvest the neighboring latifundia, a revolutionary ideology based on control of production by workers and peasants might seem very rational.[128]

To borrow E. P. Thompson's phrase, Kaplan sought to rescue the Andalusian anarchists from the 'condescension of posterity' Hobsbawm had bestowed upon them. The pathologization of Spanish anarchism went further than Hobsbawm, Woodcock and Joll's shared views on millenarianism, however. As we have seen, scholars of syndicalism ascribed the purchase of revolutionary unionism in both France and Spain in part to racist caricature – 'the Latin temper' as Ridley put it.[129] Syndicalism was of profound significance in Spain and would arguably realize some of its finest achievements in the work of the CNT before and during the anarchist revolution, but this had less to do with any stereotypical issues of national character and more to do with political culture and the international dimensions of Spanish anarchism, not least the abiding Bakuninst influence but also the reciprocal relations with syndicalist and revolutionary unionist movements abroad.[130]

In September 1881 the Federacion de Trajabadores de la Region Espanola (FTRE) was founded out of the remnants of the old FRE at a Congress in Barcelona.[131] This 'represented a triumph of the syndicalist forces' as Esenwein put it, with a more cohesive structure and propaganda operation.[132] In particular, the newspaper La Revista Social, published between 1881 and 1885, was 'popularly identified as the official mouthpiece of the FTRE'.[133] The FTRE had nearly 58,000 members by the time of the Seville Congress a year after its foundation and had diversified the base of the movement, with 'two-thirds of the FTRE's membership . . . in Andalusia' as opposed to traditional anarchist centres such as Barcelona.[134] As Esenwein chronicles, the FTRE – having surged to relative prominence – declined almost as precipitously, not least due to the impact of state repression in the wake of the *Mano Negra* ('Black Hand') affair, when a number of murders of property-owners in Andalusia were attributed to an alleged underground anarchist conspiracy by this name associated with FTRE members.[135] The anarchist movement in Spain then split along collectivist and communist lines.[136] This did not mean an end to anarchist activity and revolt; in 1892 there was a famous rising in Jerez, where – Jose Peirats and George Woodcock both claim – 'more than 4,000 peasants took over the city, shouting "Long live anarchy!"'[137] Woodcock adds that they were 'armed with scythes'.[138] Kaplan is more circumspect citing 'five to six hundred peasants' having attacked Jerez on the evening of January 8, spurred by a wave of repression which saw anarchists imprisoned for attending a congress.[139] The repression which characterized the 1880s and 1890s saw an anarchist turn to propaganda of the deed, which paralleled developments in a range of nations including France, Italy and the United States. In 1906, Mateo Moral attempted to assassinate the King and Queen of Spain on their wedding day.[140]

But syndicalism was again to play a dominant role in the development of the movement upon the foundation of the CNT in Barcelona in 1910. The decision to found a new national confederation of syndicalist unions was initially prompted by a Catalonian regional syndicalist organization, *Solidaridad Obrera*.[141] In 1909 *Solidaridad Obrera* had played a key role in the *Semana Tragica* ('Tragic Week') events in Barcelona, which took place in the last week of July. They had called a general strike in opposition to the government's call-up of reserves to put down a revolt in Morocco. The military was then sent in, leading to savage repression. It was in the wake of Tragic Week that Francisco Ferrer, the founder of the libertarian school movement, was arrested and executed supposedly for organizing the uprising. Peirats attributes the subsequent founding of the CNT to 'a kind of guilt complex', since the syndicalists believed that 'the lack of a national organization had hindered the cause of the rebels of 1909 and facilitated the Ferrer trial and execution'.[142] Between 1911 and 1914 the CNT was subject to repression, but in the course of the First World War – in which Spain remained neutral – the CNT gained strength and Spanish anarcho-syndicalists were even involved, much to the chagrin of the British government, in radicalizing workers in the naval dockyard in Gibraltar.[143] By the end of the war Peirats claims that the CNT 'had more than a million members'.[144] This followed a successful propaganda tour in 1918 and a series of general strikes including one against price rises in 1916, which had seen 'syndicalism . . . [gain] great power and even a certain cachet'.[145]

With the advent of the Russian Revolution the Spanish anarchist movement in general and the CNT in particular was faced with the question of how to relate to Soviet Russia. The Red International of Labour Unions – the Soviet-sponsored 'Profintern' – was founded in 1921 and sought to bring syndicalist organizations into its orbit, including the CNT. This led to a divide between CNT leaders. Peirats argues that the initial equivocation on whether to collaborate with the Soviets owed a good deal to the lack of understanding – as yet – of the fate of anarchism in Russia. That would change with the publication of a range of works (including those of Goldman and Berkman) in the ensuing years, but the attitude of the CNT would also change due to first-hand experience of Soviet tactics.[146] The CNT ultimately withdrew from cooperation with the Soviets and participated in the founding of the International Workers' Association (IWA), which claimed the spiritual mantle of the First International and which survives as an anarcho-syndicalist international to the present day.[147]

In the 1920s the syndicalists in Spain found themselves locked in increasingly bitter struggles with employers' associations, who engaged gunmen (pistoleros) to assassinate CNT leaders. Under the dictatorship of Primo de Rivera (1923–30), the CNT was again proscribed and faced a wave of persecution. de Rivera himself had been born in Jerez, the site of the anarchist uprising of 1892, of an aristocratic family and intrinsically hostile to the movement (though he attempted – successfully – to secure the cooperation of other socialist elements through a corporatist economic model derived from Fascist Italy). Under the dictatorship, the CNT continued to meet and organize clandestinely, and in 1927 the Federacion Anarquista Iberica (FAI) was founded in order to ensure a continued anarchist 'orientation' in the CNT's strategy.[148] In 1930 de Rivera left office in the midst of economic crisis and then in the course of 1930 to 1931 his crown-appointed successor Damaso de Berenguer failed to stabilize the situation. The Second Republic was inaugurated on the departure of King Alfonso XIII following the defeat of the monarchists in local elections by Republicans in April 1931.[149]

The troubles of the Second Republic between 1931 and the outbreak of the Civil War are well documented, and much ink has been spilt in the historiography on the culpability (or otherwise) of the anarchist movement in these events. What is undeniable is that in the period before the Civil War the CNT and the wider anarchist movement had participated in risings against the government – beginning in 1932 at Alt Llobregat, continuing at Casas Viejas in the historic anarchist heartland of Andalusia in 1933 and culminating in the famous Asturias rising of 1934. These uprisings – a 'cycle of insurrections' as described by Peirats – took place along shifting political dynamics within the Republic and as factions within the CNT sought to establish how to progress to an anarcho-syndicalist society, though there were specific causes in each case.[150] CNT militants – including future war leader Buenaventura Durruti – viewed uprisings as consciousness-raising: a form of 'revolutionary gymnastics' (as it was described in a celebrated phrase) which would train the wider working class for the coming revolution.[151] Durruti, Juan Garcia Oliver and Francisco Ascaso were a part of the *Nosotros* group which sought militant revolutionary action through the CNT.[152] They were opposed from August 1931 by 'gradualists' known as *trientistas* – so named for the number of the signatories to the 'Manfiesto of the Thirty' which advocated a less immediate approach to the question of revolution. As Evans shows in his account, by 1933 'the split was formalised' with the foundation of 'the syndicalist Opposition Unions which would remain outside the CNT until 1936'.[153] In 1932 the CNT was outlawed by the Republican government.[154] In the 1933 legislative elections, the CNT – following an anarchist line – supported abstentionism, with a view to launching revolutionary action in the event of a right-wing victory and as a response to the Casas Viejas incident where government forces had 'massacre[d] . . . twenty-two villagers' following an anarchist insurrection.[155] The right were victorious, with the new Confederation of the Autonomous Right (CEDA) gaining over 100 seats and providing political support to the new right-wing government. For Peirats, there was 'no doubt that the rout of the Left was caused by the CNT's widespread abstentionist campaign, under the banner of Casas Viejas'. As he recalls:

On the eve of the election a monster rally was held in the Plaza de Toros Monumental in Barcelona, at which 100,000 persons listened to popular speakers like Domingo Germinal, V. Orobon Fernandez and Buenaventura Durruti. The theme of the meeting was 'Instead of elections, a social revolution'.[156]

In concert with the Union General de Trajabadores (UGT), the Socialist Party-affiliated union and other forces, the CNT launched an uprising in the Asturias region in October 1934, which was savagely put down by government forces, as the Left was faced with the reality of repression in what was known to posterity as the *bienio negro* ('two black years'). The constant repression and violence had a cost for the CNT, not least in terms of loss of members, and upon the February 1936 election of a left-wing coalition, the grounds for a reconciliation with the *trientistas* were clear. Despite the CNT's militancy in the period between 1931 and 1935, and its espoused commitment to anarchist ideas, these values were not always reflected in its practice, particularly in relation to gender. In 1935, Lucia Sanchez Saornil, Mercedes Comaposada and Amparo Poch y Gascon 'initiated' *Mujeres Libres*, an organization and journal dedicated to 'address[ing] the specific subordination of women in the movement'.[157] Notwithstanding the CNT's explicit restatement of its belief in sexual and gender equality in the Confederal Conception of Libertarian Communism at the Zaragoza Congress in 1936, many anarchist militants failed to reject patriarchal social relations.[158] Mujeres Libres' conception of women's empowerment differed significantly from that of later militants, explicitly rejecting 'feminism' which they regarded as the domination of women over men, succeeding a domination of men over women, a view described by one critic as 'reactionary'.[159] It also created tensions in attempts by subsequent Spanish feminists to engage with members of Mujeres Libres to draw inspiration from the group; as Ackelsberg recounts, 'such meetings which did take place had often been characterised by arguments and misunderstandings'.[160] Instead, the 'initiators' of Mujeres Libres envisioned their project as ensuring that the emancipation of women did not remain a goal capable of indefinite postponement in a movement dominated by men and patriarchal attitudes but instead became a lived reality.[161] Part of this project was, as Ackelsberg chronicles, using the CNT infrastructure of revolutionary education as a model to 'enculturate' the movement, not merely men but also women who they regarded as participating in their own subordination.[162] The Mujeres Libres spanned different political tendencies within the CNT; whereas Sanchez Saornil and Comaposada identified with the militant line pursued by the organization in 1931 to 1935, Poch y Gascon was a *treintista*.[163] All shared the critique that women had been marginalized within the movement, whatever its stated beliefs. This was a view Emma Goldman herself shared. Sanchez Saornil, in a series of articles for CNT newspapers, put forward the idea of a separate, autonomous women's organization and met resistance, but as Ackelsberg notes even before the foundation of Mujeres Libres local women's groups were emerging which challenged male-dominated spaces.[164] Ackelsberg shows that Mujeres Libres 'demanded that the call for recognition and respect for diversity include women as well as men'.[165] Their views and ambitions were not those of the later anarcha-feminist movement, but the organization and its members played a key role in women's empowerment within the CNT.

1936–37: Revolution, 'collaboration', the May Days

The outbreak of the anarchist revolution in Spain, itself a response to the attempt of the forces of reaction to destroy the Second Republic, was not, then, a 'millenarian' or 'irrational' outburst of primitive rebels but a considered, committed response to specific circumstances. As Danny Evans has shown, the Spanish anarchists of 1936 had learned their lessons from history as they saw it, but this meant not just the fate of anarchism in Russia but also the fate of the left in general in Germany in 1933 and Italy prior to that.[166] In Evans's account, the CNT, notwithstanding its own factional divides, was determined not to suffer the fate of the Communist Party of Germany (KPD) in the event of an attempt by the forces of reaction to overthrow the Republic – an attempt which the anarchists regarded as inevitable.[167] Instead, the CNT had practised and planned for the eventuality of a revolutionary situation, including, famously, at the Congress of Zaragoza in May 1936, two months before the military uprising.[168] This did not mean that the CNT sought in 1936 to overthrow the Republic itself in the short term. As Jordi Getman-Eraso has argued, by 1936 the CNT had shifted position; it was not true that 'anarcho-syndicalists were crucial contributors to the breakdown of the Second Republic, and the outbreak of war'.[169] Though as we have seen they had been involved in number of uprisings in the years prior to 1936, Zaragoza represented a moment when the CNT offered a *rapprochement* to those who had been exiled from it, including members of the 'moderate' *treintista* wing. It became famous for its explicit esposual and definition of a libertarian communist programme, described in Murray Bookchin's words as 'the most important discussion of a libertarian communist society to ever occupy a major working-class organization'.[170]

The Congress has also been criticized for the extent to which it did not represent a blueprint for a militarized response to a potential coup, but the reality was that the period between the foundation of the Second Republic had given the CNT the opportunity to develop its capacity in this regard significantly. Though the uprisings had been defeated and had led to internal dissent within the CNT and the wider anarchist movement, the foundation of the defence committees in 1931 had been a pivotal moment. Their foundation, as Evans recounts, 'was in response to a prescient concern that the Confederation would be called upon to defend the Republic in the event of coup attempts from the right'.[171] In 1936 this 'revolutionary pessimism' was vindicated.[172]

The new Republican government had anticipated a coup; to frustrate this Francisco Franco, a senior army general known to harbour nationalist views who had been responsible for previous repressive action in Spain, was transferred to a more distant command in the Canary Islands, though on the eve of the coup he returned to Morocco where the rising began on 17 July 1936.[173] When the fighting spread to Spain itself anarchists fought alongside socialists and loyalist military forces with the defence committees firmly at the heart of the action and with anarchist forces in Barcelona and Catalonia, amongst other places, decisive. Though a number of militants including Ascaso were killed in the fighting in Barcelona, the anarchists, through the CNT and its associated militias, were the effective power in Catalonia, a situation recognized by the President of Catalonia Lluis Companys, who offered the anarchists the opportunity for power or collaboration with the state.[174]

Two principal questions have characterized the historiography of anarchism in the Civil War: the nature of the anarchist social revolution and the question of anarchist collaboration with the state. The two are inextricably linked. As discussed earlier, with the anarchists occupying a dominant position militarily in Catalonia and parts of Aragon, collectivization began in earnest. Augustin Souchy noted later the concern the anarchists in particular had with Kropotkin's principal fear in terms of revolutionary failure: the shortage of bread. As Souchy put it, 'the immediate task of the revolutionaries the day after the revolution is to feed the people' and to this end 'the distribution of basic food supplies . . . [was] undertaken by the Comites de Asbastos [supply committees]'.[175] In Souchy's account as parsed by Dolgoff, 'the food unions, together with the hotel and restaurant workers, opened communal dining halls in each neighbourhood' in true Kropotkin style. In the words of Broué and Témime also cited by Dolgoff, this amounted to 'feeding up to 120,000 people a day in open restaurants on presentation of a union card.'[176] The anarchists effectively took over much of the administration of the city, represented in the famous photographs of Barcelona trams resplendent in CNT-FAI livery. On the industrial side, as Yeoman notes, '3000 enterprises were collectivised in Barcelona in the first months of the war'.[177] This led at least in some measure to the egalitarianism Orwell sensed on his arrival later in 1936, for as Yeoman states 'in many firms salaries were levelled and workers' rights and conditions improved dramatically'.[178] In the countryside, 'many communities took control of agricultural production following the outbreak of war' with 'the clearest expression of the anarchist revolution in rural Spain . . . in Eastern Aragon',

where in some areas all land, tools, livestock, and produce was collectivised, alongside other sectors of the village economy, such as barbers, masons, and furniture-makers. Money was abolished, education provision was increased, vices – gambling, alcohol, and prostitution – were suppressed, and the freedoms of women were extended. Collectivisation was popular with poorer sections of the peasantry and rural proletariat, giving them an unprecedented degree of 'power and dignity' and bringing substantial improvements in their material conditions. It also provoked resentment and violence, particularly in areas where the land was poor.[179]

In Dolgoff's assessment, 'rural collectivisation of land was far more widespread and far more thorough than urban collectivisation', in part because the CNT met less opposition in rural areas and in part because collectivization was, in some places, already underway.[180] Yet as the final line of the quote from Yeoman on Aragon indicates, rural collectivization – as with collectivization in general – was hardly an uncontroversial business. This leads to the other aspect of the prevailing historiography – the question of collaboration with the state. The anarchists engaged in this effectively from the beginning in Catalonia with their participation in the CCMA, but this became more formal when in September 1936 the CNT joined the Catalonian regional government – the Generalitat – and infamously still more so in November when four anarchist ministers joined the cabinet of the socialist Prime Minister Largo Cabellero.[181] In a speech given in Barcelona, Federica Montseny, who took the health portfolio, defended the anarchist participation in government on the basis of the exigencies of war, but also tried to claim consistency with the anarchism of the past:

> we anarchists . . . have never changed our position. We are Anarchists as of old and still pursue the same ideals . . . an ideal which becomes stagnant, which has no flexibility, which has no adjustability, which cannot react and whose representatives cannot react in accordance with circumstances, such an ideal is destined to be set apart, to be put in a corner to be substituted by other ideals.[182]

In a commentary on the speech which appeared in *Spain and the World* in February 1937, it was stated that 'some have said of Federica Montseny that she seems to be more a disciple of Pi y Margall than Bakunin, and had more in her of classic liberalism than anarchism'. The commentator further noted that 'she disavows Pi y Margall in no way, the thinker whose federalism represents a new political interpretation of Spain. Even Russia is a federation of socialist republics'.[183] This did not convince a wide range of critics such as Jose Peirats and Emma Goldman or indeed those who formed the Friends of Durruti group to save the anarchist revolution following Durruti's death in November 1936.[184] For his part, Camillo Berneri – an Italian anarchist volunteer fighting in the conflict with the Errico Malatesta Battalion (and father of key Freedom Group figure Marie-Louise Berneri) – penned a devastating open letter which was later reprinted in *Spain and the World*.[185] On 19 May, in an edition covering the Barcelona May Days, an obituary was printed for Berneri who the paper reported had been arrested following accusations by the Communist Party that he was a counter-revolutionary. According to the Red Cross, his body and that of a companion were found, apparently killed by 'revolver shots fired from behind'.[186]

The month before his death, Berneri had stated bluntly to Montseny in his open letter that he had 'not been able to accept calmly the identity – which you affirm – as between the anarchism of Bakunin and the Federalist Republicanism of Pi y Margall'. He did not 'forgive' Montseny for 'writing that Lenin was not the true builder of Russia, but rather Stalin, with his practical realism'. Most of all, he did not forgive Montseny for joining the government; the consequence, Berneri argued, was that in some parts of the country, 'Counter Revolution oppresses and threatens to crash everything'. His conclusion was powerful and succinct: 'The problem for you and the other comrades is to choose between the Versailles of Thiers and the Paris of the Commune.'[187]

A month later Berneri was dead and anarchists fought Republican forces in the streets of Barcelona, when government troops sought to disarm anarchist militias and seize the Telefonica building which the anarchists had occupied since the beginning of the war. The standard anarchist account of the Barcelona May Days as they became known has argued for the determination of Communist forces to crush anarchist opposition, and the role of Stalin and the Soviet Union in dictating the policy of the Republican government, in return for military and economic support. The presence of NKVD (Soviet state security) officers has been cited in connection with a perceived programme of assassinations and torture, not only of anarchists but of dissident Marxists such as the leadership of the Partido Obrero de Unificacion Marxista (POUM: Workers' Party of Marxist Unification), the militia with which Orwell fought.[188] Andreu Nin, a leading figure in the POUM, was killed on the orders of a Soviet NKVD officer a month after the Barcelona May Days in June 1937.[189] This account has not gone unquestioned, with Paul Preston in particular taking issue with the anarchist narrative (particularly given its purchase in the Anglophone world through Orwell's *Homage to Catalonia* and Ken Loach's film *Land and Freedom*).[190] It was not for nothing, however, that the May Days became entrenched in anarchist memory as a 'Spanish Kronstadt'.[191] That the CNT was split on how to respond to the actions of state forces in Barcelona was an inevitability based on what had gone before. With CNT leaders in the government and imploring CNT and anarchist forces in Barcelona to lay down their arms, local CNT and militias had been acting on their own initiative, before they were eventually compelled to give in. Elements of the 26th Division of the Republican Army – which had formerly been the Durruti Column – considered withdrawing from the front to fight alongside their comrades in Barcelona against state forces. Though ultimately they stuck to their posts, as Morris Brodie has recently shown some international volunteers were 'on leave in Barcelona when the fighting began . . . and became embroiled in subsequent events', events which included the death of Berneri.[192]

The aftermath of the May Days was cataclysmic for the anarchist movement in Spain. Vilified in the pro-Soviet press as counter-revolutionaries – Barcelona was described as an alliance between fascists and anarchists by a number of Communist-inspired accounts – they faced the disbandment of their autonomous military formations, completing a process of militarization which Durruti himself had objected to shortly before his death. The social revolution – collectivization – had already had the brakes applied to it by legislative measures which in theory added a measure of legitimacy but which in practice made further collectivization harder to achieve as the government sought to assert control. Jose Peirats, known to us in this chapter as an historian of the revolution, was also a prominent participant and objector to 'collaboration' who was influential in the Libertarian Youth organization of the CNT and who repeatedly voiced his opposition at a series of CNT gatherings and in CNT papers. Some months after the May Days, he went to the front, in despair at his lack of ability to achieve anything more in terms of the social revolution.[193]

But Peirats' subsequent reflections on the fate of the anarchist revolution are of huge significance as a starting point for subsequent historiography. By the 1960s when Peirats penned his book on the revolution, a dividing line had been established between those who thought collaboration with the state was necessary and those who believed that the anarchists should have stayed outside the government and gone 'all out' for the social revolution, inspiring – possibly – a revolutionary war effort fought by a united peasantry and urban proletariat. The exogenous factors – the reality of the neutrality of those powers whose support the Republic needed, including Britain, as opposed to the very real commitment of Fascist Italy and Nazi Germany – mattered hugely, as did the fact that the Republican government became so dependent on Moscow for arms and other support. But in one respect a consensus has emerged; even in its own terms collaboration in the national Republican government was a disaster. The four anarchist ministers had no significant political experience and were effectively used and manipulated by their fellow ministers and the Republican leadership to legitimize decisions made there rather than making any significant contribution of their own. It was no coincidence that once the anarchist movement had effectively been subordinated to the ambitions of the state, the anarchist ministers were removed from the government. They had outlived their usefulness.[194]

By mid-1937 the anarchist revolution was over, though anarchists continued to fight against the fascists until the eventual defeat of the Republic in 1939, at which point many fled into exile – Peirats became general secretary of the CNT in exile – whilst the movement still in Spain went underground, as Franco exacted terrible repression against anarchists, socialists and republicans who had dared oppose his coup.[195] Some participated in rebel attacks as part of the *maquis* against the dictatorship, such as the famous Sabaté brothers.[196] The anarchist revolution in Spain was short-lived as its predecessor in the Ukraine had been, but it became a pivotal reference point in anarchist memory, even as it was (briefly) obscured from history.

Conclusion: Anarchies in action

Paul Preston, writing in his acclaimed history of the Spanish Civil War, remarked:

There is a curious pattern in Spain's modern history, arising from a frequent *desfase*, or lack of synchronization, between the social reality and the political power structure ruling over it . . . the Civil War of 1936-9 represented the ultimate expression of the attempts by reactionary elements in Spanish politics to crush any reform which might threaten their privileged position. The recurring dominance of reactionary elements was a consequence of the continued power of the old landed oligarchy and the parallel weakness of the progressive bourgeoisie.[197]

At a superficial level, it might be easy to say that Preston could as easily have been writing of Russia, the other major nation which witnessed an anarchist revolution in the period before the Second World War. Such an assessment fits with what Paul Avrich – a sympathizer to the anarchist cause – regarded as the 'backwardness' of Russian society. In Preston and Avrich's shared analysis, Russia and Spain had failed on the path to modernization, their polities out of sync with their societies, reaction and revolution were outcomes in both countries with different trajectories – but both had undergone the tumult of political uprisings as the tectonic plates of the political order sought to adjust themselves.

A hint that this author does not share Preston and Avrich's perspective is given in the use of the word 'superficial'. As Konishi showed earlier in this chapter, such a framing posits one, and only one, acceptable modernity as a yardstick to judge by and forswears any possibility of an 'anarchist modernity'. Spanish anarchism, as we have just seen, had deep roots in Spanish society but was pluralistic and was not reducible, as Hobsbawm argued, to the work of 'primitive rebels', nor was it the work of the 'lunatic fringes' as Preston puts it.[198] The cases, though grouped together here for comparison, were different, though they were linked through an international anarchist milieu which they in turn influenced. Dealt with in chronological sequence here, we have seen how the Russian experience – and the ultimate political triumph of the Bolsheviks – both fostered 'lessons' which anarchists brought to the Spanish experience (sometimes literally so; some veterans of the Revolutionary Insurrectionary Army fought against fascism in Spain in the Durruti column[199]) and shaped the constellation of forces with which the anarchists in Spain were forced to deal as they pursued their own revolution. The debate over Spain is dissimilar in nature to that over Russia. Whereas – in Maximov's view – the anarchists were 'taken in' in Russia by Lenin's rhetoric in 1917, and learned their lesson at great cost, the decisions taken by anarchists in Spain on how to pursue the revolution in time of war – or war in time of revolution – were the cause of a rupture within the anarchist movement itself. The anarchist historiography of the Russian experience is largely unanimous in its interpretations. The anarchist historiography of Spain is not, and as the insightful recent work of Chris Ealham and Danny Evans has shown, the key question of 'collaboration' – the anarchist engagement with the Republican state and its ambitions, including the critical issue of participation in its government – remains an open one.[200]

Spain in particular lends itself to counterfactual questions which now, as Preston acknowledges, characterize the framing of some of the historiography but which also frame the self-understanding of the contemporary anarchist movement. Spain and Russia – in particular the Ukraine – are considered 'usable pasts' for contemporary anarchism, not because of the likelihood of mass mobilizations on that scale in the imminent future but because of the plausibility of anarchism as a form of social organization which contemporary anarchists adduce from these examples of 'anarchy in action'. The anarchist propagandists of the contemporary age do not tire of reference to the two revolutions which saw anarchist societies become something of a reality, accompanied by anarchist armies prepared to fight for them. In particular, references to the Spanish Civil War in the context of the Rojava Revolution in northern Syria have been both commonplace and divisive in contemporary anarchism, with the International Freedom Battalion of volunteer fighters including explicitly anarchist formations and more broadly seeking to replicate the (non-anarchist) framing of the Communist-sponsored International Brigades which fought in Spain. This abiding interest and mobilization of the Spanish experience-as-anarchist past is of significance in how anarchist myth-making has developed over the course of the second half of the twentieth century and the first-quarter of the twenty-first century. But these 'case studies' were of value to the global anarchist movement in their own time and were appropriated and remade in different contexts and for different purposes around the world. More than this, though this chapter is entitled 'European Anarchisms?' the question mark is significant. Both Russian and Spanish anarchism were international phenomena in their own right, in both how they influenced other movements and how they were influenced *by* other movements. Diego Abad de Santillan, an influential figure in the Spanish movement, had only returned from Argentina three years before the Civil War erupted. In Argentina he had worked for the anarcho-syndicalist FORA and represented it in the IWA.[201] In Santillan's case, this resulted in an attempt to 'steer the Spanish movement to what the Argentines thought was their purer form of anarchism'.[202] The debate over 'pure anarchism' was not one restricted geographically to Europe, nor was it necessarily defined by movements within it. Whilst the Spanish and Russian cases were and remain prominent examples of 'anarchies in action', they were not the only ones, and an increasing focus within the historiography has been the proliferation of 'anarchies' around the world. It is to these global anarchisms we turn to next.

Further reading

Russia and the Soviet Union

The work of Paul Avrich remains essential for an understanding of the development of Russian anarchism and anarchism's place in the Russian Revolution, in particular his *Russian Anarchists* (1967), though his *Anarchist Portraits* (1988) also contains interesting biographical essays of Makhno and Zhelezniakov. His *Kronstadt, 1921* (1970) is an even-handed account which unlike some accounts does not overplay anarchist involvement but notes the significance of the Kronstadt events for anarchist historical memory. For the Russian Revolution more generally, Sheila Fitzpatrick's updated edition of her *Russian Revolution* (2017) is an accessible starting point to the wider history. For anarchism in the Ukraine, Alexander Skirda's biography of Makhno, *Nestor Makhno: Anarchy's Cossack* (1999), is valuable if at times hagiographic, while Makhno's own published writings including *The Struggle Against the State* (republished in a 1996 AK Press edition) are also useful. For an overarching anarchist take on the revolution by a participant, Voline's *The Unknown Revolution, 1917-1921* remains indispensable and has recently been reissued by PM Press with an introductory essay by Iain McKay (2019). For the anarchist memory of events, Emma Goldman's *My Further Disillusionment in Russia* (1924) is a foundational text and is available via the Internet Archive Books Collection.

Spain

For anarchist participation in the Spanish Civil War, the classic histories of Jose Peirats including his *Anarchists in the Spanish Revolution* (available in a 1998 Freedom Press edition) and his three-volume history of the CNT in the revolutionary moment are vital. They are particularly notable for the fact that though composed by a significant figure in the events themselves and an opponent of the 'collaboration' policy, they are marked by even-handedness and even self-criticism. In terms of secondary assessments, the recent *Revolution and the State* by Danny Evans is an essential new contribution to the Anglophone literature on anarchism in the Spanish Civil War which addresses critically the role anarchism played through the conflict. The special edition of the *International Journal of Iberian Studies* on approaches to Spanish anarchism (September 2016) edited by Evans and James Michael Yeoman is also extremely useful, as is the overview essay on anarchism and the Spanish Civil War by Yeoman in the *Palgrave Handbook of Anarchism*. Martha Ackelsberg's *Free Women of Spain* (1991) is critical to an understanding of the Mujeres Libres.

4

Global anarchisms
Japan, India and beyond

Introduction: Anarchism in two modes

On 13 April 1929, the *Illustrated London News* reported a 'RED OUTRAGE AT DELHI' which had taken place five days earlier.[1] Under the headline 'BOMBS IN THE LEGISLATIVE ASSEMBLY', the paper recounted how 'two bombs were hurled from the Visitors' Galleries towards the Government Front Benches':

> Seats and tables were wrecked; a deep hole was made in the floor; and a number of those present were injured . . . Copies of a Communist leaflet were also thrown. This leaflet began: 'It takes a loud voice to make the deaf hear'; ended with 'Long Live the Revolution!'; and was signed 'Commander-in-Chief' of the 'Hindustan Socialist Republican Army.'[2]

The perpetrators Bhagat Singh and B. K. Dutt were arrested at the scene.[3] Bhagat Singh was a committed revolutionary, dedicated to the cause of Indian independence, and an intellectual who drew on both anarchist and Marxist ideas. When he was executed in 1931 – not for the Assembly bombing but for his earlier participation in the assassination of a police officer – Singh was only twenty-three years old. Yet he had developed his own revolutionary thought, synthesizing elements of anarchism and Marxism in the process to offer an alternative idea of a possible modernity to that offered by Western colonialism.[4] In 1926 in the journal *Kirti* he had sketched a defence of anarchism across a series of articles.[5] His attack on the Legislative Assembly is widely acknowledged to be modelled on Auguste Vaillant's attack on the French Chamber of Deputies in 1893 – even down to the slogan on the leaflet that fluttered in the air as the smoke cleared from the blast, 'it takes a loud voice to make the deaf hear'. Vaillant had uttered those same words in his courtroom speech in 1894 (later reproduced as the 'Red Pamphlet', the leaflet explicitly credited 'the French anarchist, Valiant' [*sic*]).[6]

Singh had learned of Vaillant's speech through reading Upton Sinclair's *A Cry for Justice*.[7] It made a powerful impression on him, as Ramnath shows, with Singh citing it on several occasions – in the *Kirti* articles, in the statement on the assassination of a police officer (discussed further in what follows), in the leaflet dropped at the bombing and in his courtroom defence when on trial.[8] He was politicized from an early age, having been born into a family with 'tight Ghadar movement links', Ghadar being an independence movement associated with the anarchist Har Dayal that had organized Indian workers internationally, particularly in the United States (where Dayal had been active in the IWW in San Francisco for a time).[9] As Ole Birk Laursen has chronicled, the Indian independence movement of the early 1900s was anchored in international politics, with a nexus centred on India House in London, founded by the Indian lawyer Shyamji Krishnavarma in 1905.[10] He further notes that Dayal joined Goldman for her tour of the West Coast of the United States the year before he founded the Ghadar Party in 1913.[11] Singh for his part was of the next generation but drew on Ghadar's legacy, the journal *Kirti* in which he published his articles on anarchism having been founded by 'returned Ghadar revolutionaries'.[12] Singh's politics were 'an ever-evolving, flexible, innovative synthesis', in Ramnath's view.[13] This meant that though towards the end of his life as he awaited execution he appeared to be moving towards Marxism-Leninism, Ramnath argues that 'it is hard to imagine him limiting or reducing his thinking to [Marx, Engels, and Lenin] let alone to the mandates of some party claiming to speak in their name'.[14]

M. P. T. Acharya by contrast was a declared anarchist for much of his adult life and saw part of his project as the elucidation and development of anarchist theory and practice.[15] In this he paralleled Hatta Shuzo, a former Christian pastor who was – in John Crump's assessment – 'a gifted and original thinker'. He was a key part of an interwar intellectual milieu in Japan which ensured that 'in contrast to what happened in Europe, anarchist communist theory did not stagnate'.[16] The stories of Singh, Shuzo and Acharya, which will be discussed in what follows, highlight at an individual level anarchism in two modes. Firstly, as a resource to be drawn upon, its vocabularies and praxis to be deployed and used, and secondly as an explicit revolutionary identity, to be reformulated and theorized in different spatial contexts. 'The transnational turn' in anarchist studies, as Constance Bantman and Bert Altena have termed it, is a real and meaningful development.[17] There is an increasing awareness within the Anglophone historiography of anarchism as a global entity, not simply in terms of the reality of anarchist movements and schools of thought around the globe but also of the interconnectivity between movements and the lived reality of anarchism as an internationalist ideology in the decades after 1880. As discussed in earlier chapters, anarchism had a prominence on the international left in the decades prior to the First World War that has often been obscured in the historiography, and the legacy of this was still keenly felt around the world in the interwar period. As Benedict Anderson puts it:

> Following the collapse of the First International, and Marx's death in 1883, anarchism, in its characteristically variegated forms, was the dominant element in the self-consciously internationalist radical Left. It was not merely that in Kropotkin . . . and Malatesta . . . anarchism produced a persuasive philosopher and a colourful, charismatic activist-leader from a younger generation . . . notwithstanding the towering edifice of Marx's thought, from which anarchism often borrowed, the movement did not disdain peasants and agricultural labourers in an age when serious industrial proletariats were mainly confined to Northern Europe.[18]

In his study of anarchism in China Arif Dirlik echoes this assessment, citing Hobsbawm's claim that the 'bulk of the revolutionary left was anarcho-syndicalist' before the First World War.[19] Dirlik notes that 'there was no Marxist left to speak of in China until 1920-21' and highlights that 'most of those who were to emerge as leaders of the Communist movement in China went through an anarchist phase before they became Marxists'.[20] Dirlik notes the influence of anarchists in Tokyo and Paris on the early Chinese anarchist movement, a reflection of the intrinsic transnationalism of the anarchist movement.[21]

Anarchism and anarchists, were, for Anderson, part of a 'vast rhizomal network' that spanned the globe.[22] But the increasing recognition of this within anarchist studies has also led to a critique of what Raymond Craib has described as a 'diffusionist line' – the view that anarchism was simply a revolutionary gospel exported from Europe around the world, 'a script to be mimicked'.[23] Instead, Craib argues, there is a growing focus on the 'plural origins' of anarchism.[24] For Ilham Khuri-Makdisi, writing on the radical networks that linked Eastern Mediterranean cities in the late nineteenth century into the twentieth, the international networks that made and remade socialist and anarchist ideas did so in a less ideologically dogmatic and constrained fashion than has been assumed by historians writing after the triumph of Marxism-Leninism in the Soviet Union. Khuri-Makdisi speaks instead of 'radicalism', which in her view captures 'the lack of orthodoxy and rigid boundaries that was a key characteristic of the *fin-de-siecle*'.[25]

The 'diffusionist line' parallels a tendency to appropriation which has characterized anarchist propaganda at least since Kropotkin. In Jason Adams's widely read pamphlet *Non-Western Anarchisms*, an argument is made that anarchism is not, in its fundamentals, of European origin. Instead, Adams argues that 'anarchism has ways been derived more of the East/South than of the West/North' citing the Bakunin/Kropotkin influence on the development of anarchism as evidence of its status as an 'eastern' form of socialism.[26] Outlining a 'wave theory' of anarchism's historical development (similar in periodization to feminist wave theory), Adams laments the absence of 'non-Western' figures and movements from the historiography of the first and second waves of anarchist thought and praxis as he defines them. But one of the problems in Adams's approach is that his lens is too inclusive, including, for example, Gandhi within its ambit. Acknowledging that 'in India anarchism never took on much of a formally-named "anarchist" nature', Adams's attempts to sketch an anarchist lineage within Indian political culture and religious tradition.[27] Adams claims that Gandhi's 'passion for collective liberation sprang first and foremost from a very anarchistic notion of individualism'.[28] In this, he echoes Peter Marshall, who described Gandhi as the 'outstanding libertarian in India' of the early twentieth century.[29] Whilst scholars such as Laursen recognize Gandhi's 'anarcho-pacifist' tendencies, an unproblematic inclusion of Gandhi within a new anarchist canon militates against the successful investigation of the nature and fortunes of anarchism within India and reflects a general trend.[30]

In the case studies which follow, India and South Asia, and Japan and East Asia, attention is paid to the ways in which these were truly 'global' anarchisms, operating in a number of modes, in dialogue with anarchist movements around the world. An attempt is made here to historicize and avoid the 'universalism' which Arif Dirlik critiques in many attempts to broaden the popular understandings of the origins and development of anarchism as a social movement and body of thought.[31] The cases of India and Japan are significant contrasts. Though Indian independence activists adopted anarchist praxis and in a limited number of cases were influenced by anarchist ideas – ably historicized in Ole Birk Laursen's work – those who were influenced by anarchism did not create a significant movement in India. In Japan, the anarchist movement was marginal, but it *was* an identifiable movement which did identify with the wider anarchist movement around the globe. Both were connected through networks to other hubs of revolutionary activity, in the case of Indian anarchism, London and Paris, and in the case of Japanese anarchism, Tokyo itself was a radical hub for East Asia as a whole.

India and Japan have also been selected here in part due to recent developments in the historiography, where new work by Laursen and Maia Ramnath has asserted the significance of India for anarchist studies and where Sho Konishi's account of *Anarchist Modernity* has offered a pathbreaking analysis of anarchist 'cooperatism' building on earlier work by John Crump. Konishi's account itself highlights transnational links and exchanges between Russia and Japan. So in this chapter 'global' anarchism is understood as anarchisms (both movements and ideas) operating within global networks, building on the approach discussed in Chapter 2 – though it is important to be mindful of Khuri-Makdisi's assessment that these networks were pluralistic and 'radical', rather than 'anarchist'.[32] Addressing anarchism in a global perspective is part of an important and necessary project to 'decolonize anarchism', which has been eloquently discussed by Ramnath.[33] Part of that project in historical terms must be to critically evaluate how the 'anarchist tradition' was operationalized in global spaces. Ramnath describes the 'anarchist tradition' as 'a continuously unfolding discourse – meaning not just the writings and rhetoric of anarchism but also its body of practices and history of performative acts'.[34] Anarchist performance – the 'performance' of propaganda of the deed, including its martyrology and courtroom stagings – was appropriated and remade by a range of nationalist and independence movements, including in India. At times, individuals who were not anarchists masqueraded as such to gain support from figures within the movement and at times those involved in nationalist movements found themselves demonized as 'anarchists', irrespective of any ideological conviction. Moreover, in similar fashion to the transferences highlighted in Chapter 2, anarchism-as-discourse was, at times, more influential than the declared movement itself, with lasting resonances even as individual movements faded into history.

But as this chapter will aim to show, decolonizing the *history* of anarchism – restoring the agency of actors within that history beyond the 'traditional' Eurocentric 'canon' – is a separate project from the anarchist propagandist's (equally necessary) task of decolonizing anarchist theory and praxis. However, that latter project too is itself a subject for historical analysis. The two projects do, however, intersect at points, such as in the attempts of Black radicals to draw on and decolonize anarchist theory in the 1960s and 1970s as part of the Black liberation struggle. Due to the chronology, that decolonization will be discussed again in the next chapter. The book as a whole has sought to adopt a global perspective on anarchism; in what follows it seeks to trace through its case studies how anarchism's own global perspectives have been, and are being, historicized.

India and South Asian Anarchism

Anarchism in India and the wider Indian diaspora after 1900 existed in the context of the cause and movement for Indian independence.

As Laursen has shown, the networks of radicals that brought Indian independence activists into contact with anarchists and anarchist ideas also facilitated the travels of other ideas including Marxist communism and a wider range of nationalisms. In this last connection, discussion of anarchism's relationship to Indian nationalism and nationalists has been an ever-present staple of both scholarship and contemporary comment. As Emma Goldman recounted of her meeting with Acharya's friend and comrade, Virendranath Chattopadhyaya (known as 'Chatto'), 'He called himself an anarchist, though it was evident that it was Hindu nationalism to which he had devoted himself entirely.'[35] Krishnavarma's establishment of India House in London placed potential future leaders of the independence movement into the same intellectual revolutionary milieu as the anarchists of the Freedom Group. India lay under British imperial rule; Krishnavarma founded the Indian Home Rule Society in London in 1905 and the *Indian Sociologist* followed, becoming increasingly radical over time.[36] As Ramnath shows, Krishnavarma – a lawyer who had studied at Oxford and who had been called to the bar at the Inner Temple – collaborated with figures from within the wider socialist movement. Henry Hyndman of the Social Democratic Federation, who had collaborated with Charlotte Wilson years earlier, initially co-edited the *Indian Sociologist* and was present at the opening of India House as a lodgings for Indian students in London.[37]

The Krishnavarma enterprise was also strongly influenced by the philosophy and sociology of Herbert Spencer; Ramnath notes that 'quotations from Herbert Spencer crowned the masthead' of the *Indian Sociologist*, including 'resistance to aggression is not only justifiable but imperative'.[38] This echoed Auguste Vaillant, who had cited Spencer in his courtroom speech in Paris in 1894 when on trial for his life. It also highlighted the confused world in which turn of the century anarchism found itself – anarchists and revolutionaries of different kinds adopting a thinker in Spencer renowned for his social Darwinist views (it was in fact Spencer – not Darwin – who coined the term 'the survival of the fittest').[39] As we have seen, the Kropotkin project was in many respects set against social Darwinism, as Proudhon's project had been set against Malthus. As Ruth Kinna has argued, Kropotkin's 'claim – made against social Darwinists like Spencer – [was] that cooperation is as potent a factor as competitive struggle in determining species fitness'.[40] Nonetheless, as with Kropotkin's anarchism, the Indian independence movement in London located itself in a paradigm of science and social science.

As Laursen chronicles, Chatto came to Britain in 1902 to study, eventually being called to the bar at the Inner Temple where Krishnavarma was a member.[41] Acharya arrived some years later, and the two were to become closely connected.[42] Acharya would, over time, become a convinced and dedicated anarchist, by way of the Communist Party of India; Chatto would 'only briefly fully embrace anarchism in 1920s Berlin', but Laursen has argued strongly for anarchist resonances in the movements which followed.[43] They were part of a long list of independence activists and revolutionaries who were based at India House in the short years it was open before its enforced closure in 1910, a list which included Har Dayal.[44]

In 1905 Bengal was partitioned by the order of the British Viceroy, Lord Curzon.[45] This caused a backlash, with Curzon resigning before the year was out amid media controversy.[46] As Ramnath shows, the reaction to the partition – which divided the state on supposed ethno-religious lines – including the arrival of the 'Swadeshi movement' – was a 'flash-point of unrest'.[47] Ramnath shows how the 'militants' were demonized as 'anarchists'; Laursen argues that the nationalist movement increasingly adopted 'anarchist and nihilist principles of organisation'.[48] Ramnath and Laursen concur that central to this was propaganda of the deed with 'India . . . swept by a series of assassinations of British officials'.[49] In 1909 an India House resident, Madan Lal Dhingra, shot dead Sir William Curzon-Wyllie on the steps of the Imperial Institute in South Kensington.[50] Curzon-Wyllie was a career army officer with extensive service in India, serving as an aide to the Secretary of State for India at the time of his death. According to Ramnath's account, Lal Dhingra was a member of an 'inner circle' called *Abhinava Bharat* which had 'taken up target practice at a shooting range on the Tottenham Court Road'.[51] He was executed the following month, having used the courtroom to advance his cause, delivering 'a much republished courtroom speech'.[52] Krishnavarma had already moved to Paris over two years before Lal Dhingra assassinated Curzon-Wyllie; and it was from there that the *Indian Sociologist* was published.[53] In 1909 the publication was suppressed by the authorities in Britain following the Curzon-Wyllie killing, and the anarchist Guy Aldred agreed to print it, which ultimately landed him in prison.[54]

The Indian nationalists had adopted the form of anarchist propaganda of the deed; in the course of the war years to follow this would culminate in a series of plots, both real and imagined, against the British state. During the First World War, the purported 'Indo-German conspiracy' would see Indian nationalists ally both with Germany and with a range of other groups, including Italian anarchists, to wage war against Britain for the cause of independence.[55] But as Gajendra Singh has recently shown, Ghadar – which was seen by British elites as being behind the conspiracy – was politically far more ambiguous than scholarship linking it to Irish or anarchist radicalism sometimes admits.[56] So though Bhagat Singh's career as an revolutionary activist began, as we have seen, in the context of a Ghadarite family, his interest in anarchism was his own. In the 1920s, when Singh became active in the Hindustan Republican Association (which underwent a Singh-inspired name change to the Hindustan Socialist Republican Association, HSRA), the internationalist left within the Indian independence movement faced some of the same crises as left movements elsewhere. The original Communist Party of India was founded in late 1920, inspired by the Soviet revolution, and Acharya was its first chairman.[57] But Acharya was opposed to affiliating with the Communist International and adopting a straightforwardly Leninist line, and was ousted from the party in 1921. In 1922 he attended the initial meeting of the IWA in Berlin and from then on (in his own words) became a 'convinced anti-Bolshevik'.[58] From 1923 to the end of his life, Acharya was unambiguously an anarchist.[59]

Singh's involvement with the HSRA led to an escalation in propaganda of the deed, including his role in the assassination of a police officer, J. P. Saunders (who was not the intended target), in reprisal for the death of Lal Lajpat Rai.[60] The statement issued after the act was entitled 'Beware, Ye Bureaucracy' and lamented the death of Saunders at an individual level – 'Sorry for the death of a man' – but cited his status as an 'agent of authority' in terms of justification.[61] Ramnath cites a contemporary witness to attest that in the base of operations for the HSRA in Lahore, 'pictures of Kropotkin and Bakunin . . . [hung] . . . on the walls'.[62] While Singh was awaiting execution by the British in 1930, he requested amongst other texts that a friend send him Kropotkin's *Mutual Aid* and *Fields, Factories and Workshops*.[63] Singh's anti-imperialism was rooted in Indian nationalism, but it was also rooted in a pluralistic anticapitalist socialist critique, while his praxis in terms of propaganda of the deed explicitly drew on an anarchist 'mode' and situated itself in its lineage. It was not for nothing that Singh described Vaillant as a 'martyr'.[64]

Acharya's progress as an anarchist took him to a different direction – to pacifism.[65] Over the next three decades from 1923 Acharya published a number of essays on anarchism and critiques of Bolshevism, including his 'What Is anarchism?' in the *Whither India* collection edited by Iqbal Singh and Baja Rao following India's independence.[66] Acharya's anarchism emphasized pacifism and in that respect – if not others – offered an approach more compatible with Gandhi and more amenable to a Gandhian audience.[67] Acharya's death in 1954 did not lead to an anarchist movement in India; he had consistently been at the margins.[68] But the influence of anarchism in the context of the Indian independence movement is not to be assessed in these terms; rather, anarchism offered a mode of praxis and a series of networks which were of use for the militant wing of the nationalist movement, as we have seen. More than this, though, the impact on Gandhi was greater than simply his affection for Tolstoy. As Durba Ghosh has recently argued, Gandhi's condemnation of violence still meant that his own ideas existed in dialogue with that mode of revolutionary praxis.[69] Anarchist praxis, if not anarchist ideas or movements, played a role in India, even if that role was – at times – to be defined against the dominant approach to the independence struggle. In Japan and East Asia the story was different.

Japan and East Asian Anarchism

Traditional historiographies of Japan have seen the Mejii Restoration of 1868 as a pivotal moment in 'Japan's turn to the West', when the decision was taken to 'devote its full energy towards the realization of one goal – the establishment of a modern nation-state'.[70] This thesis, which regards the end of the Tokugawa shogunate and the establishment of a centralized bureaucracy as an 'aristocratic revolution' which transformed Japan largely out of recognition, has generally obscured the significance of dissenting movements and competing modernities.[71] Yet, as Sho Konishi has shown, there was a competing 'anarchist modernity' in Japan in the period prior to and following the Restoration, one which drew on extant cultural links with Russia.[72] By the early twentieth century, a formal anarchist movement would develop in Japan, split between anarcho-syndicalists and 'pure' anarchists who, Crump argues, offered an evolution in anarchist communist thinking on the nature of a future anarchist society. This movement was again the creation of travels and exchanges around the world. Kotoku Shusui, a key figure in the development of Japanese anarcho-syndicalism, had – like Har Dayal – been active in the United States and, also like Dayal, more specifically in San Francisco and the IWW there.[73]

Kotoku had been a journalist in Tokyo before resigning his post over his newspaper's support for the Russo-Japanese War of 1904–5 and travelling to the United States, from whence he returned in 1906. According to George Elison:

> Kotoku's greatest – and, in a sense, lasting – significance lies in that very anarchist overtone he brought back from the United States. This overtone is a rejection of parliamentarianism. The rejection of parliamentarianism is, of course, but corollary to an outright rejection of government, to anarchism . . . His anarchism had best be placed under a syndicalist label . . . Kotoku introduced into Japanese ranks the idea of substituting industrial action for political activity.[74]

But, as Crump noted, the story was not so straightforward as the importation of anarchist ideas from American sources. Instead, it was more accurate to say the trip 'brought to a head a development in his political ideas that was discernible even before he left Japan', a catalyst, rather than a point of departure.[75] A 'propagandist, not a theorist', Kotoku – with help from Osugi Sakae and Yamakawa Hitoshi – translated Kropotkin's *Conquest of Bread* into Japanese.[76] Already well known within the nascent Japanese socialist movement, Kotoku's return from the United States would change that movement, promoting an 'anarchist turn'. His translations of Kropotkin and the German syndicalist Siegfried Nacht's *The Social General Strike* (with Nacht writing under his pseudonym Arnold Roller) were, taken together, to provide the intellectual ballast for this shift.[77] *The Conquest of Bread* 'evoked a ready response in Japan' according to Crump 'due to the fact that'

> in addition to offering a vision of the future, there were very obvious similarities between the anarchist communism it portrayed and various features of traditional peasant life in Japanese villages. Rice cultivation, and the maintenance of the water system on which it depended, required a high degree of communal solidarity. Similarly, although the market economy increasingly impinged on the villages, there still remained areas of peasant life into which monetary transactions rarely intruded.

Thus, Crump argues, 'it is not difficult to see how experience of life in a peasant community . . . [made] readers . . . receptive to its arguments for a society of autonomous communes engaged in decentralised production'.[78] Put more succinctly, Kotoku's audiences recognized themselves – and their possible future selves – in Kropotkin's vision. It did not seem 'utopian' or irrational, as it was sometimes accused of being by anarchism's adversaries in other places, but plausible. Konishi highlights how the adoption of Kropotkin's thought represented a longer-term direction of travel in Kotoku's thinking rather than a sudden 'conversion' during his sojourn in the United States, citing Kotuku's membership of a direct action initiative called the *Chokkodan*, founded in 1903.[79]

Kotuku's influence would go beyond Japan. The Chinese anarchist Jing Meijiu had been 'converted . . . to anarchism' by Kotoku's lectures which he had attended whilst a student in Tokyo.[80] Dongyoun Hwang, in his study of anarchism in Korea, cites Tokyo along with Shanghai as 'nodes of . . . transnational radical networks in [the] early twentieth century'.[81] Hwang notes Tokyo's status at the beginning of the twentieth century as a 'refuge for many Eastern Asian students and radicals', one of two major 'crucibles' in East Asia in which anarchists and radicals were forged.[82]

Tensions grew rapidly in early twentieth-century Japan, however. Imperial Japan was engaged in a process of rapid state formation, with the abolition of feudal privileges in the 1870s offering the nominal possibility of a more egalitarian society, but also corresponding with the development of a centralized state bureaucracy and the imposition of a compulsory national education system spanning schools and universities.[83] As Tomoko Seto shows, in the years following the Russo-Japanese War, the Japanese socialist movement split into two factions: a legalist and an illegalist, '"direct-action" faction led by the radical intellectual Kotoku Shusui'.[84] On 22 June 1908, the Red Flag Incident took place at the Kinkikan Meeting Hall in Tokyo. A party attended by socialist and anarchist activists had just taken place to celebrate the release of a jailed activist, Koken Yamaguchi. In Seto's account, 'some of the direct-action activists left the venue singing revolutionary songs and raising red flags that read "Anarcho-Communism" and "Communism"'.[85] Subsequently attacked by the police, several were arrested and a number were jailed, including Osugi and Yamakawa, Kotoku's partners in the Kropotkin translation project.[86] The anarchist movement faced '[intense] persecution by the state', which resulted in a ratchet effect, turning the anarchist movement (as elsewhere) towards the consideration – if not the action – of propaganda by the deed.[87] In 1910 this culminated in the High Treason Incident, when Kotuku, the journalist Kanno Suga (Kotuku was Kanno's former partner), Miyashita Takichi and a number of others were arrested and charged with a conspiracy to assassinate the emperor.[88] A recent study of the incident states that Miyashita had taken it upon himself to manufacture explosives with a view to an attempt on the emperor's life 'in order to prove that the emperor was a human being just like his subjects' (rather than a god) thus 'removing the facade of legitimacy from the government'.[89] In January the following year twelve of those imprisoned were executed, including Kanno and Kotoku. In her prison diary, Kanno 'framed her life in terms of sacrifice for the anarchist cause'.[90]

Osugi Sakae survived the High Treason affair by virtue of his prior imprisonment for the Red Flag Incident. The High Treason affair inaugurated what has been described as the 'winter period' for Japanese anarchism when intense state repression made it extremely difficult for anarchists to organize and disseminate their ideas.[91] Osugi was a leading figure in 'a younger generation of anarchists' who 'shifted the ground further towards anarchist syndicalism'.[92] Unions had been banned in Japan since 1900, a situation to which

Crump attributes the relative lack of theoretical dispute between anarchist communist and anarcho-syndicalists in the period before the First World War.[93] Osugi, however, began to promote a syndicalist line within the movement as early as 1912 through a range of periodicals.[94] According to Crump, syndicalism began to rise into the ascendancy in the Japanese movement in part because of a near-universal loss of faith in Kropotkin occasioned by his infamous support for the Entente Powers in the First World War. In addition (in Crump's assessment), anarchists looked to the development of an industrial proletariat to provide the required strength to overthrow the state and were increasingly inspired by the perceived successes of the French CGT, for which Osugi acted as something of an interlocutor given his command of French.[95] Crump argues that the Japanese anarchists could view overseas debates about anarcho-syndicalism versus anarchist communism with a measure of detachment, arguing instead for a synthesis in the period before Osugi's execution in 1923.[96] In Konishi's view, this was for Osugi and his contemporaries a question of

> the balance between the individual and social . . . [being] . . . an eternal process of negotiation between the two. The individual constantly changes in response to society and his or her surroundings. In return, society and the environment are constantly reshaped in response to individuals. In other words, neither individual nor society need be sacrificed for the other. For Ishikawa, Osugi and many others, this constant negotiation between the two without sacrifice was freedom.[97]

The end of the First World War unleashed a wave of confrontation between labour and capital – notwithstanding the restrictive legislation on strikes – which led to the foundation of new labour organizations in which the anarchists could play a role. The Nihon Rodo Sodomei was founded out of the earlier Yuaikai in 1921 and had 30,000 members.[98] This was accompanied by a series of agricultural initiatives which, in Konishi's eyes, manifested a particular vision of anarchist modernity in the form of cooperatism. Such initiatives were 'at the heart of anarchist democracy'.[99] Konishi cites the establishment of a major farmers' cooperative by Arishma Takeo in 1921 as one such example of a trend and an anarchy in action which Ito Noe called 'the reality of anarchism in Japan'.[100]

In 1923 Osugi and Ito were both murdered by the authorities along with other anarchists and subversives in the wake of the Kanto earthquake, which triggered repression of thousands of activists on the grounds that they had been involved in arson and violence in the aftermath, a framing which even at the time embarrassed the authorities.[101] In the short term Japanese anarchism continued in a syndicalist direction; in 1926 the Zenkoku Jiren was founded as an explicitly syndicalist 'All-Japan Libertarian Federation of Labour Unions', in part by Ishikawa Sanshiro who, as Marshall recounts, 'had spent eight years in exile in Europe, mostly with the Reclus family in Brussels'.[102] The same year Kokuren ('Black Youth League') was founded, an anarchist federation drawing on the energy of young radicals.[103] Ultimately, these two organizations would come to reflect opposing tendencies in a theoretical dispute between anarchist communism (represented by Kokuren militants) and anarcho-syndicalists (represented by Zenkoku Jiren). With the rise of Hatta Shuzo to prominence as an advocate of 'pure anarchism' – an anarchism denuded of the 'workerism' of syndicalism – this dispute took on sharper resonances and following a period of agitation the movement ultimately split in 1928.[104]

Shuzo's anarchism sought to eradicate syndicalism and espouse a 'pure' anarchism since syndicalism (in his view) amounted to a 'taint' from 'capitalism':

as they saw it, the problem was not only for anarchism to confront external enemies, such as capitalism and bolshevism, but also to cleanse the anarchists' own ranks of any taint of capitalist or bolshevik influence.[105]

For Hatta this meant rejecting the idea of 'scientific socialism' since 'science was not a neutral technique . . . [and] was a form of knowledge which had grown up with capitalism'.[106] Syndicalism by extension was 'a mirror image of the division of labour inherent within capitalism'.[107] The desired society, for Hatta, was a 'decentralized' one 'of largely self-supporting communes engaged in both agriculture and small-scale industry'.[108] Hatta died in 1934, with the formal anarchist movement in the doldrums in the face of state persecution.[109] The formal anarchist movement waned into insignificance, but as Konishi argues, the power of cooperativist ideas continued, even into the post-war period.

Japanese anarchism also had an abiding influence in both China and Korea, both of which were linked to the Japanese movement through the status of Tokyo as a 'hub' for radical exchanges as Dirlik has acknowledged. Korea is of particular significance, since the Korean anarchist experience had its most significant manifestation not on the Korean Peninsula itself but in Manchuria, where between 1929 and 1931 two million Koreans lived in an autonomous communal federation administrated by the League of Korean Anarchists in Manchuria (LKAM) and its successor, the United Society of All Korean People (USAKP).[110] In Hwang's assessment, the LKAM was

a 'practical . . . organization' to deal with the livelihood of the Koreans in Manchuria, who numbered about two million at the time of its establishment in 1929. However practical it was, the LKAM's platform nevertheless reveals that it was indeed an anarchist organization with anarchist principles and goals. In the platform its defined goal was to realize a society of 'no rule,' in which human dignity and individual freedom were all completely ensured.[111]

China has been in the midst of civil war between nationalist government *Guomindang* forces and those of the Communist Party since 1927. The LKAM/USAKP in Manchuria, more prosaically referred to in many anarchist texts as the Shinmin Autonomous Region, was a 'self-governing network of co-operatives, prefiguring anarchist principles'.[112] As Ramnath recounts, one of its senior military figures, Kwa Jwa-Jin, was known to posterity in anarchist circles as 'the "Korean Makhno"'.[113] Though the autonomous region was ultimately destroyed by conflict from 1931, another large-scale experiment along anarchist lines was conducted there – though how 'anarchist' the region actually was is a question still up for scholarly debate.[114]

Dirlik contends that though formal anarchism was all but eradicated with the triumph of Maoist Communism, anarchism left its mark in the Chinese revolutionary settlement in a number of ways, arguing that the 'significance [of anarchism] in Chinese radicalism derives, at least in part, from the diffusion of anarchist ideas across the ideological boundaries that divided radicals'.[115] He cites the presence of former anarchists amongst the revolution's early leaders, but also the development of the Maoist regime in certain aspects that deviated from the Soviet example, including the 'integration of agriculture and industry' in the 'people's communes' of the 1950s, which were to remind Colin Ward . . . of Kropotkin's industrial villages'.[116] Such an analysis is no reversion to the 'culturalism' which Dirlik argues pervades attempts to tie anarchism to Daoism (though it should be noted John A. Rapp's work is more sophisticated than this[117]), but instead a recognition of how anarchist ideas could be sublimated into a broader socialist milieu, in China as elsewhere.[118]

Conclusion: Global anarchism?

Reviewing Steven Hirsch and Lucien van der Walt's *Anarchism and Syndicalism in the Colonial and Postcolonial World*, the Marxist historian Bryan Palmer takes them to task on the plausibility of their view that anarchism was a truly 'global' endeavour in the period before the Second World War:

> To take the historiographical question first: how convincing is their claim that the global anarchist movement 'emerged simultaneously and transnationally' across three continents? The case studies themselves seem to contradict it. As they show, it was Italian immigrants and exiled French communards who introduced anarchism to Argentina, founding the Buenos Aires branch of the IWMA in the early 1870s. Waves of Spanish anarchists fled abroad to escape Canovas's ferocious repression in 1896; it was this generation that founded the first anarchist papers in Cuba.

Palmer goes on to cite Errico Malatesta's famed efforts in spreading the anarchist message on his many travels around the world.[119] Though this objection to Hirsch and van der Walt's thesis of a simultaneous emergence of anarchism might at first glance be dismissed as that of a Marxist writer unsympathetic to the claims of anarchist propagandists that anarchism held a greater appeal for societies around the world which had yet to develop a substantial industrial proletariat, this would be mistaken. In a perceptive essay included in Hirsch and van der Walt's collection, Arif Dirlik offers a more substantive criticism of the problems of 'deterritorializing anarchism':

> While historically speaking anarchism is clearly a product of European modernity, anarchists have been quick to discover anarchism in all kinds of places, from small-scale tribal societies in Africa to ancient Chinese philosophies. This has served to reinforce anarchist universalism but also rendered anarchism ideologically ahistorical. Anarchist universalism not only flies in the face of historical evidence, but is no longer tenable at a time when the legacies of universalism are under suspicion due to their entanglement in Eurocentrism.[120]

Dirlik's critique aims squarely at those writers who have sought to find anarchism in all times and in all places, to present it as an 'immanent', naturally occurring force. This is a common feature of 'classical' anarchism, from Proudhon's claim that he 'anticipate[d] history by a few days' to Kropotkin's claim that Laozi had been an anarchist.[121] It is the origin of Peter Marshall's statement in his widely read history of anarchism, Demanding the Impossible, that his project was to 'establish the legitimate claims of an anarchist tradition, since anarchism did not suddenly appear in the nineteenth century only when someone decided to call himself an anarchist'.[122] He continued on this theme with his depiction of a 'river of anarchy', flowing through history: 'anarchism was born of a moral protest against oppression and injustice . . . The first anarchist was the first person who felt the oppression of another and rebelled against it.'[123]

But, as Dirlik shows, such an approach is 'ahistorical'. It does not allow the historian to examine successfully issues of causality and contingency, driven as it is by a teleological ambition to provide ballast for the propagandist's case for anarchism. This is not to say that anarchists themselves in Japan, China, Korea, India and around the world did not seek to do precisely this. As Dirlik argues, and as we have seen, they often did try to 'domesticate the new idea' through 'translation into local idiom'.[124] As Khuri-Makdisi shows, pivotal to the success of radical political discourses in the later nineteenth and early twentieth centuries was their 'selective adaptation'.[125] The issue of place was indeed pivotal; it was 'not a matter of importing, but adapting, and adaptations cannot take place outside of the local frameworks that give meanings to novel concepts'.[126] Anarchist propagandists in Japan and India as we have seen did remake anarchist ideas and were attentive to local contexts. But it is important therefore to recognize their agency as historical actors – and as anarchist propagandists acting in a specific historical moment – and also, as Dirlik does, to note that the 'very act of translation transformed the local idiom as well'.[127] This was of course usually the intention of the translators, as with those Japanese anarchists who drew on Russian ideas to shape a new 'anarchist modernity' as described by Konishi. Indeed, Dirlik's essay notes perceptively that in attempt to leave behind 'Eurocentrism', another Eurocentrism may be reproduced in terms of adopting a vantage point that, as discussed in the Introduction, appropriates other traditions unconnected with anarchism for a social movement that was a product of a specific historical moment. Instead, decolonizing anarchism in a historiographical sense is to restore agency to a range of actors – 'forgotten' anarchists who remade anarchism and created new anarchisms such as Hatta Shuzo and M. P. T. Acharya, but also those nationalist movements which adopted anarchist praxis to further their ends. This chapter with its two case studies has not discussed the examples given by Benedict Anderson in his *Age of Globalisation*, where anarchists and nationalists in the colonial world used anarchism to forge an 'anticolonial imagination' which could resist imperialism.[128] But similar processes, as Hwang and Dirlik, Ramnath and Laursen have shown, were at play in South and East Asia. The project of decolonizing anarchist theory and praxis itself – rather than its history – was a concern for those involved in post-war radical movements at a time when 'formal' anarchism seemed to be a lost cause. Those 'last anarchists' are the subject of the next chapter.

Further reading

For anarchism in a global perspective and its relationship with wider revolutionary and liberation movements, Benedict Anderson's *The*

Age of Globalization: Anarchists and the Anticolonial Imagination (Verso, 2013) is a crucial text (previously published as *Under Three Flags* in 2005). Steven Hirsch and Lucien van der Walt (eds), *Anarchism and Syndicalism in the Colonial and Postcolonial World* (Brill, 2010) is also vital. Ilham Khuri-Makdisi's *The Eastern Mediterranean and the Making of Global Radicalism* (University of California Press, 2010) is an exemplary work which traces the intersections and connections between radical ideas and movements in a transnational context of movement and exchange.

Maia Ramnath's *Decolonizing Anarchism* (AK Press, 2011) is excellent not merely as a study of anarchism in India and South Asia but also as a methodological reflection on the decolonization project for the historiography of anarchism. Ole Birk Laursen's many articles (cited in this chapter) and his edited collection of M. P. T. Acharya's essays, *We Are Anarchists* (AK Press, 2019), are essential for understanding the connections between European anarchist movements and the Indian independence struggle.

East Asian anarchism has been better served in terms of the number of monographs available; Arif Dirlik's *Anarchism in the Chinese Revolution* (University of California Press, 1990) remains a turning point in the historiography. John Crump's *Hatta Shuzo and Pure Anarchism in Interwar Japan* (Macmillan, 1993) is, despite the emphasis on Shuzo, a good general introduction to the development of Japanese anarchism more generally. Sho Konishi's *Anarchist Modernity* (Harvard University Press, 2013) is a magisterial examination of the intellectual linkages between Japan and Russia, though it could be argued that it overestimates (given its focus on Russia) the originality of some of the 'Russian' ideas it discusses (especially in light of the significance of cooperation in Proudhon's thought).

Sam Mbah and I. G. Igariwey's *African Anarchism* (See Sharp Press, 1997) is an essential text on anarchism and contemporary Africa, though as they note 'formal' anarchist movements in much of Africa are a comparatively recent development, though anarchist movements did exist on the Mediterranean coast (as Khuri-Makdisi shows) and in South Africa amongst syndicalist organizations, as van der Walt's contribution to his co-edited collection *Anarchism and Syndicalism in the Colonial and Postcolonial World* highlights.

PART II

'The seeds beneath the snow'

Anarchism in the age of the super-powers

PART I

The seeds
beneath the
snow

A chapter in the
age of the silent
power

5

The last anarchists?

Anarchism, decolonization and protest in the Cold War world, 1945–1989

Introduction: Anarchism from the Second World War to the 'end of history'

As with the First World War, the impact of a second global conflict on anarchism as a movement was profound. For George Woodcock, himself part of the Freedom Group in London in the early post-war period, anarchism as a meaningful 'movement' had died on the battlefields of Spain, and he was not alone in this view, even amongst anarchist partisans. The challenge to the movement in the post–Second World War period was fundamentally ideological. The conflict ended with Europe divided between east and west, with Soviet communism and American capitalism locked in a Cold War with global implications and consequences for over four decades to follow. This chapter charts and analyses the debates surrounding anarchism as a series of ideas, actions and movements at a point when anarchism – even to its adherents – seemed historically to be at a low ebb, even (in the eyes of Woodcock) defeated. As Carissa Honeywell notes, 'the period from 1945 to approximately 1999 . . .

has tended to be overlooked in anarchist studies . . . there remains a rather conspicuous theoretical and historical gap'.[1] This chapter draws on a growing body of work which highlights the ways in which anarchism changed and adjusted to the social and political realities of the post-war world. It was, in truth, a period where anarchism was remade.

In the age of nuclear weapons, issues of pacifism and disarmament were to become features of the anarchist scene. As Honeywell shows, for anarchists, the 'warfare state' was a reality in both war and (nominal) peace.[2] In Britain during the war years *Freedom* (now *War Commentary*) offered an anarchist critique of the war and its conduct, and ultimately faced predictable consequences. In the early stages of the war, *War Commentary* covered the appearance of anarchists before conscientious objection tribunals which were convened to adjudicate on the legitimacy of individual objections to conscription. Anarchists could and at times did successfully cite their beliefs to avoid combatant and non-combatant service. In March 1940, two months before the Chamberlain government fell and Winston Churchill became Prime Minister, two anarchists – Godfrey Nunn and Ralph Mills – appeared before a tribunal in south-west London. In time-honoured fashion, Nunn and Mills used the formal judicial setting to expound their beliefs, with the difference that the tribunal was a more receptive audience (at least at first) than the courtrooms of the 1880s and 1890s. In a pithy statement to the tribunal, Nunn said:

> I am an Anarchist and have worked with Anarchists for the past two years. I credit you gentlemen with intelligence enough to know that an Anarchist is not one who attempts to impose his views onto others with bombs . . . You will appreciate that I do not recognise your authority to decide what I shall do, and as a matter of fact should your decision differ from my desire, it will be found that my apparent regard for your authority is apparent only. If I am asked to give oaths of allegiance to any course of action with which I disagree I might do so under very considerable duress, but I can assure you that I would try as soon as possible to make those who used force on me regret that they had done so, by making my views known to all I come into contact with and persuading them to rebel against authority.[3]

For his part, Mills cited his trade union activism and pointed up what he saw as a contradiction in the argument for conflict in terms of the state's claim to fight a war for freedom, which he saw vitiated by the infringement of his own freedom through compulsion to become 'a uniformed assassin of the state'.[4] The *War Commentary* account concluded that 'after a great number of questions, relevant and irrelevant, the Tribunal were unanimously satisfied' that both men were genuine conscientious objectors.[5]

This was not a consistent outcome, however; in April 1941 *War Commentary* remarked ruefully that the outcome of the tribunals overall had been a vindication of the aphorism 'might is right'.[6] A subsequent article in the same edition referred to the tribunals as 'a farce' and claimed that the tribunals existed as a 'screen' to provide legitimacy for the suppression of dissent.[7] In the February edition, the paper noted the suppression of the Communist Party's *Daily Worker*. While consistently unsympathetic to the Communists, *War Commentary* noted that the suppression was 'highly unlikely' to 'remain an isolated incursion on political freedom'.[8] By 1944 the state had turned its attention more directly to the anarchists themselves. As Colin Ward recollected, two contributors to *War Commentary* had been jailed for different reasons that year, the photographer John Olday and the writer and editorial board member Tom Brown.[9] In December 1944 the Metropolitan Police's Special Branch 'raided the Freedom Press office and the homes of four of the editors and sympathisers'.[10] They subsequently arrested three of the Freedom Group in January 1945 – Marie-Louise Berneri, Vernon Richards and John Hewetson – who were tried along with Philip Sansom for 'attempting to seduce soldiers from their duty'. Ward himself had been moved from a military detention camp – he was serving as a soldier at the time – to give evidence against the four based on his own subscription to *War Commentary*.[11] Berneri was acquitted on a technicality, the others jailed – with Ward and the other soldiers effectively testifying for the defence but to no avail. Nearly thirty years later, Ward puzzled over the motivations of the government in pursuing the Freedom Group – contemplating whether it could have been as simple as the 'vindictive[ness]' of the Labour Home Secretary Herbert Morrison, who sought to crush any criticism on the left from whatever source (and Morrison had in fact been behind the suppression of the *Daily Worker*). As Carissa Honeywell has since shown (drawing on material from UK state archives) the move against *Freedom* in fact came from Home Office officials acting on MI5 and Special Branch reports.[12] They were purportedly apprehensive of what they saw as the anarchists' potential influence on demobilized soldiers, though, as Ward claimed, they overestimated this.

The trial – as ever – raised awareness of anarchism and the group's plight became a *cause celebre* for civil liberties advocates and prominent intellectuals, who – as Ward noted – included George Orwell and Bertrand Russell. But the experience of the Freedom Group during the Second World War was representative of several issues that would affect anarchism as a movement in Britain and beyond in the decade that followed. The *Daily Worker* had been suppressed in 1941 ostensibly because of its opposition to British war aims, in the era when the Moscow 'line' meant defence of the Nazi-Soviet pact. Though the suppression was orchestrated by Morrison and some of the strongest opposition to the Communists came from the left, rather than the right, it foreshadowed the fact that in the post-war era communism as represented by the Soviet Union would consistently be perceived as a threat by the British state. The anarchists were much more marginal to events and despite their persecution in 1944–45, this marginalization was reflected in the lack of attention the security services paid to anarchism vis-a-vis Marxism in the period after the war. Anarchism was, for at least the first part of the post-war period, considered by the state to be an irrelevance.

Another aspect of the Freedom Group's experience during the war which was telling for anarchism generally both in Britain and beyond was their development of a critical analysis of social democratic politics. In Britain as in other European nations, the Second World War yielded (at face value) a social democratic political settlement, resting on Keynesian economics, which accepted an interventionist role for the state in the economy and the obligation on the part of the state to deliver economic outcomes such as full employment and a welfare state. As Goodway reflects, 'with the end of the war, Labour's electoral triumph and its programme of nationalization and welfare legislation, the anarchists became exceptionally isolated'.[13] Albert Meltzer recollected ruefully 'the sudden enthusiasm for a Labour government' which had seemingly opened up political possibilities far removed from anarchism at war's end.[14] More broadly, Peter Ryley notes that individualist anarchism in particular – of which more later – seemed to face real problems as the post-war period progressed: 'The twentieth century was the era of an increasingly successful social democracy. In rejecting the democratic state, individualists faced irrelevance.'[15]

The Freedom Group's response both nuanced the broader anarchist critique of the state and evolved it, but which also reflected, in many respects, the reality of the most significant challenge to anarchism in the post-war period – social democracy. Though on one level anarchist critiques of the Labour Party and other social democratic parties in the war years in Britain and beyond were simply the legatee of the divide in the First International, the *War Commentary* and *Freedom* critiques represented an acknowledgement that the state itself was changing. The war experience and the vogue for 'planning' which it represented were increasingly seized upon by Labour as vindication of the possibilities of planning for peacetime and Labour's idea of 'socialism' (even if historians have disagreed on the subsequent fortunes of 'planning').[16] Welfare capitalism would now increasingly be a foe the anarchists would be called upon to fight, but in certain respects this was more challenging than the older enemy of a *laissez-faire* non-interventionist state which had been content for millions to go without work and dignity in the 1930s. Welfare capitalism, in alliance with the trade union movement, could call on the allegiance of much of the working-class social anarchists sort to reach – at least for the first few decades after the Second World War.

Where the enemy was not a mythologized social democracy (as Dylan Riley has noted in the case of France, the triumph of social democracy was often more apparent than real[17]), it was often dictatorship and totalitarianism. In Spain, dictatorship had effectively crushed anarchism as anything other than a clandestine movement, save for periodical *maquis* raids. In the Soviet Union too, anarchism went underground and only sporadic outbursts – such as the hoisting of the Makhnovist flag in the Norilsk gulag as part of a series of uprisings on the death of Stalin in 1953 – were possible.[18] Anarchism was squeezed out; in the 1950s the Freedom Group became increasingly pessimistic as to the possibilities, if not the ideas and principles, of anarchism. Woodcock recollected later an interview for a visa when, despite his pessimism, he belatedly realized he was still an anarchist.[19] Vernon Richards throughout the 1950s charted a lonely course in the pages of *Freedom*, attacking social democracy and its 'impossibility' at every turn. Finally, Colin Ward in the early 1960s, responding to an intervention by an Australian anarchist, George Molnar, penned two highly controversial articles that assessed anarchism's 'respectability', or lack thereof.[20] Ward's verdict – that anarchism was not a desired end in terms of a fully anarchist society – lay apparently at odds with his continued claim to be 'an anarchist communist, in the Kropotkin tradition', and would invite vicious criticism that what Ward and *Freedom* increasingly offered was not anarchism at all but a form of radical liberalism.[21]

Whilst the immediate post-war period seemed a time of thoroughgoing pessimism for anarchists, by the later 1960s perspectives had changed dramatically in the wake of the 'student revolt' of 1968. Earlier still, following the 1956 Soviet invasion of Hungary, splits had begun to emerge amongst Marxists, corresponding with the rise of the New Left and new innovations in libertarian Marxism, which often did not acknowledge anarchist influences but which at least at times paralleled anarchist critiques (sometimes unknowingly). The period from the 1960s saw a process of dissolved boundaries where anarchism became more explicitly acknowledged as an influence within wider social and political thought and activism. The French philosopher Jean-Paul Sartre's thought increasingly echoed anarchist themes, to the point where William L. Renley has traced an 'anarchist philosophy' in his writing.[22] As Rosie Germain has shown, Frantz Fanon's work existed in a reflexive relationship with Sartre's existentialism; both would influence social and political movements around the world, including the rise of Black Power in the United States.[23] Lorenzo Kom'boa Ervin, a member of the Black Panthers and previously active in the Civil Rights Movement, developed the ideas later published in his *Anarchism and the Black Revolution* whilst in prison in the later 1970s.[24] As Kom'boa Ervin powerfully argued, decolonization was a project which had to take place *within* anarchism, as well as without it.

Finally, in the course of the 1970s and 1980s anarchism became influential within feminist and ecological movements, which in turn reflexively remade anarchism. Anarcha-feminism as a school of anarchist thought and practice emerged in true anarchistic fashion from practice to theory.[25] In ecological and environmental anarchism, Murray Bookchin's 1982 masterwork *The Ecology of Freedom* shifted the focus of traditionally human-centric anarchism to a broader concern with the natural environment and emphasized anarchism's opposition not merely to the state but to hierarchy as a whole.[26] It was significant and reflective of the revived and remade anarchism of the 1980s that Bookchin proposed patriarchy as a fundamental form of hierarchy which anarchism sought to contest.

In his 1973 book *Anarchy in Action*, Colin Ward argued that

> an anarchist society, a society which organises itself without authority, is always in existence, like a seed beneath the snow, buried under the weight of the state and its bureaucracy, capitalism and its waste, privilege and its injustices, nationalism and its suicidal loyalties, religious differences and their superstitious separatism.[27]

The Cold War represented a time of deep snows for anarchism, with global politics in large part structured by the imperialist rivalries of the two superpowers. A few months before the fall of the Berlin Wall – with the demise of the Soviet Union's power becoming increasingly evident – the American political theorist Francis Fukuyama infamously penned an essay entitled 'The End of History?' for the US conservative magazine the *National Interest*.[28] In Fukuyama's estimation, history could be thought to have ended because of 'the triumph of the West, of the Western *idea* . . . evident . . . in the total exhaustion of viable systematic alternatives to Western liberalism'.[29] Fukuyama viewed history in a Hegelian sense and argued that history was a clash of economic systems and ideologies, but that Western capitalism had ultimately proven victorious and had ensured the defeat of all other political ideologies, ensuring that the boundaries of the political imagination were now drawn so narrowly as to prohibit any serious possibility of state socialism (let alone anarchism, which never crossed his mind). But Fukuyama's triumphalism was to prove short-lived, not least because of the rise of an anti-(or 'alter') globalization movement which repudiated the premises of the liberal capitalism he averred. Even at the height of the Cold War in 1968, the 'seeds' had been seen – by anarchists at least – to bloom in the rebellion first amongst students and then amongst workers – in Paris and across France. The threat of nuclear Armageddon and the colonial violence meted out to independence struggles also changed anarchism's focus, as both a movement and an ideology. Though anarchism as a movement undeniably fell – at first – on hard times in the period after the Second World War, the post-war experience also did much to reshape anarchist thought and practice, and anarchist motifs and themes subverted liberal capitalism through the medium of consumer culture. But the dilemmas of the bureaucratic society balked large in the immediate post-war moment, and it is to these we turn next.

The individual and the collective in a bureaucratic age: Anarchism, libertarian socialism and 'libertarianism'

The purported social democratic consensus in Western Europe after 1945, though it promised expanded state welfare, did not vitiate the anarchist critique of the state. For anarchists, the bureaucratized welfare states of the 1950s and 1960s were still states, and their bureaucratization was a barrier to freedom. The critiques Vernon Richards advanced (to little avail) in *Freedom* echoed Proudhon's condemnation of government in the *General Idea of the Revolution*: 'we are opposed to government because all centralised authority cannot but reduce the individual to a cipher, a statistic.'[30] But though Richards was unrelenting in his attacks on parliamentary social democracy, he was also conscious that the task of the anarchist propagandist in the second half of the twentieth century was undeniably different to that of their predecessors in the late nineteenth century:

> To dub all believers in government as authoritarians, power maniacs, or sheep, as some anarchists do, is bad for our propaganda, which after all depends for its success on the good faith of those to whom we direct it. We do not find it surprising that most people use their vote (even when they do so with no more illusions than that they are opting for the lesser of two evils), if they can see no

alternative to government for the organisation of the day to day existence of the community. Anarchists on the whole, have not, unfortunately, been very effective in presenting the alternative.[31]

Colin Ward's subsequent development of a response to the changed circumstances in which post-war anarchists found themselves has been characterized by Jeff Shantz and Dana M. Williams as a form of 'sociological anarchy'.[32] Ward, who worked for the Town and Country Planning Association for a number of years, found himself a contributor to a debate that ranged beyond the confines of anarchism – the apprehensiveness many on the left felt as to the nature of the bureaucratized state. Ward's objection, like Richards' and Proudhon's, was more fundamental, but this didn't alter the fact that part of the reason Ward's essays in journals such as *New Society* and his books such as *The Child in the City* reached a broader audience was because of their resonance for this wider debate. In 1980 the Labour politician David Owen cited one of Ward's *New Society* articles in his arguments for the decentralization of power in Britain (though whether Ward would have welcomed the approbation of a politician moving rapidly to the right is questionable).[33] Ward's solution to the marginalization of anarchism, namely a focus on decentralization, and attempting to develop anarchist approaches to everyday life – to demonstrate the 'anarchy in action' which took place in everyday situations – offered influential perspectives on a range of areas covered by social policy, including education and housing. But the power of the bureaucratized state still loomed large.

A series of debates in post-war socialism around the world related to the true nature of the state. The state was, in the socialist tradition outside anarchism, accepted as a given reality. But despite the advances made by social democratic politics in the immediate post-war period, the state was at best still Leviathan, as Thomas Hobbes had once dubbed it, a titanic entity, now bureaucratized, which had the capacity to crush individual freedom on a whim. The preeminent theorist of the British Labour Party in the post-war period, Anthony Crosland – who went on to serve in the Cabinet in two Labour governments – commented:

> The most direct and obvious loss of economic power has been to the political authority, which now exerts control over a much higher

proportion of economic decisions than before the war . . . This is largely a consequence of the explicit acceptance by governments of responsibility for full employment, the rate of growth, the balance of payments, and the distribution of incomes.[34]

This was 'due mainly to a Leftward shift in the balance of electoral opinion', in Crosland's view.[35] But the expansion of the state raised problems of its own for the socialist, Crosland believed. It was no longer a question, for him, simply of the 'transfer of economic power'; instead there were 'other forms of power' which were of key importance.[36] First amongst these was 'the power of the enlarged and bureaucratic state'.[37] In trying to find a term for this new society, Crosland had called it 'statism'.[38] He later regretted it as 'a bad choice'.[39] But in the original essay where he had opted for it he had done so because it reflected in his view the fact that 'the power of the State has enormously increased . . . it is now an independent intermediate power, dominating the economic life of the country'.[40] It was true not just of Britain but of Scandinavia and other countries too, Crosland argued. Crosland claimed that 'statism' was a new society, but he simultaneously recognized that there was another possible 'successor to capitalism', namely 'the dictatorial managerial society or . . . totalitarian bureau-technocracy or pluto-technocracy'.[41] In this framing, as Crosland acknowledged, he was drawing on the work of the libertarian Marxist Lucien Laurat, whose own critique had been developed in dialogue with the work of Rosa Luxemburg, as Catherine Ellis has shown.[42]

Crosland was to become a central figure on the Right of the Labour Party, the key thinker of Labour revisionism.[43] But the critique of the bureaucratic state was to find expression elsewhere on the left, with the rise of the New Left (ironically often strong critics of Crosland) in Britain after 1956 and splits in Communist parties around the world following the Soviet invasion of Hungary that year. As Madeleine Davis has put it, the Marxists who forged the British New Left sought 'to occupy a third space between Stalinism and social democracy, rejecting the moral and political bankruptcy of both'.[44] For Davis, the early New Left 'anticipated key elements of late '60s radicalism in its antibureaucratic – even anarchic – spirit, its participatory ethos, and its experimentation with direct action'.[45] As David Goodway has shown, the anarchism of the 1960s intersected in significant ways with the development of the New Left. In the United States, explicitly anarchist groups formed at a number of universities, whilst libertarian Marxism was also a major presence. To a limited extent in the UK, anarchism enjoyed a minor revival amongst student radicals. Ward's monthly journal *Anarchy* was distributed on university campuses, with contacts for campus distributors included in the inside cover. In Oxford, the Oxford Anarchist Group met regularly, and Raphael Samuel attended. Samuel – in an insight not forgotten by Goodway – pointed out the shared inheritance of British anarchism and the first British New Left in terms of the influence of the socialist historian and theorist G. D. H. Cole, who was based at Oxford until his death in 1959.[46] Cole's ideas, particularly his thinking on guild socialism and workers' control, variously informed Colin Ward, Anthony Crosland and Stuart Hall. Cole had, as Goodway has shown, consistently been engaged through his career in dialogue with anarchism, even standing accused of being an anarchist by both the Fabian Beatrice Webb and his own wife Margaret.[47] In the United States, Paul Goodman – who Goodway grouped as a proponent of 'the "new" anarchism"' of the 1960s, along with 'Alex Comfort, Colin Ward, and Murray Bookchin' – offered an anarcho-pacifist critique which bridged the gap between anarchism and the New Left.[48] In Honeywell's assessment, 'he utilized the anarchist tradition to formulate his distinctive critique of contemporary America according to the principles of decentralization, participatory democracy, autonomy, and community' and stood in opposition to the 'managed and proscribed nature of centralized and heavily-administered societies'.[49] He played a key role in Honeywell's eyes 'in transmitting the themes and concerns of anarchism to the early New Left in America'.[50]

In France, the Situationist International (SI) offered a thoroughgoing critique of the cultural life of welfare capitalism which amplified and elaborated on Marx's critique of 'commodity fetishism', as the anarchist theorist Murray Bookchin later grudgingly acknowledged, though he criticized the critique as 'superficially' done.[51] Founded in 1957 in Paris, the SI argued against the shallowness as they saw it of life under welfare capitalism. Guy Debord, universally regarded as the 'chief theorist' of the SI, published his *Society of the Spectacle* in 1967, which was later regarded as a central text in the 1968 events which followed.[52] For Debord and his comrades, the media society of welfare capitalism offered an alienated culture, which legitimized the existing structure of power at all points: 'life is presented as an immense accumulation of *spectacles*. Everything that was directly lived has receded into a representation.'[53]

It amounted to the 'totalitarian management of the conditions of existence', where technological change facilitated human experience mediated through images and representation. For Debord, in the consumer societies of the post-war West people were no longer authentically 'living', but living in terms of engaging in spectacles, their actions and representations (and thus their political possibilities) delineated and defined by those who owned the means of production, and the bureaucratic state was key to this process:

> If the social needs of the age in which such technologies are developed can be met only through their mediation, if the administration of this society and all contact between people has become totally dependent on these means of instantaneous communication, it is because this 'communication' is essentially unilateral. The concentration of these media thus amounts to concentrating in the hands of the administrators of the existing system the means that enable them to carry on this particular form of administration. The social separation reflected in the spectacle is inseparable from the modern *state* – that product of the social division of labor that is both the chief instrument of class rule and the concentrated expression of all social divisions.[54]

But reactions against the bureaucratic state were not by any means the exclusive preserve of anarchist or left-wing critics. One substantive response to the rise of social democracy which would have profound implications for the politics of the final decades of the twentieth century and that of the first decades of the twenty-first century was that of 'libertarianism', which amounted to a fundamental critique of the social democratic state from the right. 'Libertarianism' is offered in quotation marks in these initial usages to highlight the controversy over the use of that name; for much of the second half of the nineteenth century, anarchists had referred to themselves interchangeably as 'libertarians', and such usage applied to social and communist anarchists every bit as much as every other school of the movement.[55] But, though this book has focused on the historical anarchist movement which began with the First International, there was a school of individualist anarchism primarily centred on North America which could not simply be reduced to a wing of the socialist movement. As Ryley notes, some individualist anarchists did characterize themselves as 'socialists', but the individualist tradition also owed much to classical liberalism, and the egoism of Max Stirner, whose 1844 work *The Ego and Its Own* grounded its theory in the absolute primacy of the individual, which Stirner called 'ownness'.[56]

With the Second World War having ushered in a (seeming) social democratic consensus in major Western economies, reactions against the bureaucratic state from the right took a number of forms. The Mont Pelerin Society, a group of economists and intellectuals founded in 1947, sought to fuse classical liberalism and Austrian economics in defence of what it saw as 'open societies'.[57] It should be noted, however, that the philosopher Karl Popper – who wrote *The Open Society and Its Enemies* and was a founding member of the society – was not of the right. He shared with Friedrich von Hayek a staunch opposition to Marxism, but unlike Hayek remained a believer in 'piecemeal social engineering'.[58] Nonetheless, on the left Popper has since often been conflated with Hayek in the development of 'neoliberalism', a political-economic value system which came to dominate the politics of the global North after the 1970s and much of that of the global South through the economic imperialism of Western corporations and intergovernmental organisations (IGOs) such as the World Bank and the International Monetary Fund (IMF).[59] Hayek's *Road to Serfdom* (1944) and the *Constitution of Liberty* (1960) viewed socialism and state planning as inimical to a free or open society, and advocated for strong protections for the private sphere and emphasized the significance of free markets.[60] Hayek's work in particular offered inspiration for a new, self-professed 'libertarian' movement on the right which sought a radically diminished state, which prioritized economic freedom (ostensibly as a bulwark against totalitarianism). The appropriation of the term 'libertarian' was to cause (and continues to cause) much consternation for anarchists, who viewed this as bad faith use of terminology and a wilful obfuscation of the true meaning of 'libertarianism' (the anarchist scholar Iain McKay continues to use 'proprietarianism' as a critical term for modern self-professed 'libertarianism'[61]).

A key contribution to the post-war right-libertarian milieu was the economist Murray Rothbard's development of a school of thought which ultimately became known as anarcho-capitalism.[62] Rothbard's libertarianism purported to be an anarchism on the basis both of the affinities between some of its ideas on economic competition (for example) and those of earlier individualist anarchists, and the scale of its rejection of the state. This was not simply the libertarianism or 'minarchism' of a radically limited state stripped of its welfare functions and maintaining only a residual function in defence of property and the provision of nominal security to that end. Rothbard's condemnation of government was thoroughgoing, as was his advocacy of free markets:

> the workings of the voluntary principle and of the free market lead inexorably to freedom, prosperity, harmony, efficiency, and order; while coercion and government intervention lead inexorably to hegemony, conflict, exploitation of man by man, inefficiency, poverty, and chaos.[63]

Rothbard deliberately situated himself in relation to a (select) group of anarchist thinkers; he cited Proudhon approvingly when he remarked:

> not only does the free market directly benefit all parties and leave them free and uncoerced; it also creates a mighty and efficient instrument of social order. Proudhon, indeed, wrote better than he knew when he called 'Liberty, the Mother, not the Daughter, of Order.'[64]

Rothbard also cited Tucker and Lysander Spooner amongst others.[65] In a 1981 *Cato Journal* article he famously claimed 'the State is the organization of robbery systematized and writ large':

> The State is the only legal institution in society that acquires its revenue by the use of coercion, by using enough violence and threat of violence on its victims to ensure their paying the desired tribute.[66]

'Anarcho-capitalism' as it became known, with its emphasis on freedom through economic individuality, was roundly rejected as a form of anarchism by those who identified with the historical anarchist movement.[67] However, Ryley has recently argued that 'anarcho-capitalism is the direct descendant of individualist anarchism, but shorn of many of its most radical elements'.[68] Rothbard himself in an unpublished essay answered his own question 'are libertarians anarchists?' in the negative, primarily on grounds of historical genealogy: 'those who call us anarchists are not on firm etymological ground, and are being completely unhistorical'.[69] Rothbard preferred the term 'nonarchist'.[70]

How far Rothbard's school of thought was from anarchism as historically understood was well illustrated by his direct and vituperative attack on several anarchists associated with the Freedom Group, including Herbert Read and Alex Comfort, whom he singled out for particular censure.[71] They had, to Rothbard's mind, 'made a point of rejecting logic and reason entirely'.[72] But he also paid them a backhanded compliment, characterizing them as a 'highly influential group of British intellectuals'.[73] There was an irony in this; as the British anarchist movement developed in the post-war period *Freedom* (and the intellectuals associated with it) would come under ever-more-severe criticism from class-struggle anarchists (particularly those such as Albert Meltzer and Stuart Christie, associated with the journal *Black Flag*) as not anarchist communist enough.[74]

Critiques of the bureaucratic state then, after 1945, came from both left and the right, from libertarian socialists in parliamentary politics, to Marxists on the New Left, to anarchists, to self-styled 'libertarians' – thought their critiques were different and in the last case motivated by a distinct political framing from the former. The formal anarchist movement as it had been was largely moribund, though the intellectual work of continuity groups like *Freedom* remained of significance. Ward continued to style himself as an 'anarchist propagandist' as had been the anarchists of old.[75] As he put it in 1959:

> The anarchist movement throughout the world can hardly be said to have increased its influence during the decade . . . Yet the relevance of anarchist ideas was never so great . . . For the

anarchists the problem of the nineteen-sixties is simply that of how to put anarchism back into the intellectual bloodstream, into the field of ideas which are taken seriously.[76]

But notwithstanding the critique of welfare capitalism that anarchists advanced, they remained, at the outset of the 1960s, firmly at the margins not merely of political life in general but of socialist activism in particular. Their relationship with both was to change in the course of the social upheaval in the decade which followed.

The Sixties: Decolonization and protest

Despite a historiography which has – at times – reflectively framed the 1960s in Western European societies as a time of affluence and primarily cultural change, the roots of the growth in political activism and protest which took place in that decade were deep. As David Berry has argued, 1968 – the year when protests erupted in Paris and the government seemed under threat – cannot be viewed in isolation; it is instead 'a shorthand [used] to refer to a much longer period which saw profound economic, social, political and cultural changes'.[77] These included, in his assessment, the rise of the Civil Rights Movement in the United States and the impact of the Algerian War in France.[78] In Richard Vinen's *The Long '68* he notes:

Some . . . argue the French 68 should not be confined to one place and time . . . point[ing] to a longer cycle of protest (particularly involving workers rather than just students) and to a geographical span that took in the provinces as well as Paris.[79]

The Algerian War of Independence began in 1954 when the *Front de Libération Nationale* (FLN) launched an uprising against French colonial rule and continued until 1962 when the FLN and the French government agreed terms for Algerian independence, subsequently ratified in referendums in Algeria and France.[80] The war destabilized French politics, and in 1958 the former Free French Forces commander and national hero Charles de Gaulle returned to power as a consequence of a military coup against the Fourth Republic. de Gaulle presented his return as that of a statesman fulfilling his national duty in the face of the military uprising, but despite his lack of personal complicity in the coup it was a matter of fact that he benefited from it, remaking the French constitution as he went 'creating a strong personal presidential regime' and inaugurating the Fifth Republic.[81] As Mikkel Bolt Rasmussen has argued:

> A complicated double game was being played out in which de Gaulle used the military coup to come upon the scene using the fear of a military dictatorship, all the while distancing himself from Massu's coup and making it appear as if power came to him, and not the other way around.[82]

In Bolt Rasmussen's assessment, the Situationists elaborated their argument on 'the society of the spectacle' in the context of de Gaulle's coup:

> According to them, contemporary society was characterised by the fusion of economy and state . . . the submission of social life to the spectacle has resulted in the production of a particular kind of political work and had necessitated the creation of a new kind of state, busy administrating everyday life. The invisible surveillance and administration of the population had become the most important task of the modern state form. The state had dedicated itself to controlling the population in accordance with the needs of capital.[83]

de Gaulle's use of technology and the media to govern represented the 'spectacle' par excellence: 'he used television to address the population of France directly, and thus to address it as one subject.'[84] The parallels between an anarchist critique of the state and that of the Situationists is clear, though the Situationists were not themselves anarchists. The de Gaulle coup, and the Situationists' diagnosis of it, problematizes the analysis of those such as Tony Judt who have seen in the thirty years after 1945 – the *trente glorieuses* as they popularly became known – a France in the grip of social democratic 'progress'.[85]

The Algerian War had much broader implications, not least in terms of what Todd Shephard has called the 'invention of decolonization'. In his view, it became 'the very archetype of the mid-twentieth century struggle to end Western colonialism', inspiring both radical activists and the agencies of the states which opposed them.[86] In Fanon's *Wretched of the Earth*, published in French in 1961 and in English in 1963, he acknowledged the inevitability of violence, arguing that 'decolonization is always a violent phenomenon'.[87] The 'proof of success' of decolonization

lies in a whole social structure being changed from the bottom up. The extraordinary importance of this change is that it is willed, called for, demanded. The need for this change exists in its crude state, impetuous and compelling, in the consciousness and in the lives of the men and women who are colonized. But the possibility of this change is equally experienced in the form of a terrifying future in the consciousness of another 'species' of men and women: the colonizers.[88]

For Fanon, a psychiatrist by training and a Marxist, the question of consciousness was key. Decolonization was not simply about the rejection of territorial control or physical subjugation; it was also about the construction and remaking of consciousness.[89] Fanon was himself a member of the Algerian FLN.[90]

Fanon's thought was to become influential in the Black Power movement in the United States which sought a more militant approach to the Black freedom struggle than the Civil Rights Movement which had preceded it.[91] Internationalism was key to Fanon's vision. As Vinen puts it, 'reading Fanon encouraged black militants to think of themselves as inhabitants of a colony making common cause with other parts of the Third World rather than as citizens of the United States seeking to exercise rights in their own country'.[92] Fanon also discussed spontaneity and the gulf between the urban and the rural environments in the anticolonial revolution and praised the consciousness-raising element of violence.[93] These elements of his thought have led some anarchist partisans to claim Fanon for their own, not least the alleged resemblance of some of these aspects to Bakunin's ideas.[94] As Laursen states, however, Fanon was no anarchist, but his ideas were to become influential through the Black Power movement in the Black Anarchism which developed from the early 1970s.[95]

The outbreak of mass protest in Paris in May 1968 was also, in significant part, connected with issues of decolonization. The initial incident which began the chain of events which led to the 'cobblestone beaches' of May when streets were torn up for missiles to hurl at the police and security forces was the arrest of university students for their involvement in an anti-Vietnam War protest at an American Express office in March. In Vinen's account:

> The following day, university buildings at Nanterre were occupied in protest at these detentions. From these emerged the 22 March movement, which was formed quickly in response to events. There was no accompanying ideological programme and it drew in people who had no previous political affiliation.[96]

David Berry described the movement as a 'mixture of anarchist, Trotskyist and unaligned militants' and notes the presence of the 'Nanterre Anarchist Group, who had split from the Anarchist Federation'.[97] Nanterre was a new university, constructed as an overflow from the overcrowded Sorbonne, but by 1968 tensions had begun to grow on campus.[98] Some of these related to gender segregation on campus and the policing of student sexual behaviour.[99] The anarchists for their part along with Situationists 'at Strasbourg . . . [and] Nantes' created their own syndicalist student tendency in the student unions.[100] A professor at Nanterre unsympathetic to the militants, François Crouzet claimed that the anarchists were 'conspicuous by their costume and obscene language'.[101] He also sketched an outline of one of the iconic figures of May 1968, Daniel Cohn-Bendit, who would become famous as 'Dany la Rouge' in the press.[102] For Crouzet, Cohn-Bendit was 'stocky and red-haired, a loud, coarse, but effective orator, and a skilful agitator . . . a born leader of men'.[103]

Cohn-Bendit was something else too: a declared anarchist.[104] *Freedom* in its coverage noted that Cohn-Bendit was a member of the Nanterre Anarchist Group, but he had also been a member of the *Federation Anarchiste* (FA) and was arguably the most influential figure in the 22 March movement.[105] Despite the dismissive accounts of some historians such as Vinen who have argued that Cohn-Bendit was 'largely indifferent to the theoretical debates . . . mostly interested in action . . . frantically energetic . . . a bully', Cohn-Bendit did represent a new formulation of anarchism even if that formulation made some anarchists of an older generation uncomfortable.[106] The Freedom Group worried about his supposed authoritarianism, particularly in the context of no-platforming, but this probably reflected *Freedom*'s specific brand of anarchism more than anything else.[107] There was, however, a generational split within French anarchism. As Berry notes, the May '68 'events' took the formal French anarchist movement by surprise; he cites a 'leading figure in the FA' as saying '"we jumped on a train that was already moving!"'.[108] But a commonality between the younger and the older anarchists was their anti-Stalinist views. Alexandre Hebert, a railway worker and anarchist, stated bluntly that Stalinists were 'just cops. I am totally opposed to them'.[109] The younger anarchists were more pluralistic in their influences, but it was untrue to say that they were theoretically disengaged. Despite Vinen's assessment, Cohn-Bendit – though he vigorously rejected labels and 'theoreticians' as personalities – was influenced by his elder brother Gabriel, who was deeply engaged in theoretical debate.[110]

In a later appreciation of how May '68 brought anarchism back into political currency, Anthony Arblaster noted how Cohn-Bendit and his brother Gabriel 'cited anarchist critics and historians of Bolshevism such as Ida Mett and Voline in the course of their comprehensive attack on Soviet communism'.[111] In their book *Obsolete Communism: The Left-Wing Alternative*, published in 1968, the brothers took the side of historic 'anarchistic' forces in disputes on the left, arguing that the Bolshevik Revolution had ultimately constrained the 'leftist' tendencies of the people. When the workers' soviets had become increasingly radical during 1917, in the Cohn-Bendits's assessment, it was 'Lenin [who] had to turn "anarchist", and to carry an incredulous party with him'.[112] The Cohn-Bendits's critique of orthodox Communist parties was shared by the New Left. When the revolt broke out in Paris, the black flags of anarchy alongside the red flag of socialism and the Soviet hammer and sickle adorned the walls of the Sorbonne and other Parisian educational institutions.[113]

Cohn-Bendit pointed up the significance of the Algerian War for his radicalism and his political consciousness:

> One thing affected me a lot. I was thirteen, and it was 1958. There were five or six hundred thousand people in the streets after May 13 . . . and even so the Gaullists came to power. And I couldn't understand . . . the birth of my political consciousness took place in a continuous process – the Algerian war, the things I read which made me conscious of political and social problems.[114]

When large-scale demonstrations and disturbances broke out in Paris it was the result of both long-run and short-run causes. The Algerian War had seared the consciousness of a generation and through Fanon had developed an anticolonial revolutionary critique, and the reaction of authorities to protests against the Vietnam War further escalated the situation. Vietnam, of course, also mobilized students on US campuses, particularly given the impact of conscription – the infamous 'draft' and the racial and class inequalities the draft's implementation represented.[115] Decolonization was central to the radical movements of the 1960s.

Over a matter of weeks in May–June 1968 France stood on the brink of revolution. Marches in the high hundreds of thousands took place in Paris; a general strike was called by workers in solidarity with the students. Action committees were formed across the country and in Paris in particular, and represented a resurgent enthusiasm for workers' control; syndicalism as a mass formal movement may have been over, but syndicalism as a practice was very much alive. Though the revolution that wasn't is often characterized as a failure and though, as Berry notes, it was not 'anarchist', it nonetheless played an important role in the evolution of a new anarchism distinct from the older formal anarchist movement. It offered a manifestation of a pluralist and less doctrinal anarchism, and in Julian Bourg's view represented a turn in France 'from revolution to ethics', whereby in the decades after 1968 ethics came to predominate philosophical discussion and political activism in a way they previously had not.[116] There was also a question of form and practice; direct action was normalized by May 1968, and occupations became a standard mode of student activism. In Britain, the London School of Economics

(LSE) was occupied, and at the 1968 Labour Party conference Anthony Crosland – a minister and theorist who had once claimed 'something of the anarchist and libertarian should run in the blood of socialists' – condemned the 'anarchism' that had gripped student campuses.[117] Anarchism may have influenced and corresponded with the protests of the 1960s, rather than those protests being reducible to 'anarchism', but the events of May 1968 in France were performed in a recognizable anarchist form, even as they often drew on a Marxist vocabulary.

Black Anarchism, anarcha-feminism, eco-anarchism

Black Anarchism

The anticolonial critique that radicalized sections of the Black freedom movement in the United States, resulting in part in the development of Black Power, including the foundation of the Black Panther Party (BPP) in 1966, ultimately came to play a role in a new anarchist school of theory and practice – Black Anarchism – in the course of the 1970s. Anarcha-feminism – a distinctively anarchist school of feminism and feminist school of anarchism – emerged at the same time, and both new schools came to anarchism and remade it, rather than emerging from the anarchist movement itself. For Black anarchists, as Dana M. Williams has shown, the experience of incarceration was pivotal.[118] The radicalization of the Black Power movement and the violent state repression it faced resulted in many Black activists either dead – as with Fred Hampton, assassinated by the US government during their COINTELPRO programme – or in jail.[119] As Kom'boa Ervin attested,

> The COINTELPRO conspiracy murdered at least 39 members of the BPP as well as other black militants, and jailed hundreds. People were summoned before grand juries. There was a legal, political and police offensive which disrupted the Party's work.[120]

In jail, a number of activists began to re-evaluate their strategy. Ashanti Alston's experience is representative:

I learned about anarchism from letters and literature sent to me while in various prisons around the country. At first I didn't want to read any of the material I received – it seemed like anarchism was just about chaos and everybody doing their own thing – and for the longest time I just ignored it. But there were times – when I was in segregation – that I didn't have anything else to read and, out of boredom, finally dug in (despite everything I had heard about anarchism up to the time). I was actually quite surprised to find analyses of peoples' struggles, peoples' cultures, and peoples' organizational formations – that made a lot of sense to me.[121]

Kom'boa Ervin's reminiscences echo Alston's. In an interview given to *Black Flag* magazine in the UK in 1995, he remembered how he had formulated his anarchist politics in prison, partly in response to the efforts of anarchist movements on the outside to free him:

The real political conversion came from contacts with anarchists around the world. In Europe there was a campaign to get my freedom, by the Anarchist Black Cross (Stuart Christie, Albert Meltzer and Miguel Garcia) and Help A Prisoner Oppose Torture in the Netherlands. This sharpened my beliefs and made me more serious about anarchism as a force for black revolution. I never saw myself as a token black anarchist, but as someone to apply anarchism to the black community.[122]

Kom'boa's Black Anarchism, as defined in his *Anarchism and the Black Revolution*, was fundamentally rooted in anticolonial critique and a challenge to white supremacy. He put it clearly: 'Blacks (or Africans in America) are colonised. America is a mother country with an internal colony.'[123] For his part, Alston argued that the Black Power movement and the Panthers in particular had become too hierarchical and that his own loyalty to the leaders of the movement was representative of a more fundamental problem. As he became more critical of the movement's organization and strategy, he became more engaged with anarchism and 'wrote to people in Detroit and Canada who had been sending me literature and asked them to send more'.[124] Kom'boa Ervin and Alston both argued for a rapprochement between anarchism and some forms of nationalism, which as Williams notes caused anarchists within the existing movement considerable discomfort.[125] But Kom'boa Ervin's and Alston's understandings of nationalism were close to Fanon's, as a potential force *against* the state.[126] As Kom'boa Ervin put it, the colonial status of Blacks in the United States 'requires the Black Liberation movement to liberate a colony, and this is why it is not just a simple matter of Blacks just joining with white anarchists to fight the same type of battle against the State'.[127]

In his later revised 1993 edition of *Anarchism and the Black Revolution*, Kom'boa Ervin noted that 'the ideals of Anarchism are something new to the Black movement . . . put simply it means the people themselves should rule, not governments, political parties, or self-appointed leaders in their name'.[128] This echoed the anti-authoritarian International's positions on the true nature of the class war in the 1870s: that the emancipation of the working class should be the task of the workers themselves, and they required no intermediary. Kom'boa Ervin's Black Anarchism echoed Bakuninist themes, particularly on the nature of the revolution itself and the role of the anarchist activist. Activists and revolutionaries were not to become 'leaders', nor were any anarchist organizations intended to be permanent (as with 'a vanguard political party or a labour union').[129] Instead, the role of the anarchist group was to 'act as a catalyst to revolutionary struggles . . . which try to take the people's rebellions . . . to a higher level of resistance'.[130] Kom'boa Ervin's argument espoused federalist organization and direct action without electoralism in the context of building 'dual power' and offered specific strategic direction, including tax resistance ('a Black Tax Boycott'), rent strikes and squatting. He proposed the boycotting of businesses and ultimately a general strike.[131] He also advocated for the assassination of the leaders of white supremacist groups such as the Ku Klux Klan, though on military grounds rather than on the grounds of propaganda of the deed as such. He declared his support for the commune as a form of governance and offered a devastating critique of the endemic reality of white supremacy under capitalism.

Kom'boa Ervin's anarchism was still emphatically class-struggle anarchism, but it acknowledged that oppressions could not be understood exclusively in class terms, though it also focused on the economic nature of the institution of slavery and the relationship of racism to capitalism. For Alston, Black Anarchism rested on going beyond nostalgia for past radicalisms: 'you should never be stuck in old, obsolete approaches and always try to find new ways of looking at things, feeling, and organizing.'[132] In the course of the early 2000s, the Anarchist Peoples of Color (APOC) conferences brought activists together to try to develop new approaches to organizing.[133] Both Kom'boa Ervin and Alston saw Black Anarchism as intersectional, opposing all oppressions, not merely focused on one aspect of struggle but instead recognizing patriarchy and homophobia as enemies to be fought. Alston remembered a split amongst the ex-Panthers when he tried to press an 'anti-sexist' line in the revived *Black Panther* newspaper, which led him to work more formally 'with anarchist and anti-authoritarian groups, who have really been the only ones to consistently try to deal with these dynamics thus far'.[134]

In his recent *Anarcho-Blackness: Notes towards a Black Anarchism*, the literary scholar Marquis Bey has sought to offer a new approach to anarchism and Blackness, which seeks 'an anarchic social life in that it is delinked from oppressive forms of governance and rule'.[135] Integrating anarchism, Blackness, queer and feminist liberation, Bey seeks to elaborate a Black Anarchism not as a prescriptive movement but with a 'focus on the anarcho' as 'a world-making sensibility'.[136] Bey draws on Alston's writings in claiming that 'on one register, Black communities are, one might say, anarchist communities' given the Black experience in the United States being represented by a necessary self-organization of communities and practices of mutual aid in light of the omnipresence of white privilege and racism.[137] Central to Bey's anarcho-Blackness is abolition, a central focus of the Black Lives Matter movement which emerged as a response to police murders of Black people following the killing of Travyon Martin in 2012.[138] Abolition – the abolition of institutions of the carceral state – from police to prisons is regarded by Bey as 'fundamentally anarchic'.[139] Citing Proudhon's famous quotation – 'to be governed is to be watched over, inspected, spied on' – Bey highlights the specificity of the Black experience of state oppression while also noting its affinities with those of other oppressed groups:

> Those who are surveilled with the most scrutiny ('watched over, inspected, spied on. . .') are Black, nonnormatively gendered, and femme, and thus to seek the liberation of those who live through these nexuses requires the promotion of a Black anarchic ungovernance. The insurgent history of slave uprisings, wayward movements, racial and gender 'passing,' and illicit sexualities is a swerve away from being regulated and registered. They are the people who did not have papers, but traversed colonized territories in search of land they could live with.[140]

For Bey, anarcho-Blackness incorporates the historic Black Anarchism of Kom'boa Ervin and Alston, and he draws inspiration from the Black Panthers. But he also finds antecedents for anarcho-Blackness in the response of those discriminated against according to gender binaries as opposed to skin colour or both simultaneously. In rejecting gender binaries Bey centres trans and queer sexualities along with feminism in his anarcho-Blackness, drawing historically on the Panthers and also on the lived experience of transgender figures such as Marsha P. Johnson and Sylvia Rivera in the Street Transvestite Action Revolutionaries (STAR) movement which they founded in 1970.[141] Anarcho-Blackness as theorized by Bey represents a fundamental opposition to all hierarchies and an abolitionist project which seeks not to prescribe a plan for a post-revolutionary society but which seeks instead to embrace the beauty of being 'ungovernable'. Bey's anarcho-Blackness is fundamentally anticapitalist, tracing the discourse of abolition to the abolition of slavery, emphasizing that

> one cannot assert the ills of private property without noting that not only is the factory or storefront over there 'property' but there are people who have historically been property, and the descendants of those people – or those who might optically or politically be placed in proximity to those people – are living with the effects of, as it were, property's afterlife.[142]

Thus Bey's anarcho-Blackness is opposed to property and the institutions of the state at a fundamental level, arguing that 'abolition is always both abolition of racism/white supremacy and capitalism', since the two are constitutive of one another.[143] Bey's thought is heavily influenced by feminist theory and praxis, and it is to the connections between anarchism and feminism as they evolved from the 1970s that we turn next.

Anarcha-feminism

Like Black Anarchism, anarcha-feminism was a new anarchism that came to the anarchist movement from another activist movement – in this case second-wave feminism. Anarchist contributions to the feminist movement during first-wave feminism have been documented in Chapter 2, but a distinct tendency within the movement self-identifying as 'anarcha-feminism' (as opposed to feminists working within anarchism or anarchist feminists working within feminism) did not emerge until the 1970s. According to Julia Tanenbaum, the 'term "anarcha-feminist" . . . first appeared in an August 1970 issue of the Berkeley-based movement newspaper, *It Ain't Me Babe*'.[144] In Tanenbaum's account:

> Anarcha-feminism was at first created and defined by women who saw radical feminism itself as anarchistic. In 1970, during the rapid growth of small leaderless consciousness raising (CR) groups around the country, and a corresponding theory of radical feminism that opposed domination, some feminists, usually after discovering anarchism through the writings of Emma Goldman, observed the 'intuitive anarchism' of the women's liberation movement.[145]

Drawing on Goldman for a 'usable past', though a pivotal figure in the rise of anarcha-feminism in terms of how she was engaged with by radical feminists in the late 1960s and early 1970s, posed challenges for second-wave feminism and the feminist movement as a whole. As Clare Hemmings has noted, Goldman's views were often not those of her feminist successors, exhibiting a 'disidentification with contemporary feminism'.[146] They were not even those of her feminist contemporaries, rejecting as Goldman did as an anarchist the suffrage movement and the pursuit of the vote.[147] She did, however, offer much else to 'feminists strugg[ling] to reclaim women's history', not least her 'advocacy of birth control, free love, and personal freedom'.[148] Just as Black Anarchism had emerged as a consequence of Black activists' experiences with the Civil Rights and Black Power movements, anarcha-feminists became such due to 'their experiences in the women's liberation movement'.[149]

Peggy Kornegger, who penned an influential essay on anarcha-feminism in 1979, grounded her definition of anarchism in a citation of Goldman.[150] She then turned – after a discussion of the Spanish Revolution – to recent events to establish anarchism's viability, namely May '68. According to Kornegger,

> [the] May-June events . . . proved that a general strike and takeover of the factories by the workers, and the universities by the students, could happen in a modern, capitalistic, consumption-oriented country. In addition, the issues raised by the students and workers in France (e.g. self-determination, the quality of life) cut across class lines and have tremendous implications for the possibility of revolutionary change in a post-scarcity society. [151]

Kornegger argued that 'women now hold the key to new conceptions of revolution, women, who realize that revolution can no longer mean the seizure of power or the domination of one group over another'.[152] For Kornegger, anarcha-feminism was not simply a feminist politics that made use of anarchist praxis; it was a new form of anarchism which offered a wholesale critique of societal oppression. It established patriarchy as the critical structure of domination not just in humanist terms but also in ecological terms:

> It is domination itself which must be abolished. The very survival of the planet depends on it. Men can no longer be allowed to wantonly manipulate the environment for their own self-interest, just as they can no longer be allowed to systematically destroy whole races of human beings. The presence of hierarchy and authoritarian mindset threaten our human and our planetary existence.[153]

That anarcha-feminism was its own form of anarchism which encompassed a broader critique (and indeed other anarchist critiques) is not universally agreed by anarchists or even anarcha-feminists. As Ruth Kinna shows, some anarcha-feminists explicitly reject the idea that anarcha-feminism is 'a sect of anarchism like anarcho-syndicalism of anarcho-primitivism, for an anarcha-feminist can have affinity with these and other sects', in the words of the *Anarcha Library* web site which Kinna cites.[154] As Kinna also shows, despite the attempts by some in anarchist movements to claim that anarchism was by definition anti-patriarchal, this was not the experience of women who organized in anarchist spaces either in the 1970s or historically, as the Mujeres Libres in Spain had known only too well.[155] Nor was it the case that anarchist theory was consistently anti-patriarchal; Proudhon's thinking rested on patriarchal not to mention outright misogynistic views of women and their role in society.[156] Anarchist spaces could in fact be dangerous; 'manarchism', as Kinna describes it, included 'male predatory behaviors, uninvited protectionism premised on norms of dependency, sexual violence and the casual dismissal of gender politics'.[157] Judy Greenway, an anarcha-feminist active in the anarchist movement from the 1960s, recollected an incident where she was nearly sexually assaulted by a male anarchist at a party; when the assailant was fought off, his rejoinder was 'call yourself an anarchist?'[158] As Greenway noted, 'this attitude that sexual freedom meant women on demand was one of the factors a few years later propelling us into the first Women's Liberation groups'.[159]

In the 1970s Greenway, along with Lynn Alderson, undertook a research project interviewing anarcha-feminist women about their lives and politics.[160] One interviewee, Susan, stated that male anarchists had at times 'been very unsympathetic to sexual politics, and some I find it hard to communicate with'.[161] Susan's was unequivocally an anarchist but 'relate[d] to the women's movement as a whole more than I do anarchism'.[162] Susan identified anarchist possibilities in taking direct action in the here-and-now – she was involved in the squatting movement. She thought women's liberation become more anarchistic over time:

I think when the WLM *[Women's Liberation Movement]* becomes more broad-based, it will inevitably take on a much more anarchist structure, because I don't think the majority of women will allow themselves to be led. I really believe in a basic anarchism in all women, because of their experiences. Women being more at home, more in small groups, more tradition of gossip and small political intrigue – I think that's something that excludes hierarchical structure.[163]

Susan's anarchism was representative of a process whereby 'anarchist women interpreted the anarchist critique of authority through the lens of their experience as a *women*', as Donna Kowal puts it.[164] Anarcha-feminism developed in the course of the 1970s and 1980s through publications, conferences and small groups including 'leaderless affinity groups in which each member could act as an individual'.[165] Affinity groups offered an intersection between feminist praxis and anarchism, where prefiguration – activism conducted through means and processes which made the future society 'real' within the group – was possible.[166]

Greenway's anarcha-feminism criticized the patriarchal biases prevalent in anarchist historiography, noting that a classic attempt to address the absence of women's stories within that historiography was an 'additive approach', which simply added a new canon of women to be 'included' but which fought shy of a genuinely feminist perspective.[167] In particular she criticized what she called 'the Emma Goldman short-circuit', a mechanism by which opponents of anarcha-feminism rejected engaging with critiques in the present by citing a supposed lack of originality, claiming instead that 'Emma said it all before'.[168] Indeed, the way Goldman has been written into history often obscures as much as it reveals. As we have seen, Hemmings has highlighted the complexities of Goldman's relationship with the anarcha-feminist tradition; her politics are not synonymous with that of later anarcha-feminism, however significant a role her memory and myth played in the evolution of the early anarcha-feminist movement.

But anarcha-feminism as it evolved from the 1970s had a transformational effect on anarchist theory and practice, just as Black Anarchism had done, and in similar vein emerged from debates and movements *outside* anarchism, rather than from within the anarchist movement. It overlapped with the concerns and praxis not merely of extant anarchist schools – which it in turn remade – but also with the nascent school of 'eco-anarchism', which it heavily influenced. It is that ecological anarchism to which we turn next.

Eco-anarchism

In 1982, Murry Bookchin published his masterwork, *The Ecology of Freedom: The Emergence and Dissolution of Hierarchy.*[169] It was a pivotal moment in the development of what Bookchin called 'social ecology' and what others called 'eco' or 'green' anarchism.[170] Born in New York in 1921, Bookchin was a former Marxist and trade union shop steward who in the course of the 1950s and 1960s had become an anarchist. Raised in a Communist tradition, he broke with state socialism following his experiences in industrial conflict as a trade unionist. As his fellow social ecologist and partner Janet Biehl recollected, it had been his trade union activism which had convinced Bookchin of the bankruptcy of the Marxist theory of class struggle and the inevitable destruction of capitalism:

> In 1948, as a member of the United Auto Workers and a shop steward, Murray participated in a large United Auto Workers strike against General Motors that resulted in the workers winning quarterly cost-of-living increases, company-paid health insurance and pension funds, and extended paid vacations – in exchange for abjuring walkouts for two years. That outcome convinced him that the working class, as such, was not going to be the primary revolutionary agent. Contrary to Marxist predictions, capitalism was not going to so 'immiserate' the working class that it rose up in rebellion against it. Rather, workers were going to try to make improvements in their working conditions within capitalism.[171]

As Biehl notes, Bookchin did not drop his commitment to anti-capitalism, but he did move away from Marxism, if not 'the notion of the dialectic unfolding of history'.[172] Bookchin still sought an explanation of societal development writ large; what he aimed to do, as Andy Price shows, is address 'everything that had been missed by Marx'.[173] In the 1960s Bookchin was a member of the Libertarian

League and in the 1970s was involved in an affinity group called *Anarchos* which published a regular journal.[174] In the essays he wrote in the 1960s and 1970s – many of which were collected in *Post-Scarcity Anarchism* in 1971 – he sketched the outlines of an anarchism which made positive use of technology to develop a society in harmony with nature, advocating for a decentralized society organized on libertarian lines.[175] He was, in the words of his sometime collaborator Brian Tokar, 'a leading theoretical progenitor of the many currents of left ecological thought'.[176]

A corollary to the critiques of the bureaucratic state widely advanced by the 1960s from points across the political spectrum was an increasing concern with the relationship between technology and the environment. The immediate post-war period saw radical protest around the world focus on the anti-nuclear movement, and anarchism itself underwent an 'anarcho-pacifist' turn in the United States and the UK which complemented this.[177] The fear of nuclear annihilation was only one aspect of the growing attention to environmental concerns amongst radicals, however; the increased use of nuclear power globally heightened concerns, with incidents such as the 1957 fire inside the Windscale nuclear reactor in England calling into question the safety of nuclear plants and the possible consequences of containment failure.[178] In 1962 – the same year as the Cuban Missile Crisis – Rachel Carson's *Silent Spring* was published in the United States, which offered a thoroughgoing critique of the potential risks associated with the increasing use of pesticides in agriculture.[179] It 'ignited a national, and eventually, an international furore and debate'.[180] As is well known in anarchist circles, Bookchin had in fact published a book addressing environmental concerns shortly before Carson, under a pseudonym – Lewis Herber – entitled *Our Synthetic Environment*, which had failed to reach a broad audience.[181] Bookchin too had been concerned about pesticides and additives, and the book developed ideas which had first been outlined in his earlier essay under the same pseudonym, 'The Problem of Chemicals in Food', which had appeared in 1952.[182] Whilst his first book did not have the same impact on the zeitgeist as Carlson's, his subsequent work existed in the context of the growing environmental movement even as it criticized liberal environmentalism in favour of a more radical social ecology.

The essentials of this ecology were apparent even in Bookchin's early essays. 'Ecology and Revolutionary Thought', published in 1965, highlighted the way in which the wonder of science had given way to the use of science as a form of domination.[183] Bookchin claimed that 'we have begun to regard science itself as an instrument of control over the thought processes and physical being of man' and that 'the branches of science that once tore at the chains of man are now used to perpetuate and gild them'.[184] Ecology, Bookchin argued, retained the 'critical edge' that other sciences had lost.[185] Concerned with 'the balance of nature', ecology was an 'integrative and reconstructive science'. This in turn meant it was anarchistic by nature:

> This integrative, reconstructive aspect of ecology, carried through to all its implications, leads directly into anarchic areas of social thought. For, in the final analysis, it is impossible to achieve a harmonization of man and nature without creating a human community that lives in lasting balance with its natural environment.[186]

Anarchism by contrast was not intrinsically ecological, but Bookchin took inspiration from the utopian possibilities which classical anarchism had offered, citing Kropotkin in this connection (but also the anti-parliamentary socialist William Morris).[187] In *The Ecology of Freedom*, Bookchin recognized his debts to classical anarchism when he stated that 'Kropotkin is unique in his emphasis on the need for a reconciliation of humanity with nature, the role of mutual aid in natural and social evolution, his hatred of hierarchy, and his vision of a new technics based on decentralisation and human scale'.[188] A central tenet of Bookchin's thought was that ecological crisis was the consequence of social crisis and not merely a crisis-in-itself. After sketching the dangers of pollution and the greenhouse effect in the early pages of 'Ecology and Revolutionary Thought', Bookchin stated bluntly that 'the imbalances man has produced in the natural world are produced by the imbalances he has produced in the social world'.[189] He was a critic of urbanization, and the scale of industrial society, which had led to a 'crisis in social ecology'. It was no longer simply about the ownership of the means of production – though this was still critical – it was also about 'the size of the firms themselves – their enormous proportions, their location in a particular region, their density . . . their requirements for raw materials and water'.[190] Bookchin's critique intersected with the broader critique of the bureaucratic state examined earlier in this chapter:

> Modern society, especially as we know it in the United States and Europe, is being organized around immense urban belts, a highly-industrialized agriculture and, capping both, a swollen, bureaucratized, anonymous state apparatus.[191]

Critically, Bookchin's anarchism broadened the focus of anarchist anti-authoritarianism away from merely the state to what the modern bureaucratized state represented – hierarchy and a principle of domination which was omnipresent in society.[192] This meant that the state was a consequence of this social principle and a key element in its implementation, but not its cause. As Bookchin put it, 'the patriarchal family planted the seed of domination in the nuclear relations of humanity', and the urge to dominate had only been intensified when 'organic community relations . . . dissolved into market relationships'.[193] Unlike anarcho-primitivists such as John Zerzan who would follow later, Bookchin did not reject technology and seek a return to an imagined prehistoric utopia – indeed Bookchin was heavily critical of Zerzan and his followers.[194] Instead, Bookchin sought a 'liberatory technology' which would facilitate a society based on decentralized, non-hierarchical, autonomous communities linked through voluntary confederalism.[195] Bookchin described his anarchism as 'social ecology', and in 1974 he co-founded the Institute for Social Ecology in Vermont to promote his ideas. His ideas – often appropriated by others without credit – offered a substantive theoretical basis for an ecology that went liberal environmentalism and which sought an end to capitalism and hierarchy as a whole. At the same time, the 'mainstream' environmental movement increasingly adopted the praxis of anarchism, if not its ideas – direct action chief amongst them. Bookchin himself was involved in direct action in 1977 in the occupation of the Seabrook nuclear installation alongside members of the Clamshell Alliance.[196] 'Green' anarchism would continue to be a prominent feature of anarchist ideas and movements into the twenty-first century.

Conclusion: 'New' anarchisms?

In 1989, history ended, for Francis Fukuyama at least. Western capitalism had won the argument in terms of political possibility; the impending defeat of Soviet communism meant the debate between conflicting political ideologies and systems was over. That was never true, and the belief in Western liberal-democratic hegemony looks, from a contemporary viewpoint, not merely misplaced but fundamentally ahistorical. Even during the age of the superpowers, other political systems and ideas had been available and deployed against the master-narratives of liberal capitalism and Marxist-Leninism. But the post-war period also remade some of these oppositional ideas, as we have seen.

A number of historians, including Goodway and Honeywell, have seen 'new' anarchisms emerging after 1945. For Goodway, the 'new' anarchisms were encapsulated in the work of Ward, Comfort, Goodman and Bookchin as described earlier in this chapter; for Honeywell, there were new anarchisms emergent at the end of the century, with the birth of the alter-globalization movement and the arrival of postanarchism. It was significant that Woodcock, in an article for the American magazine *Commentary* in 1968, changed his mind on anarchism. It wasn't dead, and it hadn't, after all, failed. But it had changed. Woodcock's comment – that the 'new anarchism' was a 'moral-economic movement appropriate to the age' – had something in it. As Bourg has shown, amongst French intellectuals, the social revolution of May '68 – though it had not toppled the French state – had resulted in an 'ethical' turn and a prioritization of ethical issues over straightforwardly political ones in both intellectual work and activism.[197] The various schools of poststructuralist and postmodernist thought which emerged in French theory in the course of the 1970s and 1980s would ultimately interact with anarchist theory in the confluence which became known as 'postanarchism' in the 2000s. But the 'ethical turn', as far as anarchism was concerned, also raised questions. Whilst the feminist movement had espoused the slogan the 'personal is political' to advocate for transformational social change, some anarchists feared that a narrower reading of personal politics than that which the feminist movement argued for – a retreat to ethics – might result in an abandonment of the revolution and of the necessary structural change required to usher in a free society. In Britain this split found expression in the often-bitter conflict between the Freedom Group and *Black Flag* magazine after 1970, with the latter group identifying more explicitly with 'class-struggle anarchism', as Class War was also to do in the course of the 1980s. Class-struggle anarchists, who in some cases identified directly with the pre-1939 anarchist tradition, were wary of the idea of 'anarchizing' spaces or the creation of Temporary Autonomous Zones as Hakim Bey argued for in the 1980s. 'Anarchization' (as Ruth Kinna later described it) was not enough; in their view anarchism at a societal level and realized through revolution remained the desired goal, a goal which Ward for one had explicitly and publicly abandoned in the early 1960s.

Though these divisions of opinion were real and bitter, they obscure the fact that there was no single new anarchism, but there were new *anarchisms* (even as propagandists fighting for one position or another consciously created straw-men out of their opponents). Black Anarchism and anarcha-feminism never abandoned any idea of a revolution, though understandings of what revolution meant varied (as did the timescale on which the revolution might take place). Class-struggle anarchists' dismissals of 'new' anarchisms were at times exclusionary and rooted in prejudice – as anarcha-feminists and Black anarchists knew only too well. Class first, what was sometimes described as 'identity politics' second, where second had a tendency to mean not 'second' but 'never', was rightly unacceptable to Black and feminist anarchists.

The diversity of anarchisms which developed in the post-war period breathed new life into anarchist organizing and helped to shape – through 'permeation' – wider debates about social issues from education, to housing, to the environment. Ward and Bookchin's contributions here remain significant. The praxis of anarchism – direct action, non-hierarchical organizing, the search for consensus within groups – would also become defining characteristics of organizing across radical movements, as increasing numbers of groups adopted prefigurative approaches. After the 1970s, the rapid acceleration of globalization – the increasing interconnectedness of the world at an economic and political level, governed by free-market ideology – provided a new target for anarchists and those like them opposed to hierarchy and united in the defence of social freedoms. This saw the rise of the most iconic 'anarchist' mobilizations of the era of the millennium – the rise of the alter-globalization movement and the appearance of the 'Black Bloc'. It is to these we turn next.

Further reading

General reading

Historical literature on post–Second World War anarchism is understandably less developed than for the pre-war period, with a significant lack of single-volume histories to parallel such work. However, for France David Berry's edited special edition of the journal *Modern and Contemporary France* 24, no. 2 (2016), '"Y'en a pas un sur cent et pourtant ils existent. . .": Anarchists and Anarchisms in France since 1945', offers essays on a range of topics including one by Berry introducing French anarchism and sources on French anarchism after 1945. Benjamin Franks has provided a history of British anarchism since 1945 as part of his broader philosophical work *Rebel Alliances: The Means and Ends of Contemporary British Anarchisms* (AK Press, 2006). Some work still in print is more primary source than historiography but is useful to the student nonetheless, for example David E. Apter and James Joll's edited collection *Anarchism Today* (Macmillan, 1971, available digitally from Palgrave) which gives an interesting first-hand look at anarchism in the wake of 1968. US anarchism since 1945 receives some attention in the Pacific Street Films production *Anarchism in America* (1983), which is available on DVD and also online, and which was produced by members of the 1960s student left.

1968

The 1968 events in France and their relationship to anarchism are well surveyed in an edition of Freedom Press' *Anarchy* journal (*Anarchy* 69, edited by Colin Ward) produced a year after the revolt and available at the libcom.org online archive (https://libcom.org/library/anarchy -099). David Berry's essay 'Anarchism and 1968' in the Carl Levy and

Matthew S. Adams's *Palgrave Handbook of Anarchism* (Palgrave, 2019) is a valuable survey and point of orientation for the student seeking to understand the specific connections between anarchism and 1968. Julian Bourg's *From Revolution to Ethics: May 1968 and Contemporary French Thought* (MQUP, 2007), though it says little specifically about anarchism, is extremely useful on highlighting the points of fracture within French society that were central to May '68 and what he sees as an 'ethical' turn in radical theory which followed.

Anarcha-feminism and Black Anarchism

Anarcha-feminism has received increasing attention and has been the subject of excellent essays in the *Palgrave Handbook of Anarchism* (by Donna Kowal) and *Brill's Companion to Anarchism and Philosophy* (2017, by Ruth Kinna). An invaluable starting point is *Anarcha-Feminisms*, issue 29 of *Perspectives on Anarchist Theory* (2016), which is available as a single volume (with some of its essays, including the historical account by Julia Tanenbaum drawn on here, available online at the Institute for Anarchist Studies website – www.anarchiststudies.org). Also vital for an understanding of the rise of anarcha-feminism within the anarchist and feminist movements is the Dark Star Collective's anthology *Quiet Rumours* (AK Press, 2012) which includes writings from famous historical figures such as Goldman and Wilson alongside essays from within the anarcha-feminist movement of the 1970s on from authors such as Peggy Kornegger and the work of radical collectives such as RAG Dublin. For Black Anarchism, Lorenzo Kom'boa Ervin's *Anarchism and the Black Revolution* remains a critical text and has been updated several times; it is available as part of the Black Rose Federation's essential *Black Anarchism* reader (2016, available online at https://blackrosefed.org/black-anarchism-a-reader/).

General anarchist thought

Arguably the most two major anarchist thinkers of the post-war period, Murray Bookchin and Colin Ward, have received considerable scholarly attention. Their main works are worthy of consultation directly. For Bookchin, the student may wish to read *Post-Scarcity Anarchism* (Ramparts Press, 1971) and *The Ecology of Freedom: The Emergence and Dissolution of Hierarchy* (Cheshire Books, 1982, now available in a revised AK Press edition). Bookchin is a controversial figure in anarchist circles, not least for his apparent repudiation of anarchism towards the end of his life, but the short book by Andy Price, *Recovering Bookchin: Social Ecology and the Crises of Our Time* (New Compass Press, 2012), offers a helpful critique. For Ward, *Anarchy in Action* (Allen & Unwin 1973, now available in a revised Freedom Press edition) is the best summary of his 'sociological anarchism'. A Colin Ward reader collating representative examples of his wider writing entitled *Autonomy, Solidarity, Possibility* and edited by Chris Wilbert and Damian F. White is available from AK Press (2011). Ward was the subject of a special issue of the journal *Anarchist Studies*, 19, no. 2 (2011) edited by Carl Levy, which was subsequently republished as a book, Carl Levy (ed.), *Colin Ward: Life, Times and Thought* (Lawrence and Wishart, 2014).

PART III

Anarchist 'turns'
Anarchism in the age of postmodernity

Conclusion

Anarchism and history in a second anarchist moment

Since there are very good reasons why an anarchist anthropology really ought to exist, we might start by asking why one doesn't – or, for that matter, why an anarchist sociology doesn't exist, or an anarchist economics, anarchist literary theory, or anarchist political science.

–DAVID GRAEBER, *Fragments of an Anarchist Anthropology* (2004)[1]

History never contains truth; it is the past transformed to resemble the present.

–ANDREW M. KOCH, 'Post-structuralism and the Epistemological Basis of Anarchism' (1993)[2]

[P]olitics without history is directionless . . . attempts to renegotiate an alignment between red and black would benefit from a sense of historical precedent rather than more theory.

RUTH KINNA AND ALEX PRICHARD, 'Introduction' in Alex Prichard, Ruth Kinna, Saku Pinta and David Berry (eds.), *Libertarian Socialism: Politics in Black and Red* (2012)[3]

Introduction: 'The new anarchists'

In 2002, the anthropologist David Graeber published what would become a well-known and highly influential article in the emerging field of anarchist studies. Entitled 'The New Anarchists', it appeared in the Marxist journal *New Left Review*. In the piece, Graeber offered a sketch of the eponymous 'new anarchists', who in his view had not received enough credit from the broader left-intellectual milieu. '[I]n a mere two or three years', Graeber wrote, the alter-globalization movement had 'managed to transform completely the sense of historical possibilities for millions across the planet'.[4] As he knew – and reminded his audience – the movement of which he spoke was demonized as an 'anti-globalization movement' by hostile critics, critics which included even some of those who styled themselves as radicals.[5] In 1999 the World Trade Organization (WTO) summit in Seattle had been met by mass protests, including direct action activism and a heavy-handed police response to the protestors, becoming known to posterity (and to Hollywood) as 'the Battle in Seattle'.[6] But the media coverage's (purposeful and misleading) emphasis on violence obscured in Graeber's view what the movement really represented. The movement was not straightforwardly 'anti-globalization'. In fact, in Graeber's view, it was an *authentic* globalization movement, made up of peoples from around the world, working together in new networks of resistance and cooperation, to fight the economic imperialism of neoliberal globalization as promoted by states in the global North and enforced by international economic and financial institutions such as the International Monetary Fund, the World Bank and the WTO. Graeber argued that globalization as generally advocated for by Western governments was reducible to trade in commodities and little else:

> activists have been trying to draw attention to the fact that the neoliberal vision of 'globalization' is pretty much limited to the movement of capital and commodities, and actually increases barriers against the free flow of people, information and ideas – the size of the US border guard has almost tripled since the signing of NAFTA. Hardly surprising: if it were not possible to effectively

imprison the majority of people in the world in impoverished enclaves, there would be no incentive for Nike or The Gap to move production there to begin with.[7]

Instead, the globalization of the supposedly 'anti-globalization' movement – which preferred to be known as the alter-globalization movement – was one which had concerns of justice and equality at its core, and, in Graeber's assessment, 'anarchism is at the heart of the movement, its soul; the source of most of what's new and hopeful about it'.[8] Graeber was uninterested in quibbling over whether this was 'formal' anarchism or not; as far as he was concerned it was enough that this was a direct action movement operating outside electoral politics, one that was a question not simply of a Western-dominated movement but on where the world as a whole was engaged in resistance, with much of the drive coming from the global South. Taking a longer historical view, this echoed for Graeber what we have seen earlier in this book: that in the pre-1914 period, 'anarchism and anarcho-syndicalism were the centre of the revolutionary left'.[9] The contemporary movement, for Graeber, had its 'origins with the Zapatistas ... and other movements in the global South'.[10] On 1 January 1994 the Zapatistas – Ejército Zapatista de Liberación Nacional (EZLN; the Zapatista Army of National Liberation) – launched an uprising in the Chiapas region of Mexico. Chiapas had been on the front line of neoliberal globalization after the 1970s, with economic transformation including rapid growth in cattle farming (at a huge environmental cost) promoted by both the Mexican government and the World Bank.[11] In 1992, as the Mexican government prepared to join the North American Free Trade Agreement (NAFTA), the constitution was altered to ensure the availability for sale of community-owned land.[12] Indigenous communities were subjected to disenfranchisement and discrimination by federal authorities over an extended period, leading Burbach to conclude that '[th]e rebellion in Chiapas is the product of a quarter-century of capitalist modernization and resistance by peasant and Indian organizations'.[13] Crucially for Graeber it was a decentralized rebellion, which opposed electoralism and used direct action in its attempt to seize both territory and the agenda from the Mexican government. As Graeber recounted, the People's Global Action (PGA) group which 'put out the first summons for planet-wide days of action such as .... N30 ... the original call for protest against the 1999 WTO meetings in Seattle . . . owe[d] its origins' in part to a conference hosted by the Zapatistas in 1996, 'the International Encounter for Humanity'.[14] Though the Zapatistas did not define themselves as anarchists, for Graeber at least this paralleled the ways in which in the pre-1914 period, as Benedict Anderson had argued, anarchism had often found its fullest expression outside Europe and the United States, where it was remade.[15]

Graeber's anthropological background influenced his assessment. Anarchism was for Graeber a practice and anti-authoritarian way of being and mode of action that existed in other cultures and which did not necessarily have to relate in specific terms to the movement which was born in Europe in mid-nineteenth century. In 2006, Graeber appeared on *Charlie Rose* to defend his approach to anthropology and to anarchism, which he saw as intrinsically linked.[16] For Graeber, the recognition of the vitality of anarchism flowed from his anthropological studies; the 'credibility gap' which many ascribed to anarchism was resolved by the reality of witnessing 'anarchy in action', something Graeber had done during his fieldwork in Madagascar and elsewhere.

This informed Graeber's theorization of anarchism in 'The New Anarchists' and how it could be viewed categorically. He differentiated between 'capital-A anarchist groups' and 'small-a anarchists', in a schema that was to be taken up by Maia Ramnath and others subsequently. Capital-A groups identified with the historical anarchist tradition, and Graeber regarded them as 'sectarian', akin to Marxist groups.[17] Instead, the 'ideology' of the small-a anarchists was 'immanent in the anti-authoritarian principles that underlie their practice, and one of their more explicit principles is that things should stay this way'.[18] Graeber went on to write a series of major histories, including volumes on debt and bureaucratization, and an ethnography of direct action in the global justice movement.[19] He remained both an academic and an activist, with his *Democracy Project*, published in 2013, offering an account of the Occupy movement, with which he was closely associated.[20]

Graeber's view of the 'new anarchism' saw it as the animating force in popular protest from the later 1990s into the 2010s, even if it was not conscious of itself as anarchism, and this allowed Graeber to incorporate other movements (such as the 'Rojava revolution' in northern Syria) into his account of political change. But in his emphasis on anarchism as a practice rather than an identity, he echoed Kropotkin's naturalistic arguments for anarchism in *Mutual Aid*; anarchism was a 'sensibility', timeless and 'immanent'. As Graeber put it:

> there are two different ways one could tell the history of anarchism. On the one hand, we could look at the history of the word 'anarchism' which was coined by Pierre-Joseph Proudhon in 1840 and was adopted by a political movement in late-nineteenth-century Europe, becoming especially strongly established in Russia, Italy, and Spain, before spreading across the rest of the world; on the other hand we could see it as a much broader political sensibility.[21]

Though Graeber attempts to do justice to both perspectives, his sympathy is clearly with the sensibility. The problems with this as we have seen is that anti-authoritarian movements outside of Europe become defined by a European anti-authoritarian vocabulary not their own; in addition the genuine relationship and influence of global movements to and on the specific anarchist movement is obscured. This perspective, which echoes Kropotkin's propagandizing, leads Graeber to claim:

> In this sense there have always been anarchists: you find them pretty much any time a group. Of people confronted with some system of power or domination imposed over them object to it so violently that they begin imagining ways of dealing with each other free of such forms of power or domination.[22]

Graeber then cites ancient Chinese history, including 'a philosophical movement that came to be known as the "School of the Tillers"' and 'the Taoist philosophy of Lao Tzu and Chuang Tzu' as anarchist precursors. He then approvingly cites James C. Scott, another scholar with an anthropological academic background, who has written *longue duree* histories of stateless societies in Southeast Asia.[23] Scott's histories range widely and echo anarchist themes, focusing as they do not merely on statelessness itself but also on subtle forms of resistance and the failures of state socialism.[24] Scott has claimed that his 'interest in the anarchist critique of the state . . . [was] born of disillusionment and dashed hopes for revolutionary change'.[25] He located this in the failures of the 1960s rebellions around the world, not merely the student movement which he had been involved in but also 'peasant wars of national liberation'.[26] The 'anarchist critique', for Scott, paralleled his recognition that 'virtually major successful revolution ended by creating a state more powerful than the one it overthrew'.[27] Unlike Graeber, Scott was not an anarchist himself in terms of his personal politics; in his historical work he advocated for an 'anarchist squint', a way of seeing the historical past which allowed for the detection of 'anarchism as praxis' in the behaviour of previous societies.[28] As he made clear, what he was looking for was anarchism in what he regarded as a Proudhonian sense: 'mutuality or *cooperation without hierarchy or state rule*'.[29] Critically, though, he did not repudiate the state. He did not believe it is 'everywhere and always the enemy of freedom', noting that it has been the US armed forces acting on federal government orders which had desegregated the Arkansas school system in 1957.[30] Scott argued that 'both theoretically and practically, the abolition of the state is not an option. We are stuck, alas, with Leviathan.'[31] The boundaries of Scott's 'anarchism' are thus narrowly drawn; the definitional aspect of anarchism, the outright rejection of the state, is itself rejected.

Yet for all that, Scott's histories offer an opportunity to recover a past which has been obscured by the state-centricity of the historical discipline. In addition, his view of anarchism as essentially a vehicle for driving radical democracy touches on (even if it is clearly not the same as) themes in Graeber's work and Murray Bookchin's too. Graeber envisioned Occupy as a 'democracy project', and Bookchin had advocated for participation in local government – but not national government – to make local democracy real, as part of a process of creating an authentic, participatory democracy. But, as Markus Lundstrom has recently reminded us, the equation of anarchism with 'democracy' is a highly contentious one.[32] As discussed in the Introduction to this volume, the academy saw an 'anarchist turn' in the early twenty-first century as Jacob Blumenfeld, Chiara Bottici and Simon Critchley claimed in their edited volume of the same name, with anarchist approaches and anarchism as an object of study becoming of greater significance in a number of disciplines.[33] The extent to which developments in anarchist ideas paralleled developments within movements is, however, a contentious one. For some such as Burbach, the Zapatista uprising was itself a 'postmodern' rebellion; this was the age of postmodernity, when the certainties of the 'modernist' paradigm had been shattered. This meant a need for differentiated, decentralized action, not the vanguardism of the past. The Zapatistas for Burbach represented that decentralized, postmodern revolt.

Within the academy, an intellectual project to address correspondences and conjunctures between anarchist ideas and postmodernist and poststructuralist theories developed in earnest amongst philosophers and other scholars after the early 1990s. As Jason Adams and Sureyyya Evren detail in their separate accounts, postanarchism developed in a complex relationship with the alter-globalization and new social movements which had developed since the 1990s, offering a critique of classical anarchism whilst embracing anarchist modes of praxis. For some activists though there was no relationship at all, with 'postanarchism representing an approach that unconsciously plays the game of neoliberalism'.[34]

The remainder of the concluding chapter will trace the outlines of the postanarchist debate and its relationship (or lack thereof) to the anarchistic movements which Graeber has chronicled. It will then conclude with final reflections on assessing historical debates on anarchism in the early twenty-first century, a time Andrej Grubacic described as, we saw at the opening of this book, a 'second anarchist moment'.

The modern legacy of '68?: A postanarchist 'moment'

Postanarchism and 'lifestyle anarchism'

When the philosopher Todd May published his *Political Philosophy of Poststructuralist Anarchism* in 1994, history was not foremost on his mind. As May recalled, his attention had been called to anarchism when in a conversation with a fellow philosopher about poststructuralism on a train in the late 1980s, his colleague informed him that poststructuralism 'sounded like anarchism to me'.[35] In the book which followed, May took the fall of Soviet communism as a point of departure but in a radically different way than Fukuyama had done. May argued that the collapse of the Soviet Union meant that 'political philosophy is now in crisis'.[36] This was not, May continued, because of excessive faith in the Soviet Union itself – quite the contrary – but because

> the discourse of Marxism still seemed to provide enough hope and enough sense to political philosophy that its shortcomings – both in theory and in reality – appeared reparable. However, the rejection by its subjects of the entire spectrum of Marxist thought and intervention laid waste to that appearance.[37]

The demise of Marxism in part represented the demise of modernity; Marxism's purported universal truth and scientific socialism having been repudiated, the age of the postmodern was no longer merely a cultural phenomenon but also a political one. May explicitly rejected Fukuyama's claim that the fall of the Soviet Union meant 'capitalism is triumphant'; instead he advocated for a new 'framework' which could incorporate poststructuralist critiques which had emerged in the previous several decades and translate them into action.[38] This could be done, he argued, by 'grafting poststructuralism onto a tradition in whose light it has not been grasped – the anarchist tradition'.[39] Poststructuralism – understood in May's account as a combination of insights and theories derived from three principal thinkers, Michel Foucault, Jean Francois-Lyotard and Gilles Deleuze – offered a more nuanced understanding of power than classical anarchism had done, allowing for 'tactical' political interventions in arenas ranging across the whole of society.[40] This came in part from the 'the poststructuralist critique of representation', a signal feature of three thinkers May grouped together.[41] For May this meant 'a refusal of the vanguard, of the idea that one group or party could effectively represent the interests of the whole.[42]

Jason Adams, an anarchist and scholar active in the alter-globalization movement, saw postanarchism as the philosophy of that movement. In an essay published in 2003, Adams stated that it was 'no surprise' scholars such as May had come to see affinities between anarchism and poststructuralism.[43] In fact, for Adams the postanarchist moment of the late 1990s and the 2000s was a legacy of May '68, as were the ideas and theories of poststructuralism itself. Whereas Bourg had seen the failure of the political revolution in May '68 as inaugurating a 'turn to ethics' amongst prominent French theorists, Adams historicized the picture differently. The affinities between anarchism and poststructuralism were present in part because of poststructuralism's own genealogy; in Adams's reading of May '68, anarchism had been at its heart, claiming as he did that 'it is well-known that anarchism was a major element of the events'.[44] He cited Raoul Vanigem's critique of hierarchy and Foucault's critique of power to emphasize that 'poststructuralism emerged out of a much larger anti-authoritarian milieu'.[45] As Benjamin Franks has critically noted, there is a distinction between Adams's account and May's; anarchism was always present in poststructuralism for Adams, and so there was no need for 'grafting [it] onto' anarchism.[46]

Adams's account arguably overemphasizes the centrality of anarchism to May '68 though May '68 was certainly important for anarchism, as the account in this book has endeavoured to show. But whilst he based poststructuralism's character on an anarchist inheritance, his argument then turned to an attack on the alleged sectarianism of historic anarchist schools. Tomas Ibanez, a participant in the May '68 events, writing in his 2014 book *Anarchism Is Movement*, summarized the most fundamental criticism of classical anarchism put forward by postanarchists such as Saul Newman, namely that classical anarchism was fundamentally an Enlightenment project which had at its heart the 'modern vision of an autonomous subject'. What this meant in practice was that anarchism held that there was an 'essential' human nature which could be liberated, when in fact – following the poststructuralist line which sees subjects 'moulded and constituted by relations of power' – there could be no return to 'its fundamental nature, for this last is to be found nowhere, given that *it simply does not exist*'.[47] Dave Morland responded at some length to these charges, offering an insightful assessment of human nature in classical anarchism.[48] Ibanez further noted that some of the postanarchists (including Newman) had responded to criticisms that they had failed to grasp the diversity of classical anarchist attitudes to human nature and refined their critiques accordingly.[49]

Adams for his part had incorporated the work of Hakim Bey (real name Peter Lamborn Wilson), who as we have seen since the 1980s had been arguing for temporary autonomous zones and realizing autonomy at a personal level.[50] Bey is an immensely controversial figure in anarchist studies, for two principal reasons. Firstly, because of his support of adult sexual relations with adolescent boys (pederasty) and writing for the publications of an advocacy group aiming to change the US legal settlement to facilitate this, namely the North American Man-Boy Love Association (NAMBLA).[51] Simon Sellars, in an article seeking to rehabilitate Bey's work on the temporary autonomous zone, has claimed that the reaction to the disclosure of these views and activities amounted to a 'moral panic' on the part of anarchists and other activists, which does not 'bode well for a movement seeking to overturn government and society on the grounds of historical irrelevance'.[52] Sellars's defence of Bey, arguing that his interventions are 'satirical' and the reaction to him is a 'manifestation of institutionalised homophobia', is unconvincing, not least because it rests on the distinction between pederasty and paedophilia and a case of whataboutery, citing a number of famous historical figures who had exhibited sexual desire for adolescent boys.[53] Critics of Bey such as the historian of anarchism Robert P. Helms have argued that Bey's entire theory of anarchist praxis – the temporary autonomous zone – is constructed in order to facilitate Bey's sexual desires.[54]

The temporary autonomous zone, and Bey's work more generally, was controversial for a second reason, however, which as Ibanez notes prefigured later critiques of postanarchism. This was Bey's espousal of what Murray Bookchin dubbed 'lifestyle anarchism'.[55] Bey's theory was undeniably hugely influential; as Sellers chronicles, the idea of the temporary autonomous zone and the creation of spontaneous anarchic spaces and interventions cohered well with the emergent 'cyberculture' of the 1980s, the world of online 'bulletin boards' which preceded the internet, even though that was only in Bey's words 'an adjunct to the TAZ'.[56] Sellars shows how Bey's temporary autonomous zone succeeded to Debord's ideas from the *Society of the Spectacle*, rebooting Situationism for the 1980s and 1990s, but also extrapolated from Debord's ideas that an actual revolution was doomed to inevitable defeat:

> Absolutely nothing but a futile martyrdom could possibly result now from a head-on collision with the terminal State, the megacorporate information State, the empire of Spectacle and Simulation. Its guns are all pointed at us, while our meagre weaponry finds nothing to aim at but a hysteresis, a rigid vacuity, a Spook capable of smothering every spark in an ectoplasm of information, a society of capitulation ruled by the image of the Cop and the absorbent eye of the TV screen.[57]

As Grindon notes, Bey's views were 'influential amongst rave youth culture and a range of anarchist countercultures'.[58] These included 'Reclaim the Streets, a global organization dedicated to unsanctioned events that typified anti-globalization activism in the 1990s'.[59] It was not for nothing that the cover of James Bowen and Jonathan Purkis's edited collection *Twenty-First Century Anarchism* (published in 1997) featured a photograph of a web address with a Circle-A symbol.[60] As they put it in their introduction to the volume, 'anarchy is back in action . . . sometimes bleary-eyed at a computer terminal riding the electronic waves'.[61] Bowen and Purkis dismissed classical anarchism in terms redolent of the revisionist dismissals of Marxism earlier in the twentieth century:

> The terrains of theory and action have changed, and now there are generations of activists operating in many fields of protest for whom the works of Kropotkin, Malatesta and Bakunin are as distant in terms of their description of the world as the literary classics of writers such as Charles Dickens . . . Anarchist theory also rarely travelled beyond the confines of the nascent industrial West.[62]

The last statement as the account given earlier in this volume has shown was not true; anarchism was a global phenomenon in the 'classical' period and was remade and reformulated around the world. Nonetheless, it was never quite the case that there was a straightforward elision, in any event, between postanarchist theory and 'postmodern' rebellious practice. Whilst it was true, as Jude Davies has noted, that anarchism in the 1990s was engaged extensively on the terrain of popular culture, it was also true that much of this activity was independent of postanarchist theorization and (as Davies did) could be linked to classical anarchist ideas just as easily in any event. What postanarchism had, undeniably, achieved in ways which paralleled the anticapitalist movement, as Morland argued, was force anarchism to confront its own complacency in terms of sites of resistance at a theoretical level and offer new tools and vocabularies for critique.[63] Whatever the divide between 'social' and 'lifestyle' anarchisms, it was not true to say that the latter was simply the same as postanarchism. Instead, it was important to recognize, as Morland did, that in the 2000s a new 'social anarchism' was emerging and that it was 'a project that now possesses a distinctively poststructuralist dynamic.'[64] In the course of the 2000s, however, material conditions were to change in ways which would alter anarchist discourses still further and render the vocabularies of social anarchism more explicit.

From 9/11 to Occupy

The authoritarian turn in Western politics which followed the 9/11 attacks in New York and Washington in 2001 came as a shock to many liberals who railed against the infringements of civil liberties enshrined in the Bush Administration's PATRIOT Act and the Blair government's series of anti-terror bills passed in the UK Parliament. Yet the international politics of the post-9/11 era came as less of a shock to countries in the global South which had long been forced to contend with the military adventures of Western capitalism. The war in Afghanistan which erupted immediately following the 9/11 attacks was framed within a broader context of a 'war against terror', which also framed the subsequent invasion of Iraq in 2003, though no evidence of any link to the 9/11 attacks was ever produced for that invasion, and the ostensible justification – the supposed presence of weapons of mass destruction (WMDs) – turned out to be based on fraudulent 'intelligence' which the media in interventionist states had done far too little to challenge.[65] The invasion of Iraq, however, did trigger mass protests around the world, including in London and New York. The military intervention itself destabilized Iraq and ultimately the whole Middle East. The British government had, under Tony Blair's tenure as Prime Minister, forged relations with Bashar al-Assad, the Syrian president, and Muammar Gaddafi, the Libyan leader, during the war against terror. In the case of Libya, this meant collusion in torture. When in 2010 the Arab Spring broke out – a series of political revolutions against corrupt regimes in the Middle East and North Africa – many of the rebellions were popular insurrections against US client regimes, as in Egypt. As Nader Hashemi put it in 2012:

What the Arab Spring has done is help clarify what Middle East scholars have known for a long time – that the fundamental political chasm in the Middle East that shapes internal politics is not between pro-Western and anti-Western forces nor is it between Shia and Sunni or Arab and Jew, but rather it is the enormous gulf that separates longstanding authoritarian regimes from the people they rule over.[66]

The Arab Spring was not an anarchist phenomenon, but as Clifford Baverel has shown, there were 'anarchistic features', such as 'anticapitalism and antistatism'.[67] In the medium term, the revolution in Syria against the Assad regime created space for the Autonomous Administration of Northern and Eastern Syria, known to the international public as Rojava. The Rojava Revolution as it has been characterized has been a point of significant controversy amongst anarchists. Rojava is often presented as a society organized on libertarian socialist principles, derived from the teachings of the imprisoned Kurdish leader Abdullah Ocalan, who is held in custody by the Turkish government and who during his imprisonment has developed a political system known as Democratic Confederalism, which draws inspiration from the writings of Murray Bookchin.[68] Bookchin's social ecology developed in tandem with his libertarian municipalism – decentralized communities, autonomous, with power devolved to the lowest possible level.[69] For some such as Debbie Bookchin and David Graeber, Rojava represents a fundamental 'democracy project', inclusive, democratic and feminist. For others in the anarchist community, it has been seen as nation-state in all but name, and the debate continues. Notwithstanding that debate, anarchists such as the British activist Anna Campbell (Kurdish name: Hêlîn Qereçox) have fought and died for the Rojava Revolution and its promise of a decentralized, free feminist society.[70] The Occupy movement which emerged in the United States in 2011 had in part (in John L. Hammond's assessment) 'been inspired by the Arab Spring', with the initial call for action referring to the mobilization in the Egyptian Revolution at Tahrir Square.[71] The impact of the 2008 North Atlantic financial crisis had been felt around the world.[72] In the financialized societies of Europe and the United States, its impact was particularly acute; though a number of left thinkers argued that this was, in quasi-Marxian terms, a crisis of capitalism which would present opportunities for progressive social change, what resulted instead was an explosion in inequality in Western nations and a further financialization of their societies.[73] In the UK, mass demonstrations erupted in 2010 to 2011 when the coalition government, ostensibly as part of its austerity agenda, used the cover of the debt crisis to further marketize and financialize its university system – which as recently as 1998 had been 'free' at the point of delivery for entrants to higher education. As Joseph Ibrahim has shown, this cut across a 'moral economy' of higher education which was embedded in the social realm, and led to mass protests and an attack on Conservative Party headquarters.[74] In Matt Myers's first-hand account, it was a 'student revolt' which played a key role in radicalizing younger activists who had been disillusioned by the Conservatives' coalition partner, the Liberal Democrats, and their behaviour in reneging on a pledge not to raise fees.[75] Less than a year later, riots swept Britain's cities in response to the police killing of Mark Duggan, a young Black man in Tottenham.[76]

Occupy was arguably pivotal to the revival of interest in classical anarchism which took place in the 2010s and the fusion of postanarchist praxis with classical anarchist goals. Whilst early 'post-left' anarchists had argued that an outright revolution was impossible, after the 2008 financial crisis and the example of the Arab Spring, revolution became, once again, a legitimate subject for discussion. As Hammond notes, when, on 17 September 2011, activists responded to a call from the radical magazine *Adbusters* for an occupation in the Wall Street financial district of New York, ultimately settling on

Zuccotti Park, they were not by and large conscious anarchists.[77] Instead, anarchism was their praxis – non-hierarchical assemblies, consensus decision-making, inclusivity: 'it was anarchist in spirit and sensibility; anarchists (whether declared or not) set the tone'.[78] Daniel Cohn-Bendit, speaking of the 1968 events, had preferred that he was referred to not as a 'leader' but as a 'megaphone'. In Occupy's meetings, when the power was cut to public address systems, the speakers were amplified by the repetition of their audiences, a practice referred to as 'the people's microphone'.[79] For two months the occupiers maintained their horizontally organized community, setting the '99%' against the '1%', before the agents of the state eventually drove them out. As Nathan Schneider, a participant in Occupy Wall Street (OWS), put it:

> One couldn't call the Occupy movement an anarchist phenomenon per se . . . Still, the mode of being that Occupy swept so many people into with its temporary autonomous zones in public squares nonetheless left them feeling, as it was sometimes said, anarcho-curious.[80]

For young American anarchists, Schneider claimed, 'anarchism is the political blank slate of the early twenty-first century'.[81] It had not been defined for them by their elders. It was an opportunity for them to 'affirm the values we had learned on the Internet – transparency, crowd-sourcing, freedom to, freedom from. We can be ourselves'.[82] Occupy was prefigurative, attempting to build the new world in the ruins of the old and using the postmodern techniques of rebellion which has passed through the social movements which had preceded it. But it was also, as Schneider chronicled, an awakening. For him, an 'anarchist amnesia' had 'overtaken radical politics in the United States':

> Such amnesia can be useful because it lends a sense of pioneering vitality to our undertakings that the rest of the history-heavy world seems to envy. But it also condemns us to reinvent the wheel. And this means missing out on what makes anarchism worth taking seriously in the end: the prospect of learning how to build a well-organized and free society from the ground up.[83]

Schneider continued his reflections by noting that the amnesia was not an accident: 'it has also been imposed on us through repression against the threat anarchism was once perceived to pose'.[84] In the ensuing pages of a series of reflections which introduced a collection of Noam Chomsky's writings to a new audience, he referenced Godwin, Proudhon, Orwell's account of the anarchist revolution, Anonymous and the legacy of the Paris Commune.[85] It was an inheritance he – and other new anarchists – sought to assert, rather than forget.

Conclusion: A tale of two anarchisms

On 24 April 2018, a new channel appeared on the web platform Reddit. *BreadTube* as it is titled is a reddit which brings together discussions of videos hosted on the YouTube website which aim to educate and explain left-wing politics to a broad audience. By its own admission, its name derives from an allusion to Kropotkin's *Conquest of Bread*, a book known in activist circles as 'the Bread Book'.[86] Three years previously, the 'Bread Book' itself had been republished by Penguin Classics and in the introduction the historian David Priestland made explicit the connection to the Occupy movement:

> though Occupy's ideological influences were diverse and disparate, most important by far was anarchism, and particularly the ultra-democratic version of anarchism propounded by the Russian anarchist prince, Peter Kropotkin.[87]

It was a time of ironies and contradictions. Also in 2015 the historian David Goodway lamented the closure of *Freedom* the year before in the following terms:

> This is an odd situation since there must be a greater number of conscious anarchists today than at any previous time in British history, while in addition there are many more natural anarchists, people who, though not identifying themselves as anarchists, think and behave in significantly anarchist ways.[88]

By the index applied by the Freedom Group in the 1960s, anarchism certainly mattered again in Britain, as elsewhere. The police, after all, were watching them once more. As the internet age developed, more and more young people became interested in libertarian socialism and anarchism. In 2015, the anarchist group Class War, in a radical break with anarchist practice, stood candidates at the UK General Election as members of the Class War Party. They maintained that it was consistent with anarchist principles because this was in truth not electoralism but propaganda of the deed – they had no intention of winning or taking office but sought instead to use the spotlight of General Election coverage to get their message across.[89] Later that year, Jeremy Corbyn's election as leader of the Labour Party led to Ruth Kinna noting the arrival of 'anarcho-Corbynism' as the British left reorganized itself, a phenomenon where self-declared anarchists flocked to the Labour Party seeking a libertarian socialist alternative.[90] In 2019, a libertarian socialist caucus was founded in the party, calling itself Black Rose, the name already used by a North American anarchist federation. It published a reading list, which prominently featured Kropotkin, Goldman and Chomsky.[91] Whatever the merits of anarchists involving themselves in electoral projects, the reality was that anarchism was, as it had been in the past, an influence within the British Labour movement.

The same year, as we saw at the opening of the book, former officers of the Metropolitan Police in London called for a crackdown on 'anarchists' in London in the context of the Extinction Rebellion (XR) environmental protests. A year later, in 2020, as the Black Lives Matter (BLM) movement sought justice in the United States, President Donald Trump and other US politicians including the presumptive Democratic presidential nominee Joe Biden condemned 'anarchists' and called for their incarceration. One Republican Senator, Tom Cotton of Arkansas, called for the deployment of the armed forces to destroy antifascists and anarchists, saying there should be 'no quarter' for them.[92] As a number of nations around the world became 'reactionary democracies' in Aurelien Mondon and Aaron Winter's pithy phrase, anarchists once again were wheeled out as the villains of the piece for authoritarian regimes seeking to crush political dissent.[93]

At the time of writing at the height of the Covid-19 pandemic, with nations and communities under lockdown around the world, anarchism might seem very far from reality. And yet, anarchist modes of practice are ever-present realities. In Britain, as we have already noted, mutual aid groups sprang up across its constituent nations and communities in the absence of effective state action to support the vulnerable. With pandemics occurring with increasing frequency due to deforestation and the destruction of natural habitats bringing animals and humans into ever-closer contact, social ecology has arguably never been more necessary, to foster a society which is able to promote a viable future for the planet. Another aspect of the Covid crisis which brought the relevance of anarchism to the fore was the behaviour of nation-states, including highly financialized ones such as the United States and Britain, which sought to preserve economies first and lives second. The Hobbesian social contract argument in favour of state authority – that the sovereign's powers were granted in order to guarantee the security of the people – was shown to be false. Arguably of greater explanatory value was the Proudhonian analysis that the state in fact existed to guarantee the rights of property, or, in Marx's terms, capital. Looking upon the present with Scott's anarchist squint, as on the past, yields vastly different insights than the ones available through traditional liberal lenses.

As liberal democracy enters a period of widely acknowledged crisis, there has arguably never been a more pressing urgency to understand the history of anarchism, the foundational objection not merely to the nation-state but to unjustified political authority, which in its modern iteration has embraced the rejection of all unjustified hierarchy and (in part through the recent contribution of the postanarchists) offered a sophisticated analysis of power. Looking back over the history and historiographical debates charted in this book, it is clear that there is no 'one' anarchism to examine but many. However, it is also clear that there is a substantive historical dividing line between periods which gives this final short section its title. This tale of two anarchisms has first the anarchism of the Bakuninst era, when the movement he founded promoted and developed the ideas first explicitly stated by Proudhon into a series of schools of thought and practice. This movement and its ideas, for a time, gained the ascendancy on the global radical left and offered genuinely internationalist socialisms which were remade and altered in widely disparate geographical and social contexts. The second broad anarchism is the anarchism of the post–Second World War period, which drew on the vocabularies and ideas of the older movement and in some cases maintained a lineal relationship with the older movement (though this was in the minority). This is at the core of Goodway's puzzle over *Freedom*'s demise; the new anarchisms of the 2000s did not necessarily relate straightforwardly to those organizations and publications which survived from the era of 'classical anarchism' and often forged their own, new directions via the internet and social media. But it is critical to note *Freedom*, far from being dead, survives and flourishes online, alongside newer publications like libcom.org and communities like BreadTube. It is also critical to note that whilst relations between the new anarchisms and the old have never been straightforward or uncomplicated, the new anarchism increasingly lays claim to the classical heritage, even as it seeks to decolonize and reframe it.

As this book has shown, there is a growing scholarship on anarchist history within the academic historical writing, and some of this has reached wider audiences. The publication of Ruth Kinna's *The Government of No-One* – though not exclusively a 'history' of anarchism – by Penguin in 2019 represents publishers' recognition of the wider interest in anarchism characteristic of this 'second anarchist moment'. Anarchism is neither dead as a movement, or more properly a series of movements, nor is it any longer seen as unworthy of academic historical investigation. The historical study of anarchism, like all historical study, is – to paraphrase Scott – at its best subversive of the present. The present is the creature of everyday myth and stories told by power; the historical past is, by contrast, studied interrogatively, a challenge to that present rather than a comfort blanket. The past may not yield 'lessons' in the straightforward sense commonly assumed, but what it can do is show that the present is contingent and that other worlds were, and are, possible. The historical study of anarchism is of paramount importance, then, not merely in its own right but also for what the anarchist perspectives of the past tell us of the contingency of our present. Many of the battles waged by the classical anarchists in the nineteenth century, for a more nuanced and less monolithic understanding of science, for a rejection of crude Malthusianism, for an egalitarian society which, in Kropotkin's phrase, promised not just work but well-being for all, are battles still relevant today. It is important that we know those battles and all-too-often forgotten contributions those anarchists around the world made to broader political, social and cultural developments. At a time when the narrowing of the political imagination in many societies articulates politics in increasingly nationalist terms, the authentic values of anarchism, of mutual aid, of cooperation, of internationalism and of opposition to all hierarchies, urgently need further historical reassertion.

Further reading

For an understanding of anarchism in the early twenty-first century David Graeber's 'The New Anarchists', *New Left Review*, 13 (2002), remains a vital 'primary source' starting point. For postanarchism, an essential resource for the student and scholar is Duane Rousselle and Sureyyya Evren's anthology *Post-Anarchism: A Reader* (Pluto, 2011), which has an excellent introduction by Evren and features representative excerpts from many key postanarchist texts, in addition to including pieces critical of postanarchism.

For the Occupy movement, Graeber's *The Democracy Project: A History, a Crisis, a Movement* (Penguin, 2013) is an essential account which mixes first-hand participation with scholarly analysis.

For anarchism and the Arab Spring and Rojava in particular, it is worth consulting the following articles. Yagmur Savran's 'The Rojava Revolution and British Solidarity', published in *Anarchist Studies*, 24, no. 1 (2016), gives a standard sympathetic account of Rojava and appeals for solidarity. Enrique Galvan-Alvarez's 'Rojava: A State Subverted or Reinvented?', *Postcolonial Studies*, 23, no. 2 (2020), offers a more thorough, critical perspective. A 2017 Mouvement Communiste/Kolektivně proti Kapitálu polemic against Rojava's status as a lineal descendant of anarchism is available at libcom.org at https://libcom.org/files/LTMC1744ENvF-Rojava.pdf.

Notes

Introduction

1 Charlotte Wilson, 'Anarchism', in Fabian Society, *What Socialism Is* (London: Fabian Society, 1886), reprinted in Charlotte Wilson, *Anarchist Essays* (London: Freedom Press, 2000), 53.

2 The Social Democratic Federation was a British socialist organization led by H. M. Hyndman, a friend of Wilson's (though increasingly opposed to anarchism).

3 'An English Anarchist' [Charlotte Wilson], 'Anarchism' [1884], in Wilson, *Anarchist Essays*, 19.

4 Nicolas Walter, 'Introduction', in Wilson, *Anarchist Essays*, 8–9.

5 Ibid., 7.

6 For Wilson's politics, see Walter, 'Introduction' and Susan Hinely, 'Charlotte Wilson, the "Woman Question", and the Meanings of Anarchist Socialism in Late Victorian Radicalism', *International Review of Social History* 57, no. 1 (2012): 3–36.

7 Wilson, 'Anarchism', 19.

8 Ruth Kinna, *The Government of No-One: The Theory and Practice of Anarchism* (London: Pelican, 2019), 11.

9 Colin Ward, *Anarchy in Action* (London: Freedom Press, 1973), 31.

10 Anthony Arblaster argues this returned as a trope in the late 1960s. Anthony Arblaster, 'The Relevance of Anarchism', *Socialist Register* 8 (1971): 157–84.

11 Robert Booth, 'Anarchists Should Be Reported, Advises Westminster Anti-Terror Police', *The Guardian*, 31 July 2011.

12 Bob Rivett, 'Extinction Rebellion Protesters Aren't Anarchists – We Just Want to Save Our World', *The Guardian*, 19 July 2019.

13 Ibid.

14 Discussed eloquently by Ruth Kinna on the BBC's BOOKTalk programme, 26 October 2019.

15 Andrej Grubacic, 'The Anarchist Moment', in Jacob Blumenfeld, Chiara Bottici and Simon Critchley (eds), *The Anarchist Turn* (London: Pluto Press, 2013), 198.

16 Colin Ward, 'Self-Help Socialism', *New Society* 44, no. 811 (1978): 140–1.

17 Nick McAlpin, 'It's a Shame It's Taken Something Like This for Us to Start Acting in This Way', *Byline Times*, 18 March 2020. Available online: https://bylinetimes.com/2020/03/18/the-coronavirus-crisis-it s-a-shame-its-taken-something-like-this-for-us-to-start-acting-in-this -way/ (accessed 7 May 2020).

18 John Hammond, 'The Anarchism of Occupy Wall Street', *Science and Society* 79, no. 2 (2015): 288–313.

19 David Graeber, *The Democracy Project: A History, A Crisis, A Movement* (Harmondsworth: Penguin, 2013).

20 Cited in Arblaster, 'Relevance of Anarchism', 161.

21 James Joll, *The Anarchists*, 2nd edn (London: Methuen, 1979), 110.

22 Matthew Filsfelder, 'Mr. Robot: Season 1, and Mr. Robot: Season 2', *Science Fiction Film and Television* 11, no. 1 (2018): 143–7.

23 Karl Marx, *Capital*, vol. 1 [1867] (Harmondsworth: Penguin, 1990).

24 Jacob Blumenfeld, Chiara Bottici and Simon Critchley (eds), *The Anarchist Turn* (London: Pluto Press, 2013).

25 For a summary of postanarchism, Duane Rousselle and Sureyyya Evren (eds), *Post-Anarchism: A Reader* (London: Pluto Books, 2011), is indispensable.

26 Scott has produced a significant body of work, but representative examples include James C. Scott, *Domination and the Arts of Resistance: Hidden Transcripts* (New Haven, CT and London: Yale University Press, 1990); *Seeing Like a State: How Certain Schemes to Improve the Human Condition Have Failed* (New Haven, CT and London: Yale University Press, 1998). For Scott's methodological perspective, see his *Two Cheers for Anarchism: Six Easy Pieces on Autonomy, Dignity, and Meaningful Work and Play* (New Haven, CT and London: Yale University Press, 1998).

27 Dongyoun Hwang, *Anarchism in Korea: Independence, Transnationalism, and the Question of National Development, 1919-1984* (Albany, NY: SUNY Press, 2016); Constance Bantman, *The French Anarchists in London, 1880-1914: Exile and Transnationalism in the First Globalisation* (Liverpool: Liverpool University Press, 2013); Carissa Honeywell, *A British Anarchist Tradition: Herbert Read, Alex Comfort and Colin Ward* (London: Bloomsbury, 2011); Matthew S. Adams, *Kropotkin, Read, and the Intellectual History of British Anarchism: Between Reason and Romanticism* (Basingstoke: Palgrave, 2015); Maia Ramnath,

Decolonizing Anarchism: An Antiauthoritarian History of India's Liberation Struggle (Oakland, CA: AK Press, 2011); Ole Birk Laursen, 'Anti-Colonialism, Terrorism and the "Politics of Friendship": Virendranath Chattapadhyaya and the European Anarchist Movement, 1910-1927', *Anarchist Studies* 27, no. 1 (2019): 47–62.

28 Ramnath, *Decolonizing Anarchism*; Arif Dirlik, 'Anarchism and the Question of Place: Thoughts from the Chinese Experience', in Steven Hirsch and Lucien van der Walt (eds), *Anarchism and Syndicalism in the Colonial and Postcolonial World, 1870–1940: The Praxis of National Liberation, Internationalism, and Social Revolution* (Leiden: Brill, 2010), 131–46.

29 Andrej Grubacic, 'The Anarchist Moment', in Blumenfeld, Bottici and Critchley (eds), *The Anarchist Turn*, 187–201. Citation at 188–9.

30 Sho Konishi, *Anarchist Modernity: Cooperatism and Japanese-Russian Intellectual Relations in Modern Japan* (Cambridge, MA: Harvard University Press, 2013), 6.

31 Contrast with Michael Bentley's survey of the English historical profession. Michael Bentley, *Modernizing England's Past: English Historiography in the Age of Modernism, 1870-1970* (Cambridge: Cambridge University Press, 2009).

32 Scott, *Two Cheers for Anarchism* (Princeton, NJ: Princeton University Press, 2012), xii.

33 Matthew S. Adams, 'The Possibilities of Anarchist History: Rethinking the Canon and Writing History', *Anarchist Developments in Cultural Studies* 1 (2013): 33–63, esp. 37–8.

34 Noam Chomsky, 'Part II of *Objectivity and Liberal Scholarship*', in Noam Chomsky, *On Anarchism* (London: Penguin, 2013).

35 Ian Forrest, 'Medieval History and Anarchist Studies', *Anarchist Studies* 28, no. 1 (2020): 46.

36 Ibid. Original emphasis.

37 Ibid., 35.

38 Robert Graham, *We Do Not Fear Anarchy, We Invoke It: The First International and the Origins of the Anarchist Movement* (Oakland, CA: AK Press, 2015).

39 Eric Hobsbawm, *Primitive Rebels* [1959] (Manchester: Manchester University Press, 1971), 82. This refers to 'utopianism' used pejoratively by anarchism's opponents; recent scholarship in anarchist studies has accentuated the importance of utopianism in the imagining of different possible futures otherwise unimaginable in the political logics of particular times. See Ruth Kinna,

'Anarchism and the Politics of Utopia', in Laurence Davis and Ruth Kinna (eds), *Anarchism and Utopianism* (Manchester: Manchester University Press, 2009).

40 Adams, 'Possibilities of Anarchist History'.

41 Walter, 'Introduction'.

42 Hinely, 'Charlotte Wilson'.

43 Ibid., 30.

44 Peter Kropotkin, *The Conquest of Bread* [1892] (London: Penguin, 2015), 23.

45 Grubacic, 'The Anarchist Moment', 195.

46 E. H. H. Green, 'An Age of Transition: An Introductory Essay', *Parliamentary Affairs* 16, no. 1 (1997): 1–17.

47 *H. C. Deb.*, 17 February 1870, vol. 199 cols. 438–98.

48 Geoff Eley, *Forging Democracy: The History of the Left in Europe, 1850-2000* (Oxford: Oxford University Press, 2000), 4.

49 Bantman, *French Anarchists in London*.

50 See, for example, John Merriman, *Massacre: The Life and Death of the Paris Commune of 1871* (New Haven, CT: Yale University Press, 2014); Robert Tombs, *The Paris Commune, 1871* (London: Longman, 1999); Paul Avrich, 'The Paris Commune and Its Legacy', in Paul Avrich, *Anarchist Portraits* (Princeton, NJ: Princeton University Press, 1988), 229–39; Laura C. Forster, 'The Paris Commune and the Spatial History of Ideas, 1871-1900', *Historical Journal* 62, no. 4 (2019): 1021–44.

51 Karl Marx, *The Civil War in France* [1871], in David McLellan (ed.), *Karl Marx: Selected Writings* (Oxford: Oxford University Press, 2000), 584–603; Mikhail Bakunin, *The Paris Commune and the Idea of the State* [1871], in Sam Dolgoff (ed.), *Bakunin on Anarchy* (New York: Vintage Books, 1972), 259–73.

52 Louise Michel, testimony to the 'Inquiry on the Commune', *La Revue Blanche* [1897], in Mitchell Abidor (ed.), *Voices of the Paris Commune* (Oakland, CA: PM Press, 2015), 69.

53 Edith Thomas, *Louise Michel* (Montreal: Black Rose Books, 1980), 224; Matthew Thomas, '"No-One Telling Us What to Do": Anarchist Schools in Britain, 1890-1916', *Historical Research* 77, no. 197 (2004): 415.

54 Hinely 'Charlotte Wilson', 25.

55 Wilson, 'Anarchism', 27.

56 Hinely, 'Charlotte Wilson', 3.

57 Ruth Kinna, 'Anarchism and Feminism', in Nathan Jun (ed.), *Brill's Companion to Anarchism and Philosophy* (Leiden: Brill, 2017), 253–84.

58 See, for example, Emma Goldman, *Anarchism and the Sex Question: Essays on Women and Emancipation, 1896-1917*, ed. Shawn P. Wilbur (Oakland, CA: PM Press, 2016).

59 Judy Greenway, 'The Gender Politics of Anarchist History: Re/Membering Women, Re/Minding Men', paper delivered at the Political Studies Association Conference 'Anarchism and Feminism', Edinburgh, April 2010. Available online: http://www.judy greenway.org.uk/wp/wp-content/uploads/Gender-politics-of-ana rchist-history-download-1.doc.

60 Adams, 'Possibilities of Anarchist History', 34.

61 Ibid., 34–52; Matthew S. Adams and Nathan J. Jun, 'Political Theory and History: The Case of Anarchism', *Journal of Political Ideologies* 20 (2015): 244–62.

62 Ruth Kinna, *Anarchism: A Beginner's Guide* (London: Oneworld, 2005), 10–14.

63 Though in connection with the British Empire this approach has become less popular within the academy, it is still present and influential in popular culture, for example Niall Ferguson, *Empire: How Britain Made the Modern World* (London: Allen Lane, 2002).

64 Chomsky, 'Part II of *Objectivity and Liberal Scholarship*'.

65 K. Steven Vincent, 'Visions of a Stateless Society', in Gareth Stedman Jones and Gregory Claeys (eds), *The Cambridge History of Nineteenth Century Political Thought* (Cambridge: Cambridge University Press, 2011), 433–76.

66 Wolfgang Eckhardt, *The First Socialist Schism: Bakunin vs. Marx in the International Working Men's Association* (Oakland, CA: PM Press, 2016).

67 Peter Marshall, *Demanding the Impossible: A History of Anarchism* (London: Harper Perennial, 1992), 4.

68 Ibid., 3–11.

69 Patricia Crone, 'Ninth-Century Muslim Anarchists', *Past and Present* 167 (2000): 3–28.

70 George Woodcock, *Anarchism* (Harmondsworth: Penguin, 1963 edn.), 7–8.

71 David Graeber, 'Why Is the World Ignoring the Revolutionary Kurds in Syria?', *The Guardian*, 8 October 2014.

72 Graeber, *The Democracy Project*, passim.

73 David Graeber, 'The New Anarchists', *New Left Review* 13 (2002): 61–73.

74 Richard Boston, 'Conversations about Anarchism', *Anarchy* 85 (1968): 74, cited in Colin Ward and David Goodway, *Talking Anarchy* (Oakland, CA: PM Press, 2014), 9.

75 Julian Bourg, *From Revolution to Ethics: May 1968 and Contemporary French Thought* (Montreal: McGill-Queens' University Press, 2007), 26.

76 Woodcock, *Anarchism*, 443.

77 Danny Evans, *Revolution and the State: Anarchism and the Spanish Civil War, 1936-1939* (Oakland, CA: AK Press, 2020).

78 Michael Malet, *Nestor Makhno and the Russian Civil War* (London: Macmillan, 1982).

79 Iain McKay, 'Introduction: The General Idea of the Revolution in the 21st Century', in Pierre-Joseph Proudhon, *Property Is Theft! An Anthology of the Writings of Pierre-Joseph Proudhon*, ed. Iain McKay (Oakland, CA: AK Press, 2012).

80 This is discussed at some length in Iain McKay (ed.), *The Anarchist FAQ*, vol. 1 (Oakland, CA: AK Press, 2008), Section F.

81 Graeber, 'The New Anarchists', 72 n. 6; Ramnath, *Decolonizing Anarchism*, 6–7.

82 Graeber, 'The New Anarchists', 70, 72.

83 Ramnath, *Decolonizing Anarchism*, 7–8.

84 Ibid., 8.

85 Peter Kropotkin, *Mutual Aid: A Factor of Evolution* [1902] (London: Freedom Press, 2009).

86 Peter Kropotkin, 'Anarchism', *Encyclopaedia Britannica* [1911], in Peter Kropotkin, *Anarchism & the State* (London: Freedom Press, 2017), 54.

87 Ibid.

88 Ruth Kinna, 'Kropotkin's Theory of Mutual Aid in Historical Context', *International Review of Social History* 40, no. 2 (1995): 259–83.

89 Iain McKay, 'Introduction: General Idea of the Revolution in the 21st Century', in Pierre-Joseph Proudhon, *Property Is Theft! A Pierre-Joseph Proudhon Anthology*, ed. Iain McKay (Oakland, CA: AK Press, 2011), 4.

90 Adams, 'Possibilities of Anarchist History'.

91 Woodcock, *Anarchism*, 443.

92 Cited in Marshall, *Demanding the Impossible*, 541.

93 Graham, *We Do Not Fear Anarchy*.

94 Stuart White, 'Making Anarchism Respectable: The Social Philosophy of Colin Ward', *Journal of Political Ideologies* 12, no. 1 (2007): 11–28.

95 Colin Ward, 'Anarchism and Respectability' parts I and II, *Freedom*, 22:28 and 22:29 (1961), 2nd and 9th September, cited in Stuart White, 'Social Anarchism, Lifestyle Anarchism, and the Anarchism of Colin Ward', in Carl Levy (ed.), *Colin Ward: Life, Times and Thought* (London: Lawrence and Wishart, 2013), 122.

96 Richard Boston, 'Conversations About Anarchism', in Colin Ward (ed.), *A Decade of Anarchy*, 1961-1970 (London: Freedom Press, 1988), 11.

97 Murray Bookchin, *The Ecology of Freedom: The Emergence and Dissolution of Hierarchy* [1982] (Oakland, CA: AK Press, 2005).

98 Kinna, *Government of No-One*.

99 Honeywell, *A British Anarchist Tradition*.

100 McKay, 'Introduction', 2.

101 Graham, *We Do Not Fear Anarchy*.

102 Peter Kropotkin, *Memoirs of a Revolutionist* [1899] (London: Folio Society, 1978), 51–7.

103 Errico Malatesta, *The Method of Freedom: An Errico Malatesta Reader*, ed. Davide Turcato (Oakland, CA: AK Press, 2015).

104 Vadim Damier, *Anarcho-Syndicalism in the 20th Century* (Edmonton: Black Cat Press, 2009), 1.

105 Alex Prichard, Ruth Kinna, Saku Pinta and David Berry (eds), *Libertarian Socialism: Politics in Black and Red* (Basingstoke: Palgrave, 2012), 6.

106 Raymond Craib, 'A Foreword', in Barry Maxwell and Raymond Craib (eds), *No Gods, No Masters, No Peripheries: Global Anarchisms* (Oakland, CA: PM Press, 2015), 3.

107 F. F. Ridley, *Revolutionary Syndicalism in France: The Direct Action of Its Time* (Cambridge: Cambridge University Press, 1970), 11.

108 As in Lorenzo Kom'boa Ervin, *Anarchism and the Black Revolution* (1993).

109 Murray Bookchin, *Social Anarchism or Lifestyle Anarchism: An Unbridgeable Chasm* (Oakland, CA: AK Press, 1995).

110 David Priestland, 'Introduction', in Kropotkin, *The Conquest of Bread*, xxix–xxx.

Chapter 1

1 Pierre-Joseph Proudhon, *What Is Property? Or, An Inquiry into the Principle of Right and of Government* [1840] in Pierre-Joseph Proudhon, *Property Is Theft! A Pierre-Joseph Proudhon Anthology*, ed. Iain McKay (Oakland, CA: AK Press, 2011), 97.

2 Robert Graham, *We Do Not Fear Anarchy, We Invoke It: The First International and the Origins of the Anarchist Movement* (Oakland, CA: AK Press, 2015), 188.

3 Mark Leier, *Bakunin: The Creative Passion* (New York: St Martin's Press, 2006).

4 E. H. Carr, *Michael Bakunin* (London: Macmillan, 1975), 354.

5 Daniel Guerin, *Anarchism and Marxism* (Orkney: Cienfugos Press, 1981), 11.

6 Graham, *We Do Not Fear Anarchy*, 197.

7 Ibid.

8 Wolfgang Eckhardt, *The First Socialist Schism: Bakunin vs. Marx in the First International* (Oakland, CA: AK Press, 2016).

9 George Woodcock, *Anarchism: A History of Libertarian Ideas and Movements* (Harmondsworth: Pelican, 1963), 134–70.

10 Sho Konishi, *Anarchist Modernity: Cooperatism and Japanese-Russian Intellectual Relations in Modern Japan* (Cambridge, MA: Harvard University Press, 2013), 1.

11 Leier, *Bakunin*.

12 Scholars vary on precisely when: 1864 when he renounced Slav liberation movements is one date considered; 1868 and his admission to the International is another.

13 Proudhon, *What Is Property?*, 133.

14 Ibid.

15 Proudhon, *What Is Property?* Available online: https://www.marxists.org/reference/subject/economics/proudhon/property/ch05.htm (accessed 10 May 2020).

16 Proudhon, *What Is Property?*, 133.

17 Carr, *Michael Bakunin*, 128.

18 Ibid., 131.

19 Mikhail Bakunin, *Bakunin on Anarchy*, ed. Sam Dolgoff (New York: Vintage, 1971), 22.

20 Peter Kropotkin, *Memoirs of a Revolutionist* [1899] (London: Folio Society, 1978), 201–2.

21 Tomás Ibáñez, *Anarchism Is Movement* (London: Freedom Press, 2019).

22 C. Alexander McKinley, 'The French Revolution and 1848', in Carl Levy and Matthew S. Adams (eds), *The Palgrave Handbook of Anarchism* (Basingstoke: Palgrave, 2019), 307–24.

23 G. D. H. Cole, *A History of Socialist Thought, vol. 1: The forerunners, 1789-1850* (London: Macmillan, 1953), 4–5.

24 Ibid., 5–6.

25 Gerry Kearns and Charles W. J. Withers, 'Introduction: Class, Community and the Processes of Urbanisation', in Gerry Kearns and Charles W. J. Withers (eds), *Urbanising Britain: Essays on Class and Community in the Nineteenth Century* (Cambridge: Cambridge University Press, 1991), 1.

26 Martin Daunton, 'Introduction', in Martin Daunton (ed.), *The Cambridge Urban History of Britain, vol. III: 1840-1950* (Cambridge: Cambridge University Press, 2001), 2–3.

27 A. M. C. Waterman, *Revolution, Economics and Religion: Christian Political Economy, 1798-1833* (Cambridge: Cambridge University Press, 1991), 7.

28 Ibid., 15.

29 Woodcock, *Anarchism*, 57.

30 Ibid.

31 Geoff Eley, *Forging Democracy: The History of the Left in Europe, 1850-2000* (Oxford: Oxford University Press, 2002), 17.

32 Peter Kropotkin, *The Conquest of Bread* [1913 edn] (London: Penguin, 2014), 2.

33 Gareth Stedman Jones, 'Malthus, Nineteenth-Century Socialism, and Marx', *Historical Journal* 63, no. 1 (2020): 105.

34 Pierre-Joseph Proudhon, 'The Malthusians', *Le Representant du Peuple*, 10 August 1848 in Proudhon, *Property Is Theft!*, 354.

35 Ibid., 355.

36 Marx to Engels, cited in Iain McKay, 'Introduction', 6.

37 George Woodcock, *Pierre-Joseph Proudhon: A Biography* (Montreal and New York: Black Rose Books, 1987), 1–2.

38 Graham, *We Do Not Fear Anarchy*, 25.

39 Woodcock, *Proudhon*, 2; Graham, *We Do Not Fear Anarchy*, 25.

40 Woodcock, *Proudhon*, 6, 9.

41 Ibid., 12–13.

42 Ibid., 29–30.

43 K. Steven Vincent, 'Visions of Stateless Society', in Gareth Stedman Jones and Gregory Claeys (eds), *The Cambridge History of Nineteenth-Century Political Thought* (Cambridge: Cambridge University Press, 2011), 456.

44 Proudhon, *What Is Property?*, 87.

45 Ibid., 88.

46 Ibid., 89

47 Ibid., 92.

48 Ibid.

49 Ibid., 95.

50 Vincent, 'Visions of Stateless Society', 457.

51 Proudhon, *What Is Property?*, 97.

52 Vincent, 'Visions of Stateless Society', 440.

53 Proudhon, *What Is Property?*, 88.

54 Ibid., 133.

55 Ibid., 107.

56 Ibid., 137.

57 Ibid., 138.

58 Woodcock, *Anarchism*, 98.

59 Peter Marshall, *Demanding the Impossible: A History of Anarchism* (London: HarperCollins, 1992), 234.

60 Graham, *We Do Not Fear Anarchy*, 42.

61 Woodcock, *Proudhon*, 129.

62 Ibid., xiv.

63 Pierre-Joseph Proudhon, 'Letter to Karl Marx', 17 May 1846, in Proudhon, *Property Is Theft!*, 163.

64 Pierre-Joseph Proudhon, *General Idea of the Revolution in the Nineteenth Century* [1851] in Proudhon, *Property Is Theft!*, 598.

65 Woodcock, *Proudhon*, 20, 24.

66 Ibid., 21.

67 Pierre-Joseph Proudhon, *System of Economic Contradictions, Volume II: Or the Philosophy of Misery* [1846], in Proudhon, *Property Is Theft!*, 254–5.

68 Woodcock, *Anarchism*, 115.

69 Shawn P. Wilbur, 'Mutualism', in Adams and Levy (eds), *Palgrave Handbook of Anarchism*, 216.

70 Marshall, *Demanding the Impossible*, 243.

71 Graham, *We Do Not Fear Anarchy*, 60–1.

72 Samuel Hayat, 'The Construction of Proudhonism in the IWMA', in Fabrice Bensimon, Quentin Deluermoz and Jeanne Moisand (eds), *'Arise Ye Wretched of the Earth': The First International in a Global Perspective* (Leiden: Brill, 2018), 314–15.

73 Ibid., 320.

74 Ibid., 316.

75 Ibid., 321.

76 Ibid., 323.

77 Ibid., 313–31.

78 Graham, *We Do Not Fear Anarchy*, 99–108.

79 Paul Avrich, 'The Legacy of Bakunin', in Paul Avrich, *Anarchist Portraits* (Princeton, NJ: Princeton University Press, 1988), 1.

80 Bakunin, cited in Avrich, 'Legacy of Bakunin', 2.

81 Kropotkin, cited in Avrich, 'Legacy of Bakunin', 6.

82 Woodcock, *Anarchism*, 134–5.

83 Leier, *Bakunin*, xi–xii.

84 Ibid., 1.

85 Colin Ward, 'Introduction', in Kropotkin, *Memoirs of a Revolutionist*, 8.

86 Woodcock, *Anarchism*, 141–3.

87 Leier, *Bakunin*, 1–33.

88 Ibid., 56.

89 Carr, *Michael Bakunin*, 124.

90 Woodcock, *Anarchism*, 151–2.

91 Avrich, 'Legacy of Bakunin', 6.

92 Leier, *Bakunin*, 113.

93 Graham, *We Do Not Fear Anarchy*, 66.

94 Robert Graham, 'Anarchism and the First International', in Levy and Adams (eds.), *Palgrave Handbook of Anarchism*, 327.

95 Ibid.

96 Ibid., 328.

97 Graham, *We Do Not Fear Anarchy*, 77.

98 Ibid., 78–9.

99 Graham, 'Anarchism and the First International', 329.

100 Ibid.

101 Ibid., 332.

102 Ibid., 334.

103 Eckhardt, *First Socialist Schism*, 14.

104 Ibid., 12–14.

105 Ibid., 14.

106 Marianne Enckell, 'Bakunin and the Jura Federation', in Bensimon, Deluermoz and Moisand (eds), *'Arise Ye Wretched of the Earth'*, 358.

107 Ibid., 358–9.

108 Daniel Guerin, *Anarchism: From Theory to Practice* (New York: Monthly Review Press, 1970), 6.

109 T. R. Ravindranathan, *Bakunin and the Italians* (Montreal: McGill-Queen's University Press, 1988).

110 Mikhail Bakunin, 'Federalism, Socialism, and Anti-Theologism' [1867], Marxists Internet Archive. Available online: https://www.marxists.org/reference/archive/bakunin/works/various/reasons-of-state.htm (accessed 2 May 2020).

111 Ibid.

112 Ibid.

113 Graham, *We Do Not Fear Anarchy*, 65.

114 Woodcock, *Anarchism*, 338.

115 Joaquin A. Pedroso, 'Mikhail Bakunin's True-Seeking: Anti-Intellectualism and the Anarchist Tradition', *Anarchist Studies* 27, no. 1 (2019): 84.

116 Ibid., 87.

117 Marshall, *Demanding the Impossible*, 287.

118 Pedroso, 'Mikhail Bakunin's True-Seeking', 87.

119 Malatesta, cited in Max Nettlau, *A Short History of Anarchism* [1934] (London: Freedom Press, 1996), 131.

120 Marshall Shatz, 'Introduction', in Mikhail Bakunin, *Statism and Anarchy* [1873] (Cambridge: Cambridge University Press, 1990), xxx.

121 Graham, *We Do Not Fear Anarchy*, 65.

122 Eckhardt, *First Socialist Schism*, 101–20.

123 Sonvillier Circular [1871], cited in Eckhardt, *First Socialist Schism*, 108.

124 Cited in Eckhardt, *First Socialist Schism*, 356.

125 Mikhail Bakunin, 'Socialism and the Paris Commune' [June 1871] in Mikhail Bakunin, *Bakunin: Selected Texts, 1868-1875* (London: Anarres Editions, 2016), 106.

126 Louise Michel, testimony [1897] in Mitchell Abidor (ed.), *Voices of the Paris Commune* (Oakland, CA: PM Press, 2015), 67.

127 Ibid., 68.

128 John Merriman, *Massacre: The Life and Death of the Paris Commune of 1871* (New Haven, CT: Yale University Press, 2014), 18–39.

129 Enckell, 'Bakunin and the Jura Federation', 362.

130 Robert Tombs, *The Paris Commune 1871* (London: Longmans, 1999), 118.

131 Marx, *Civil War in France*, 584–5.

132 Ibid., 585, 596.

133 Merriman, *Massacre*, 249–50.

134 Ibid.

135 As discussed by Kropotkin, *Memoirs of a Revolutionist*, 99–100.

136 Constance Bantman, *The French Anarchists in London, 1880-1914: Exile and Transnationalism in the First Globalisation* (Liverpool: Liverpool University Press, 2013), 44–71.

137 John Merriman, *The Dynamite Club: How a Bombing in Fin-de-siecle Paris Ignited the Age of Modern Terror* (New Haven, CT: Yale University Press, 2016 edn), 40–1.

138 Mikhail Bakunin, 'Letter to James Guillaume, 21st April 1869', in Bakunin, *Bakunin*, 38.

139 Marshall, *Demanding the Impossible*, 434.

140 Davide Turcato, *Making Sense of Anarchism: Errico Malatesta's Experiments with Revolution, 1889-1900* (Oakland, CA: AK Press, 2015), 9.

Chapter 2

1 Davide Turcato, *Making Sense of Anarchism: Errico Malatesta's Experiments with Revolution, 1889-1900* (Oakland, CA: AK Press, 2015), 130.

2 Ibid., 45.

3 Matthew Thomas, ' "No-One Telling Us What to Do": Anarchist Schools in Britain, 1890-1916', *Historical Research* 77, no. 197 (2004): 405–36.

4 Emma Goldman, *Living My Life* (New York: Alfred A. Knopf, 1931).

5 Constance Bantman, *The French Anarchists in London: Exile and Transnationalism in the First Globalisation* (Liverpool: Liverpool University Press, 2013).

6 Ibid., 190.

7 Anthony Gorman, '"Diverse in Race, Religion, and Nationality . . . But United in Aspirations of Civil Progress": The Anarchist Movement in Egypt, 1860-1940', in Steven Hirsch and Lucien van der Walt (eds), *Anarchism and Syndicalism in the Colonial and Postcolonial World, 1870-1940: The Praxis of National Liberation, Internationalism, and Social Revolution* (Leiden: Brill, 2010), 7.

8 Dan Colson, 'Propaganda and the Deed: Anarchism, Violence and the Representational Impulse', *American Studies* 55, no. 4 (56, no. 1) (2017): 168.

9 Johann Most, 'Action as Propaganda', *Freiheit*, 25 July 1885.

10 Colson, 'Propaganda and the Deed', 168.

11 Caroline Cahm, *Kropotkin and the Rise of Revolutionary Anarchism, 1872-1886* (Cambridge: Cambridge University Press, 1989), 158.

12 James Joll, *The Anarchists*, 2nd edn (London: Methuen, 1979), 104.

13 Colson, 'Propaganda and the Deed', 168.

14 Kenyon Zimmer, 'Haymarket and the Rise of Syndicalism', in Carl Levy and Matthew S. Adams (eds), *The Palgrave Handbook of Anarchism* (Basingstoke: Palgrave, 2019), 353.

15 Alain Pengam, 'Anarcho-Communism', in Maximilien Rubel and John Crump (eds), *Non-Market Socialism in the Nineteenth and Twentieth Centuries* (Basingstoke: Palgrave, 1987), 62.

16 John Crump, *Hatta Shuzo and Pure Anarchism in Interwar Japan* (New York: St Martin's Press, 1993).

17 Carl Levy, 'Italian Anarchism, 1870-1926', in David Goodway (ed.), *For Anarchism: History, Theory, and Practice* (London: Routledge, 1989), 39.

18 Errico Malatesta, *Anarchy* [1891], in Errico Malatesta, *The Method of Freedom: An Errico Malatesta Reader*, ed. Davide Turcato (Oakland, CA: AK Press, 2014), 109–40.

19 Judith Suissa, *Anarchism and Education: A Philosophical Perspective* (Oakland, CA: PM Press, 2010), 78–82.

20 Mikhail Bakunin, 'The Reaction in Germany' [1842], in Mikhail Bakunin, *Bakunin on Anarchy*, ed. Sam Dolgoff (New York: Vintage, 1971), 57.

21 Eric Hobsbawm, *Primitive Rebels: Studies in Archaic Forms of Social Movement in the 19th and 20th Centuries* [1959] (London: Abacus, 2017 edn).

22 Geoffrey Cubitt and Allen Warren (eds), *Heroic Reputations and Exemplary Lives* (Manchester: Manchester University Press, 2000).

23 Héléne Bowen Raddeker, 'A Woman of Ill Fame: Reconfiguring the Historical Reputation and Life of Kanno Suga', in Masako Gavin and Ben Middleton (eds), *Japan and the High Treason Incident* (Abingdon: Routledge, 2013), 91–102.

24 Lewis H. Mates, 'The Syndicalist Challenge in the Durham Coalfield Before 1914', in Alex Prichard, Ruth Kinna, Saku Pinta and David Berry (eds), *Libertarian Socialism: Politics in Black and Red* (Basingstoke: Palgrave, 2012), 57–77.

25 Antony Taylor, 'The Whiteway Anarchists in the Twentieth Century: A Transnational Community in the Cotswolds', *History* 101, no. 344 (2016): 62–83.

26 John A. Merriman, *The Dynamite Club: How a Bombing in fin-de-siecle Paris Ignited the Age of Modern Terror* (New Haven, CT: Yale University Press, 2016 edn), 41.

27 Cf. Mitchell Abidor, *Death to Bourgeois Society: The Propagandists of the Deed* (Oakland, CA: PM Press, 2016).

28 Elun Gabriel, 'Performing Persecution: Witnessing and Martyrdom in the Anarchist Tradition', *Radical History Review* 98 (2007): 35.

29 Ibid.

30 *The Times*, 28 May 1885.

31 *The Times*, 1 August 1887.

32 *The Times*, 26 March 1885.

33 *The Times*, 1 August 1887.

34 Charles Malato, 'Some Anarchist Portraits', *Fortnightly Review* 333 (September 1894).

35 Ibid., 315.

36 Ibid., 322.

37 Ibid., 324.

38 *The Times*, 11 December 1893.

39 Ibid.

40 Mitchell Abidor, 'Introduction', in Abidor (ed.), *Death to Bourgeois Society*, 5.

41 Richard Bach Jensen, *The Battle Against Anarchist Terrorism: An International History, 1878-1934* (Cambridge: Cambridge University Press, 2013), 77.

42 *The Times*, 11 January 1894.

43 Ibid.

44 See pp. above.

45 *The Times*, 11 January 1894.

46 Karl Marx, *Capital*, vol. 1 [1869] (Harmondsworth: Penguin, 1990), 342. I am grateful to Michael Grant and George Cammack for pointing this out.

47 *The Times*, 11 January 1894.

48 Ibid.

49 Ibid.

50 Ibid.

51 Ibid.

52 Ibid.

53 Ibid.

54 Ibid.

55 Peter Kropotkin, 'The Scientific Bases of Anarchy', *Nineteenth Century* 283 (1887). Discussed in Iain McKay, 'Reality Has a Well-known Libertarian Bias', in Peter Kropotkin, *Modern Science and Anarchy* (Oakland, CA: AK Press, 2018), 3.

56 Alex Butterworth, *The World That Never Was: A True Story of Dreamers, Schemers, Anarchists and Secret Agents* (London: The Bodley Head, 2010).

57 Merriman, *Dynamite Club*, 9.

58 *The Times*, 11 January 1894.

59 John Merriman, 'The Spectre of the Commune and French Anarchism in the 1890s', in Levy and Adams (eds), *Palgrave Handbook of Anarchism*, 343.

60 Jensen, *Battle Against Anarchist Terrorism*, 13–14.

61 Ibid., 17.

62 Ibid.

63 Ibid.

64 Cahm, *Kropotkin and the Rise of Revolutionary Anarchism*, 100.

65 Ibid., 102.

66 Jensen, *Battle Against Anarchist Terrorism*, 341–65.

67 Joll, *The Anarchists*, 109.

68 *The Times*, 11 January 1894.

69 Joll, *The Anarchists*, 113.

70 Abidor, 'Introduction', 9.

71 Goldman, *Living My Life*.

72 Ibid. Available online: http://theanarchistlibrary.org/library/emma-g oldman-living-my-life (accessed 6 May 2020).

73 Emma Goldman, 'The Tragedy at Buffalo', *Free Society* (October 1901). Available online: https://theanarchistlibrary.org/library/emma-goldman-the-tragedy-at-buffalo (accessed 6 May 2020).

74 Errico Malatesta, 'Propaganda by Deeds' [1889], in Malatesta, *The Method of Freedom*, 80.

75 Ibid.

76 Ibid., 83.

77 Errico Malatesta, 'Anarchy and Violence' [1894], in Malatesta, *Method of Freedom*, 191.

78 Merriman, *Dynamite Club*.

79 Jensen, *Battle Against Anarchist Terrorism*, 18.

80 Benedict Anderson, *The Age of Globalisation: Anarchists and the Anticolonial Imagination* (London: Verso, 2013).

81 Constance Bantman and David Berry, 'Introduction', in David Berry and Constance Bantman (eds), *New Perspectives on Anarchism, Labour and Syndicalism: The Individual, the National and the Transnational* (Newcastle: Cambridge Scholars, 2010), 10.

82 Rob Ray, *A Beautiful Idea: History of the Freedom Press Anarchists* (London: Freedom Press, 2018).

83 Benedict Anderson, 'Preface', in Hirsch and Van der Walt (eds), *Anarchism and Syndicalism*, xvi.

84 Iain McKay, 'Kropotkin, Woodcock, and Les Temps Nouveaux', *Anarchist Studies* 23, no. 1 (2015): 62–85.

85 Ibid.

86 Paul Avrich, 'Jewish Anarchism in the United States', in Paul Avrich, *Anarchist Portraits* (Princeton, NJ: Princeton University Press, 1988), 176–99.

87 Ibid.

88 Paul Avrich, 'Mollie Steimer: An Anarchist Life', in Avrich, *Anarchist Portraits*, 214–26.

89 Carl Levy, 'Anarchism and Cosmopolitanism', in Levy and Adams (eds), *Palgrave Handbook of Anarchism*, 134.

90 Tom Goyens, *Beer and Revolution: The German Anarchist Movement in New York City, 1880-1914* (Chicago: University of Illinois Press, 2007), 93.

91 Margaret Vallance, 'Rudolf Rocker: A Biographical Sketch', *Journal of Contemporary History* 8, no. 3 (1973): 76.

92 Nancy Fraser, 'Rethinking the Public Sphere: A Contribution to the Critique of Actually Existing Democracy', *Social Text*, no. 25/26 (1990): 56–80.

93 Maxine Molyneux, 'No God, No Boss, No Husband: Anarchist Feminism in Nineteenth Century Argentina', *Latin American Perspectives* 13, no. 1 (1986): 119–45.

94 Hélené Bowen Raddeker, 'Anarchist Women of Imperial Japan: Lives, Subjectivities, Representations', *Anarchist Studies* 24, no. 1 (2016): 15.

95 Ibid.

96 Ibid., 16.

97 Ole Birk Laursen, 'Anarchist Anti-Imperialism: Guy Aldred and the Indian Revolutionary Movement, 1909–14', *Journal of Imperial and Commonwealth History* 46, no. 2 (2018): 288.

98 Ibid.

99 Ibid., 120.

100 Andy Green, *Education and State Formation: The Rise of Education Systems in England, France and the USA* (Basingstoke: Palgrave, 1990).

101 Haia Shpayer-Makov, 'Anarchism in British Public Opinion, 1880-1914', *Victorian Studies* 31, no. 4 (1988): 488.

102 Thomas, '"No-One Telling Us What to Do"', 405.

103 Paul Avrich, *The Modern School Movement: Anarchism and Education in the United States* (Princeton, NJ: Princeton University Press, 1980), 19–20.

104 Peter Marshall, *Demanding the Impossible: A History of Anarchism* (London: HarperPerennial, 1992), 194.

105 Ibid.

106 Avrich, *Modern School Movement*, 4.

107 Francisco Ferrer, *The Origins and Ideals of the Modern School* (London: Watts and Co, 1913).

108 Ibid.

109 Avrich, *Modern School Movement*, 23.

110 Ibid., 3.

111 Ibid., 3–33.

112 Thomas, '"No-One Telling Us What to Do"', 415.

113 Ibid.

114 Ibid., 416.

115 Ibid., 417.

116 Ibid.

117 Ibid., 122.

118 John Shotton, *No Master High or Low: Libertarian Education and Schooling, 1890-1990* (Bristol: Libertarian Education, 1993), 43.

119 Ibid., 44.

120 Ibid., 45.

121 David Gribble, 'Good News for Francisco Ferrer – How Anarchist Ideals in Education Have Survived Around the World', in Jonathan Purkis and James Bowen (eds), *Changing Anarchism: Anarchist Theory and Practice in a Global Age* (Manchester: Manchester University Press, 2012), 181–97.

122 Suissa, *Anarchism and Education*, 81.

123 Ibid., 61.

124 Lucien van der Walt and Steven Hirsch, 'Rethinking Anarchism and Syndicalism: The Colonial and Postcolonial Experience, 1870-1940', in Hirsch and van der Walt (eds), *Anarchism and Syndicalism*, xxxvii.

125 F. F. Ridley, *Revolutionary Syndicalism in France: The Direct Action of Its Time* (Cambridge: Cambridge University Press, 1970), 1.

126 van der Walt and Hirsch, 'Rethinking Anarchism and Syndicalism'; Ridley, *Revolutionary Syndicalism*, 15–44.

127 Mates, 'The Syndicalist Challenge'.

128 Joll, *The Anarchists*, 188–95.

129 Ridely acknowledges the debts to both Proudhon and Bakunin; *Revolutionary Syndicalism*, 28–32; 38–44.

130 Zimmer, 'Haymarket and the Rise of Syndicalism', 354–6.

131 Confédération Générale du Travail, *Charter of Amiens* [1906]. Available online: https://www.marxists.org/history/france/cgt/charter-amiens.htm (accessed 6 May 2020).

132 Lucien van der Walt, 'Syndicalism', in Levy and Adams (eds), *Palgrave Handbook of Anarchism*, 250.

133 Bob Holton, *British Syndicalism, 1910-1914: Myths and Realities* (London: Pluto, 1975).

134 van der Walt and Hirsch, 'Rethinking Anarchism and Syndicalism', xli.

135 Lucien van der Walt, 'Revolutionary Syndicalism, Communism and the National Question in South African Socialism, 1886–1928', in Hirsch and van der Walt (eds), *Anarchism and Syndicalism*, 33–94.

136 Paul Avrich, *The Haymarket Tragedy* (Princeton, NJ: Princeton University Press, 1984), 393.

137 Zimmer, 'Haymarket and the Rise of Syndicalism', 356.

138 David Cannadine, *Class in Britain* (New Haven, CT: Yale University Press, 1998).

139 Industrial Workers of the World (IWW), 'Preamble to the IWW Constitution', IWW.org.uk. Available online: https://iww.org.uk/preamble/ (accessed 26 April 2020).

140 *The Syndicalist*, cited in Ralph Darlington, *Syndicalism and the Transition to Communism: An International Comparative Analysis* (Aldershot: Ashgate, 2008), 42.

141 Anderson, *Age of Globalisation*, 2.

142 Ibid.

143 Darlington, *Syndicalism and the Transition to Communism*, 40.

144 Marshall, *Demanding the Impossible*, 455.

145 George Woodcock, *Anarchism: A History of Libertarian Ideas and Movements* (Harmondsworth: Pelican, 1963), 350. Woodcock gives the location as Seville; most authoritative sources clearly state Barcelona (e.g. Jose Peirats, *The Anarchists in the Spanish Revolution* (London: Freedom Press, 1990), 27).

146 Murray Bookchin, *The Spanish Anarchists: The Heroic Years, 1886-1936* (New York: Harper and Row, 1977), 186.

147 Woodcock, *Anarchism*, 350.

148 Rudolf Rocker, *Anarcho-Syndicalism: Theory and Practice* [1938] (London: Pluto Press, 1989), 118–19.

149 Ibid.

150 Ruth Kinna and Clifford Harper, *Michael Bakunin*, Great Anarchists no. 3 (Dog Section Press, 2019).

151 Daniel J. Kevles, *In the Name of Eugenics: Genetics and the Uses of Human Heredity* (Cambridge, MA: Harvard University Press, 1995), 70–84.

152 Patricia Bass, 'Cesare Lombroso and the Anarchists', *Journal for the Study of Radicalism* 13, no. 1 (2019): 19–42.

153 Adrian Wooldridge, 'The English State and Educational Theory', in S. J. D. Green and R. C. Whiting (eds), *The Boundaries of the State in Modern Britain* (Cambridge: Cambridge University Press, 1996).

154 Peter Marshall, 'Human Nature and Anarchism', in Goodway (ed.), *For Anarchism*, 127.

155 McKay, 'Reality Has a Well-known Libertarian Bias', 10.

156 Suissa critiques this in her *Anarchism and Education*, 1.

157 Anderson, 'Preface', xiii.

158 Kropotkin, *Conquest of Bread*, 54.

159 Peter Kropotkin, *Mutual Aid* [1902] (London: Freedom Press, 2009 edn), 19.

160 Ibid.

161 Ibid., 24.

162 Ibid., 29.

163 Ibid., 216.

164 Peter Kropotkin, *The Conquest of Bread* [1892] (London: Penguin, 2015), 33.

165 McKay, 'Kropotkin, Woodcock, and Les Temps Nouveaux'.

166 Constance Bantman, 'The Era of Propaganda of the Deed', in Levy and Adams (eds), *Palgrave Handbook of Anarchism*, 375.

167 Goodway (ed.), *For Anarchism*.

168 V. I. Lenin, *Left-Wing Communism: An Infantile Disorder* (New York: International Publishers, 1940).

Chapter 3

1 'The Russian Revolution and the Soviet Government: Letter to the Workers' of the Western World', *Labour Leader*, 22 July 1920. Available online: https://www.marxists.org/reference/archive/kr opotkin-peter/1910s/19_04_28.htm.

2 José Peirats, *Anarchists in the Spanish Revolution* [1974] (London: Freedom Press, 1998), 12.

3 Anthony D'Agostino, 'Anarchism and Marxism in the Russian Revolution', in Carl Levy and Matthew S. Adams (eds), *The Palgrave Handbook of Anarchism* (Basingstoke: Palgrave, 2019).

4 Alexandre Skirda, *Anarchy's Cossack: Nestor Makhno and the Struggle for Free Soviets in the Ukraine, 1917-1921* (Oakland, CA: AK Press, 2004).

5 George Orwell, *Homage to Catalonia* [1938] (Harmondsworth: Penguin, 2000), 2.

6 Voline, *The Unknown Revolution, 1917-1921* (Oakland, CA: PM Press, 2019).

7 Richard Pipes, 'The Trial of Vera Z', *Russian Review* 37, no. 1 (2010): 5.

8 Ibid.

9 Paul Avrich, *The Russian Anarchists* (Princeton, NJ: Princeton University Press, 1967), 3.

10 George Woodcock, *Anarchism: A History of Libertarian Ideas and Movements* (Harmondsworth: Penguin, 1963), 377.

11 D'Agostino, 'Anarchism and Marxism in the Russian Revolution', 409.

12 Ibid.

13 Woodcock, *Anarchism*, 377–8.

14 Paul Avrich, *Kronstadt 1921* (New York: W. W. Norton, 1974), 78.

15 Woodcock, *Anarchism*, 378.

16 Avrich, *Kronstadt 1921*, 176.

17 Ibid., 12, 41.

18 Robert Graham, *We Do Not Fear Anarchy! We Invoke It: The First International and the Origins of the Anarchist Movement* (Oakland, CA: AK Press, 2015), 42.

19 Isaiah Berlin, 'Herzen and Bakunin on Individual Liberty' [1955], in Isaiah Berlin, *Russian Thinkers*, 2nd edn (London: Penguin, 2013), 119.

20 Woodcock, *Anarchism*, 380.

21 Herzen, cited in Woodcock, *Anarchism*, 381.

22 Woodcock, *Anarchism*, 377.

23 Sho Konishi, *Anarchist Modernity: Cooperatism and Japanese-Russian Intellectual Relations in Modern Japan* (Cambridge, MA: Harvard University Press, 2013), 59–64. It can be argued Konishi overplays this; he negatively constructs Bakunin's anarchism as essentially destructive and fails to engage with the strong cooperativist elements present in anarchism prior to Mechnikov's travels to Japan (not least Proudhon's work).

24 Avrich, *Russian Anarchists*, 10.

25 G. P. Fedotov, 'The Religious Sources of Russian Populism', *Russian Review* 1, no. 2 (1942): 28.

26 Joaquin A. Pedroso, 'Mikhail Bakunin's True-Seeking: Anti-Intellectualism and the Anarchist Tradition', *Anarchist Studies* 27, no. 1 (2019): 87.

27 Fedotov, 'Religious Sources of Russian Populism', 28.

28 Pipes, 'The Trial of Vera Z', 1.

29 Woodcock, *Anarchism*, 176.

30 Ibid., 388.

31 Avrich, *Russian Anarchists*, 9.

32 Ibid., 13.

33 Ibid.

34 Ibid., 14.

35 Ibid., 71.

36 Rex A. Wade, 'The Russian Revolution and Civil War', in Silvio Pons and Stephen A. Smith (eds), *The Cambridge History of Communism* (Cambridge: Cambridge University Press, 2017), 74.

37 Ibid., 75.

38 Ibid., 76.

39 Sheila Fitzpatrick, *The Russian Revolution* (Oxford: Oxford University Press, 2017), 40.

40 Ibid., 50.

41 Ibid., 51.

42 Ibid., 42–3.

43 Ibid., 43.

44 Christos Memos, 'Anarchism and Council Communism on the Russian Revolution', *Anarchist Studies* 20, no. 2 (2012): 24.

45 Iain McKay, 'Introduction to the 2019 Edition' in Voline, *Unknown Revolution*, xvii–xviii.

46 Vladimir Ilyich Lenin, 'The Tasks of the Proletariat in the Present Revolution', *Pravda*, 7 April 1917. Available online: https://www.marxists.org/archive/lenin/works/1917/apr/04.htm (accessed 20 May 2020).

47 Vladimir Ilyich Lenin, *State and Revolution* [1917]. Available online: https://www.marxists.org/archive/lenin/works/1917/staterev/ch01.htm#s3 (accessed 20 May 2020).

48 Grigori Petrovitch Maximov, *Syndicalists in the Russian Revolution* [1940] (Anarchist Library Edition, 2011), 5–6.

49 D'Agostino, 'Anarchism and Marxism in the Russian Revolution', 411.

50 Paul Avrich, 'The Anarchists in the Russian Revolution', *Russian Review* 26, no. 4 (1967): 341–50.

51 Paul Avrich, 'Stormy Petrel: Anatoli Zhelezniakov', in Paul Avrich, *Anarchist Portraits* (Princeton, NJ: Princeton University Press, 1988), 107.

52 Ibid., 107, 108.

53 Ibid., 108.

54 Ibid., 109.

55 Jane Burbank, *Intelligentsia and Revolution: Russian Views of Bolshevism, 1917-1922* (New York: Oxford University Press, 1989), 99.

56 Ken Wenzner, 'An Anarchist Image of the Russian Revolution', *Revolutionary Russia* 6, no. 1 (1993): 122.

57 Avrich, 'Anarchists in the Russian Revolution', 343.

58 Maximov, *Syndicalists in the Russian Revolution*, 4.

59 Rudolf Rocker in Maximov, *Syndicalists in the Russian Revolution*, 15.

60 Colin Darch, *Nestor Makhno and Rural Anarchism in Ukraine, 1917-1921* (London: Pluto Press, 2021); Sean Patterson, *Makhno and Memory: Anarchist and Mennonite Narratives of Ukraine's Civil War* (Manitoba: University of Manitoba Press, 2020); Skirda, *Anarchy's Cossack*; Michael Malet, *Nestor Makhno in the Russian Civil War* (London: Macmillan, 1982).

61 Peter Marshall, *Demanding the Impossible: A History of Anarchism* (London: Harper Perennial, 1992), 473.

62 Paul Avrich, 'Nestor Makhno: The Man and the Myth', in Avrich, *Anarchist Portraits*, 111.

63 Marshall, *Demanding the Impossible*, 473.

64 Skirda, *Anarchy's Cossack*, 1–4.

65 Brendan McGeever, *Antisemitism and the Russian Revolution* (Cambridge: Cambridge University Press, 2019), 134 n. 103.

66 Nestor Makhno, 'The Maknovschchina and Anti-Semitism' [1927], in Nestor Makhno, *The Struggle Against the State and Other Essays* (Edinburgh: AK Press, 1996), 38.

67 Avrich, 'Nestor Makhno', 111.

68 Ibid.

69 Alexander Shubin, 'The Makhnovist Movement and the National Question in the Ukraine', in Steven J. Hirsch and Lucien van der Walt (eds), *Anarchism and Syndicalism in the Colonial and Postcolonial World, 1870-1940: The Praxis of National Liberation, Internationalism, and Social Revolution* (Leiden: Brill, 2010), 151–2.

70 Ibid., 152.

71 Avrich, 'Nestor Makhno', 112.

72 Shubin, 'Makhnovist Movement', 154.

73 Woodcock, *Anarchism*, 394.

74 Malet, *Nestor Makhno in the Russian Civil War*, 160; Shubin, 'Makhnovist Movement', 168.

75 Shubin, 'Makhnovist Movement', 153.

76 Ibid.

77 Ibid., 154–5.

78 Ibid., 157.

79 Nestor Makhno, 'Great October in the Ukraine', in Makhno, *Struggle Against the State*, 2.

80 Shubin, 'Makhnovist Movement', 164.

81 Avrich, 'Nestor Makhno', 113.

82 Ibid., 120.

83 Ibid., 116.

84 Ibid., 115.

85 Ibid., 116.

86 Alexander Berkman, *The Kronstadt Rebellion* [1922], 19–20. Available online: http://theanarchistlibrary.org/library/alexander-b erkman-the-kronstadt-rebellion.pdf.

87 Avrich, *Kronstadt 1921*, 10.

88 Ibid., 13.

89 Ibid., 42.

90 Ibid.

91 Ibid., 44.

92 Ibid., 91.

93 Ibid., 169.

94 Ibid.

95 Ibid.

96 Kathy E. Ferguson, 'The Russian Revolution and Anarchist Imaginaries', *South Atlantic Quarterly* 116, no. 4 (2007): 749.

97 Ibid.

98 Emma Goldman, *My Further Disillusionment in Russia* (New York: Doubleday, Page & Co., 1924), 87.

99 Noam Chomsky, 'Objectivity and Liberal Scholarship: Part II' [1969], in Noam Chomsky, *On Anarchism* (London: Penguin, 2014), 45.

100 Ibid., 47–101.

101 Ibid., 50.

102 Ibid.

103 Ibid.

104 Paul Preston, *The Spanish Civil War: Reaction, Revolution, & Revenge* (London: HarperPerennial, 2006).

105 José Peirats, *Los anarquistas en la crisis politica española* (Alfa: Buenos Aires, 1964).

106 This episode and its implications are well discussed in Danny Evans's recent *Revolution and the State: Anarchism in the Spanish Civil War* (Abingdon: Routledge, 2018).

107 *Freedom*, 1 August 1936.

108 Max Nettlau, 'The Truth About Spain', *Freedom*, 1 August 1936.

109 Ibid.

110 Ibid.

111 Gaston Leval, *Collectives in the Spanish Revolution* [1971] (Oakland, CA: PM Press/Jura Books, 2018), 17.

112 Woodcock, *Anarchism*, 336, 341.

113 Julián Casanova, 'Terror and Violence: The Dark Face of Spanish Anarchism', *International Labor and Working-Class History* 67 (2005): 79.

114 James Michael Yeoman, *Print Culture and the Formation of the Anarchist Movement in Spain, 1890-1915* (Abingdon: Routledge, 2020).

115 George R. Esenwein, *Anarchist Ideology and the Working-Class Movement in Spain, 1868-1898* (Berkeley: University of California Press, 1989), 35–42.

116 Ibid., 45–50.

117 Woodcock, *Anarchism*, 341.

118 Gerald Brenan, *The Spanish Labyrinth: An Account of the Social and Political Background of the Spanish Civil War* [1943] (Cambridge: Cambridge University Press, 2014 edn), 214–15.

119 Ibid., 215.

120 Ibid., 228, 229.

121 Ibid., 230.

122 Hobsbawm, *Primitive Rebel*, passim.

123 James Joll, *The Anarchists*, 2nd edn (London: Methuen, 1979), 207.

124 Ruth Kinna, 'Heretical Constructions of Anarchist Utopianism', *History of European Ideas* 46, no. 8 (2020): 1084–6.

125 Temma Kaplan, *Anarchists of Andalusia* (Princeton, NJ: Princeton University Press, 1977), 11.

126 Danny Evans and James Michael Yeoman, 'Introduction: New Approaches to Spanish Anarchism', *International Journal of Iberian Studies* 29, no. 3 (2016): 199–200.

127 Kaplan, *Anarchists of Andalusia*, 10.

128 Ibid.

129 F. F. Ridley, *Revolutionary Syndicalism in France: The Direct Action of Its Time* (Cambridge: Cambridge University Press, 1970), 11.

130 Peirats, *Anarchists in the Spanish Revolution*, 28.

131 Esenwein, *Anarchist Ideology*, 80.

132 Ibid.

133 Ibid., 81.

134 Ibid., 83.

135 Ibid., 85–90.

136 Ibid., 98–116.

137 Peirats, *Anarchists in the Spanish Revolution*, 22; Woodcock, *Anarchism*, 342.

138 Woodcock, *Anarchism*, 342.

139 Kaplan, *Anarchists of Andalusia*, 173.

140 Peirats, *Anarchists in the Spanish Revolution*, 24.

141 Ibid., 28.

142 Ibid., 27.

143 Chris Grocott, Gareth Stockey and Jo Grady, 'Reformers and Revolutionaries: The Battle for the Working Classes in Gibraltar and Its Hinterland, 1902–1921', *Labor History* 59 (2018): 692–719.

144 Peirats, *Anarchists in the Spanish Revolution*, 30.

145 Ibid.

146 Ibid., 39.

147 Vadim Damier, *Anarcho-Syndicalism in the Twentieth Century* (Montreal: Black Rose Books, 2009), 84.

148 Peirats, *Anarchists in the Spanish Revolution*, 55.

149 Julian Casanova, *The Spanish Republic and Civil War* (Cambridge: Cambridge University Press, 2010), 1.

150 Peirats, *Anarchists in the Spanish Revolution*, 87.

151 Evans, *Revolution and the State*, 19.

152 Ibid., 18.

153 Ibid., 17–19.

154 Peirats, *Anarchists in the Spanish Revolution*, 90.

155 Evans, *Revolution and the State*, 19.

156 Peirats, *Anarchists in the Spanish Revolution*, 91.

157 Martha A. Ackelsberg, *Free Women of Spain: Anarchism and the Struggle for the Emancipation of Women* (Oakland, CA: AK Press, 2005), 120.

158 Ibid., 120.

159 Ibid., 22.

160 Ibid.

161 Ibid., 88.

162 Ibid.

163 Ibid., 122.

164 Ibid., 123.

165 Ibid., 205.

166 Danny Evans, '"Ultra-Left" Anarchists and Anti-Fascism in the Second Republic', *International Journal of Iberian Studies* 29, no. 3 (2016): 241–56.

167 Ibid.

168 Philip Holgate, 'May 1936: The Congress of Zaragoza', *Anarchy* 5 (1961): 144–8.

169 Jordi Getman-Eraso, '"Cease Fire, Comrades!" Anarcho-Syndicalist Revolutionary Prophesy, Anti-Fascism and the Origins of the Spanish Civil War', *Totalitarian Movements and Political Religions* 9, no. 1 (2008): 94.

170 Murray Bookchin, *The Spanish Anarchists: The Heroic Years, 1886-1936* (New York: Harper and Row, 1977), 291.

171 Evans, *Revolution and the State*, 16.

172 Evans, '"Ultra-Left" Anarchists', 248.

173 Peirats, *Anarchists in the Spanish Revolution*, 106.

174 James Michael Yeoman, 'The Spanish Civil War', in Levy and Adams (eds), *Palgrave Handbook of Anarchism*, 431.

175 Augustin Souchy, 'Workers' Self-Management in Industry', in Sam Dolgoff (ed.), *The Anarchist Collectives: Workers' Self-Management in the Spanish Revolution, 1936-1939* (Montreal, CA: Black Rose Books, 1974), 79.

176 Sam Dolgoff editorial note 4 to Souchy, 'Workers' Self-Management in Industry', 79.

177 Yeoman, 'The Spanish Civil War', 434.

178 Ibid.

179 Ibid., 435.

180 Sam Dolgoff, 'Urban Collectivisation: Introduction', in Dolgoff (ed.), *Anarchist Collectives*, 85.

181 Yeoman, 'Spanish Civil War', 438–9.

182 Federica Montseny, 'The Anarchist Ideal', reprinted in *Spain and the World*, 22 January 1937.

183 'Militant Anarchism and Spanish Reality', *Spain and the World*, 19 February 1937.

184 Yeoman, 'Spanish Civil War', 437.

185 *Spain and the World*, 15 May 1937

186 Ibid.

187 Ibid.

188 Yeoman, 'Spanish Civil War', 438.

189 Jose Peirats, *The CNT in the Spanish Revolution*, vol. II (Hastings: Christie Books, 2005), 227.

190 Paul Preston, 'George Orwell's Spanish Civil War Memoir Is a Classic, but Is It Bad History?', *Observer*, 7 May 2017.

191 Evans, *Revolution and the State*, 89.

192 Morris Brodie, 'Volunteers for Anarchy: The International Group of the Durruti Column in the Spanish Civil War', *Journal of Contemporary History* 56, no. 1 (2021): 47.

193 Chris Ealham, *Living Anarchism: Jose Peirats and the Spanish Anarcho-Syndicalist Movement* (Oakland, CA: AK Press, 2015)., 71.

194 Yeoman, 'Spanish Civil War', 440.

195 Paul Preston, *The Spanish Holocaust: Inquisition and Extermination in Twentieth-Century Spain* (London: Harper, 2011).

196 Eric Hobsbawm, *Bandits* (London: Weidenfeld & Nicolson, 2010).

197 Preston, *Spanish Civil War*, 18–19.

198 Ibid., 18.

199 Avrich, 'Nestor Makhno', 124.

200 Evans, *Revolution and the State*.

201 James A. Baer, *Anarchist Immigrants in Spain and Argentina* (Chicago: University of Illinois Press, 2015), 93–4.

202 Ibid., 93.

Chapter 4

1 'A "Red" Outrage at Delhi: Bombs in the Legislative Assembly', *Illustrated London News*, 13 April 1929.

2 Ibid.

3 Neeti Nahi, 'Bhagat Singh as "Satyagrahi": The Limits to Non-Violence in Late Colonial India', *Modern Asian Studies* 43, no. 3 (2009): 655.

4 Simona Sawhney, 'Bhaghat Singh: A Politics of Death and Hope', in Anshu Malhotra and Farina Mir (eds), *Punjab Reconsidered: History, Culture and Practice* (Oxford: Oxford University Press, 2012), 383–4.

5 Maia Ramnath, *Decolonizing Anarchism* (Oakland, CA: AK Press, 2012), 145.

6 'Balraj' [Bhagat Singh], 'The Red Pamphlet' [1929]. Available online: https://www.marxists.org/archive/bhagat-singh/1929/04/08 .htm.

7 Aparna Vaidik, 'Was Bhagat Singh an Internationalist? Resistance and Identity in a Global Age', in Vivek Sachdeva, Queeny Pradhan and Anu Venugopalan (eds), *Identities in South Asia: Conflicts and Assertions* (Abingdon: Routledge, 2019).

8 Ramnath, *Decolonizing Anarchism*, 149.

9 Kenyon Zimmer, 'A Golden Gate of Anarchy: Local and Transnational Dimensions of Anarchism in San Francisco, 1880s-1930s', in Constance Bantman and Bert Altena (eds), *Reassessing the Transnational Turn: Scales of Analysis in Anarchist and Syndicalist Studies* (Abingdon: Routledge, 2015), 107.

10 Ole Birk Laursen, 'Anarchist Anti-Imperialism: Guy Aldred and the Indian Revolutionary Movement, 1909-14', *Journal of Imperial and Commonwealth History* 46, no. 2 (2018): 286–303.

11 Ole Birk Laursen, '"I Believe My Name Is Not Unknown in India": Emma Goldman and the Indian Revolutionary Movement, 1909-1925', 3 October 2017. Available online: https://olebirklaursen.wo rdpress.com/2017/10/03/i-believe-my-name-is-not-unknown-in-india-emma-goldman-and-the-indian-revolutionary-movement-1909-1925/.

12 Ramnath, *Decolonizing Anarchism*, 145.

13 Ibid., 146.

14 Ibid.

15 Ole Birk Laursen, 'M. P. T. Acharya: A Revolutionary, an Agitator, a Writer', in M. P. T. Acharya, *We Are Anarchists: Essays on*

Anarchism, Pacifism and the Indian Independence Movement, 1923-1953, ed. Ole Birk Laursen (Oakland, CA: AK Press, 2019).

16 John Crump, *Hatta Shuzo and Pure Anarchism in Interwar Japan* (London: St Martin's Press, 1993), xvii.

17 Bantman and Altena (eds), *Reassessing the Transnational Turn*.

18 Benedict Anderson, *The Age of Globalization: Anarchism and the Anticolonial Imagination* (London: Verso, 2013), 2.

19 Arif Dirlik, *Anarchism in the Chinese Revolution* (Berkeley: University of California Press, 1991), 2.

20 Ibid.

21 Ibid., 118–19.

22 Anderson, *Age of Globalization*, 4.

23 Raymond Craib, 'A Foreword', in Barry Maxwell and Raymond Craib (eds), *No Gods, No Masters, No Peripheries: Global Anarchisms* (Oakland, CA: PM Press, 2015), 3.

24 Ibid.

25 Ilham Khuri-Makdisi, *The Eastern Mediterranean and the Making of Global Radicalism, 1860-1914* (Berkeley: University of California Press, 2013), 3.

26 Jason Adams, *Non-Western Anarchisms: Rethinking the Global Context* (Johannesburg: Zabalaza Books, 2003).

27 Ibid., 12–13.

28 Ibid., 13.

29 Peter Marshall, *Demanding the Impossible: A History of Anarchism* (London: HarperPerennial, 1992), 529.

30 Ole Birk Laursen, '"Anarchism, Pure and Simple": M. P. T. Acharya, Anti-Colonialism and the International Anarchist Movement', *Postcolonial Studies* 23, no. 2 (2020): 241.

31 Arif Dirlik, 'Anarchism and the Question of Place: Thoughts from the Chinese Experience', in Steven Hirsch and Lucien van der Walt (eds), *Anarchism and Syndicalism in the Colonial and Postcolonial World: The Praxis of National Liberation, Internationalism, and Social Revolution* (Leiden: Brill, 2010), 131.

32 Khuri-Makdisi, *Eastern Mediterranean and the Making of Global Radicalism*.

33 Ramnath, *Decolonizing Anarchism*, esp. 1–40.

34 Ibid., 37.

35 Emma Goldman, *Living My Life* (New York: Alfred A. Knopf, 1931) cited in Birk Laursen, 'Anarchism, Pure and Simple', 253 n. 46.

36 Ramnath, *Decolonizing Anarchism*, 56.

37 Ibid.

38 Ibid., 58.

39 Gregory Claeys, 'The "Survival of the Fittest" and the Origins of Social Darwinism', *Journal of the History of Ideas* 61, no. 2 (2000): 227.

40 Ruth Kinna, *Kropotkin: Reviewing the Classical Anarchist Tradition* (Edinburgh: Edinburgh University Press, 2016), 12.

41 Ole Birk Laursen, '"The Bomb Plot of Zurich": Indian Nationalism, Italian Anarchism and the First World War', in Matthew S. Adams and Ruth Kinna (eds), *Anarchism, 1914-18: Internationalism, Anti-Militarism, and War* (Manchester: Manchester University Press, 2017), 139.

42 Birk Laursen, 'Anarchist Anti-Imperialism', 243.

43 Ole Birk Laursen, 'Anti-Colonialism, Terrorism and the "Politics of Friendship": Virendranath Chattapadhyaya and the European Anarchist Movement, 1910-1927', *Anarchist Studies* 27, no. 1 (2019): 48.

44 Birk Laursen, 'The Bomb Plot of Zurich', 139.

45 Ramnath, *Decolonizing Anarchism*, 45.

46 Chandrika Kaul, 'Washing Dirty Linen in Public: Imperial Spin Doctoring, the British Press and the Downfall of Lord Curzon, 1905', *Media History* 15, no. 4 (2009): 385–406.

47 Ramnath, *Decolonizing Anarchism*, 45.

48 Birk Laursen, 'The Bomb Plot of Zurich', 138.

49 Ibid., 138.

50 Ramnath, *Decolonizing Anarchism*, 59.

51 Ibid.

52 *Belfast News-Letter*, 12 July 1909; Ramnath, *Decolonizing Anarchism*, 59.

53 Birk Laursen, 'Anarchist Anti-Imperialism', 287.

54 Ibid., 286–303.

55 Birk Laursen, 'The Bomb Plot of Zurich', 135.

56 Gajendra Singh, 'Jodi Singh, the Ghadar Movement, and the Anti-Colonial Deviant in the Anglo-American Imagination', *Past and Present* 245 (2019): 191.

57 Birk Laursen, 'Anarchism, Pure and Simple', 246.

58 Ibid., 247.

59 Ibid.

60 Ramnath, *Decolonizing Anarchism*, 154.

61 'Balraj' [Bhagat Singh] 'Beware, Ye Bureaucracy!' [1928]. Available online: https://www.marxists.org/archive/bhagat-singh/1928/12/18 .htm.

62 Ramnath, *Decolonizing Anarchism*, 150.

63 Ibid., 158.

64 Ibid., 156.

65 Birk Laursen, 'Anarchism, Pure and Simple', 250.

66 M. P. T. Acharya, 'What Is Anarchism?' [1948], in Acharya, *We Are Anarchists*.

67 Ibid.

68 Birk Laursen, 'Anarchism, Pure and Simple', 251.

69 Durba Ghosh, 'Gandhi and the Terrorists: Revolutionary Challenges from Bengal and Engagements with Non-Violent Political Protest', *South Asia: Journal of South Asian Studies* 39 (2016): 560–76.

70 Hirakawa Sukehiro, 'Japan's Turn to the West', in Marius B. Jensen (ed.), *The Cambridge History of Japan, Volume 5: The Nineteenth Century* (Cambridge: Cambridge University Press, 1989), 432.

71 Andrew Gordon, *A Modern History of Japan: From Tokugawa Times to the Present* (New York: Oxford University Press, 2003), 62.

72 Sho Konishi, *Anarchist Modernity: Cooperatism and Japanese-Russian Intellectual Relations in Modern Japan* (Cambridge MA: Harvard University Press, 2013).

73 Adams, *Non-Western Anarchisms*, 7.

74 George Elison, 'Kotoku Shusui: The Change in Thought', *Monumenta Nipponica* 22, no. 3/4 (1967): 438–9.

75 Crump, *Hatta Shuzo and Pure Anarchism*, 22.

76 Elison, 'Kotoku Shusui', 439; Crump, *Hatta Shuzo and Pure Anarchism*, 26.

77 Crump, *Hatta Shuzo and Pure Anarchism*, 26.

78 Ibid., 27.

79 Konishi, *Anarchist Modernity*, 194.

80 Dirlik, *Anarchism in the Chinese Revolution*, 119.

81 Dongyoun Hwang, *Anarchism in Korea: Independence, Transnationalism, and the Question of National Development, 1919-1984* (Albany, NY: SUNY Press, 2016), 11.

82 Ibid.

83 Gordon, *Modern History of Japan*, 67–8.

84 Tomoko Seto, '"Anarchist Beauties" in Late Meiji Japan: Media Narratives of Police Violence in the Red Flag Incident', *Radical History Review* 126 (2016): 32.

85 Seto, 'Media Narratives of Anarchist Violence in the Red Flag Incident', 32.

86 Crump, *Hatta Shuzo and Pure Anarchism*, 25.

87 Ibid., 28.

88 Vera Mackie and Yamaizumi Susumu, 'Introduction', in Masako Gavin and Ben Middleton (eds), *Japan and the High Treason Incident* (Abingdon: Routledge, 2013), 1.

89 Ibid.

90 Hélène Bowen Raddeker, 'Anarchist Women of Imperial Japan: Lives, Subjectivities, Representations', *Anarchist Studies* 24, no. 1 (2016): 18.

91 Crump, *Hatta Shuzo and Pure Anarchism*, 30.

92 Ibid., 31.

93 Ibid., 26.

94 Ibid., 32.

95 Ibid., 33.

96 Ibid., 34.

97 Konishi, *Anarchist Modernity*, 340–1.

98 Crump, *Hatta Shuzo and Pure Anarchism*, 36.

99 Konishi, *Anarchist Modernity*, 344.

100 Ibid., 345.

101 Crump, *Hatta Shuzo and Pure Anarchism*, 43.

102 Marshall, *Demanding the Impossible*, 525.

103 Crump, *Hatta Shuzo and Pure Anarchism*, 69–70.

104 Ibid., 85.

105 Ibid., 62.

106 Ibid.

107 Ibid., 63.

108 Ibid.

109 Ibid., 66.

110 Hwang, *Anarchism in Korea*, 50.

111 Ibid.

112 Ramnath, 'Non-Western Anarchisms', in Carl Levy and Matthew S. Adams (eds), *The Palgrave Handbook of Anarchism* (Basingstoke: Palgrave, 2019), 683.

113 Ibid.

114 Ibid., 683–4.

115 Dirlik, *Anarchism in the Chinese Revolution*, 3.

116 Ibid., 296.

117 John A. Rapp, *Daoism and Anarchism: Critiques of State Autonomy in Ancient and Modern China* (London: Bloomsbury, 2012).

118 Dirlik, 'Anarchism and the Question of Place', 135.

119 Bryan Palmer, 'The Black and the Red', *New Left Review*, second series, 77 (2012): 155–6.

120 Dirlik, 'Anarchism and the Question of Place', 132.

121 Pierre-Joseph Proudhon, *What Is Property?* [1840], in Pierre-Joseph Proudhon, *Property Is Theft! A Pierre-Joseph Proudhon Anthology*, ed. Iain McKay (Oakland, CA: AK Press, 2011), 88.

122 Marshall, *Demanding the Impossible*, xiv.

123 Ibid., 3–4.

124 Dirlik, 'Anarchism and the Question of Place', 132.

125 Khuri-Makdisi, *Eastern Mediterranean and the Making of Global Radicalism* , 1.

126 Ibid., 9.

127 Dirlik, 'Anarchism and the Question of Place, 132.

128 Anderson, *Age of Globalization*.

Chapter 5

1 Carissa Honeywell, 'Paul Goodman: Finding an Audience for Anarchism in Twentieth-Century America', *Journal for the Study of Radicalism* 5, no. 2 (2011): 1.

2 The term as used here is from David Edgerton, *Warfare State: Britain, 1920-1970* (Cambridge: Cambridge University Press, 2006) and used in an anarchist context by Carissa Honeywell in her account of the prosecution of the Freedom Press anarchists – Carissa Honeywell, 'Anarchism and the British Warfare State:

The Prosecution of the *War Commentary* Anarchists, 1945', *International Review of Social History* 60 (2015): 257–84.

3 'Anarchists Face Tribunal', *War Commentary*, March 1940: 6.

4 Ibid.

5 Ibid.

6 'State Control or Workers' Control?', *War Commentary*, April 1941: 1.

7 'Putting the COs on the Spot', *War Commentary*, April 1941: 12.

8 J. H. [John Hewetson], 'The Suppression of the *Daily Worker*', *War Commentary*, February 1941: 4.

9 Colin Ward, 'Witness for the Prosecution', *Wildcat Inside Story*, 1 (1974). Available at: https://theanarchistlibrary.org/library/colin-ward-witness-for-the-prosecution.pdf.

10 Ibid.

11 Ward had also submitted his own articles to the paper by this point. David Goodway, *Anarchist Seeds Beneath the Snow: Left-Libertarian Thought and British Writers from William Morris to Colin Ward* (Liverpool: Liverpool University Press, 2006), 311.

12 Honeywell, 'Anarchism and the British Warfare State', 257–84.

13 Goodway, *Anarchist Seeds Beneath the Snow*, 326.

14 Albert Meltzer, *The Anarchists in London, 1935-1955* (London: Freedom Press, 2018), 80.

15 Peter Ryley, 'Individualism', in Carl Levy and Matthew S. Adams (eds), *The Palgrave Handbook of Anarchism* (Basingstoke: Palgrave, 2019), 234.

16 Stephen Brooke, 'Problems of "Socialist Planning": Evan Durbin and the Labour Government of 1945', *Historical Journal* 34, no. 3 (1991): 687–702.

17 Dylan Riley, 'Tony Judt: A Cooler Look', *New Left Review* 71 (2011): 31–63.

18 Lucien van der Walt, 'Detailed Reply to *International Socialism:* Debating Power and Revolution in Anarchism, *Black Flame* and Historical Marxism' (2011), 5. Available online: https://lucienvanderwalt.files.wordpress.com/2011/07/van-der-walt-detailed-reply-to-international-socialism.pdf.

19 George Woodcock, *Proudhon: A Biography*, 3rd edn (Montreal: Black Rose Books, 1987), xiv–xv.

20 See the discussion in Stuart White, 'Making Anarchism Respectable? The Social Philosophy of Colin Ward', *Journal of Political Ideologies* 12, no. 1 (2007): 11–28.

21 Richard Boston, 'Conversations About Anarchism', *Anarchy* 85 (1968): 65; Meltzer, *Anarchists in London.*

22 William L. Renley, *Jean-Paul Sartre's Anarchist Philosophy* (London: Bloomsbury, 2018).

23 Rosie Germain, 'Existentialism and the Student Critique of Colonialism', paper delivered to the 'Student Movements and (Post-)colonial Emancipations: Transnational Itineraries, Dialogues and Programmes' conference, Université Paris Diderot, 9 December 2016.

24 Lorenzo Kom'boa Ervin, *Anarchism and the Black Revolution* [1979], in *Black Anarchism: A Reader by the Black Rose Anarchist Federation* (2016), 10–71.

25 Julia Tanenbaum, 'To Destroy Domination in All Its Forms: Anarcha-Feminist Theory, Organization, & Action 1970-1978', *Perspectives on Anarchist Studies* 29 (2016): 15.

26 Murray Bookchin, *The Ecology of Freedom: The Emergence and Dissolution of Hierarchy* (Palo Alto: Cheshire Books, 1982).

27 Colin Ward, *Anarchy in Action* (London: Freedom Press, 1973), 18.

28 Francis Fukuyama, 'The End of History?', *National Interest* 16 (1989): 3–18.

29 Ibid., 3.

30 Vernon Richards, 'Room at the Top?' [1964], in Vernon Richards, *The Impossibilities of Social Democracy* (London: Freedom Press, 1978), 43.

31 Ibid.

32 Jeff Shantz and Dana M. Williams, *Anarchy and Society: Reflections on Anarchist Sociology* (Leiden: Brill, 2013), 40–50.

33 David Owen, *Face the Future* (London: Jonathan Cape, 1980).

34 C. A. R. Crosland, *The Future of Socialism* (London: Jonathan Cape, 1956), 26–7.

35 Ibid., 27.

36 Ibid., 40.

37 Ibid.

38 Ibid., 67.

39 Ibid.

40 C. A. R. Crosland, 'The Transition From Capitalism', in R. H. S. Crossman (ed.), *New Fabian Essays* [1952] (London: J. M. Dent & Son, 1970), 39.

41 Ibid., 47.

42 Ibid.; Catherine Ellis, '"The New Messiah of My Life": Anthony
Crosland's Reading of Lucien Laurat's *Marxism and Democracy*
(1940)', *Journal of Political Ideologies* 17 (2012): 189–205; Lucien
Laurat, *Marxism and Democracy* (London: Victor Gollancz, 1940),
55–62, 85–91.

43 Mike Finn, *Socialism, Education and Equal Opportunity: The
Contemporary Legacy of Anthony Crosland* (Basingstoke:
Palgrave, 2021).

44 Madeleine Davis, 'The Origins of the British New Left', in Martin
Klimke and Joachim Scharloth (eds), *1968 in Europe: A History of
Protest and Activism* (Basingstoke: Palgrave, 2008), 45.

45 Ibid.

46 David Goodway, 'G. D. H. Cole: A Socialist and Pluralist', in Peter
Ackers and Alastair J. Reid (eds), *Alternatives to State-Socialism in
Britain: Other Worlds of Labour in the Twentieth Century* (London:
Palgrave, 2016).

47 Ibid., 255.

48 Goodway, *Anarchist Seeds Beneath the Snow*.

49 Honeywell, 'Paul Goodman', 3.

50 Ibid., 2.

51 Murray Bookchin, *Social Anarchism or Lifestyle Anarchism: An
Unbridgeable Chasm* (Oakland, CA: AK Press, 1995), 33.

52 Guy Debord, *Society of the Spectacle* [1967] (Berkeley, CA:
Bureau of Public Secrets, 2014).

53 Ibid., 2.

54 Ibid., 8.

55 Peter Marshall, *Demanding the Impossible: A History of
Anarchism* (London: HarperPerennial, 1992), 641.

56 Max Stirner, *The Ego and Its Own* [1844] (Cambridge: Cambridge
University Press, 1995).

57 Daniel Stedman Jones, *Masters of the Universe: Hayek, Friedman,
and the Birth of Neoliberal Politics* (Princeton, NJ: Princeton
University Press, 2012).

58 Popper presents this position in his *The Poverty of Historicism*
[1957] (London: Routledge, 2002), 58ff.

59 David Harvey, *A Brief History of Neoliberalism* (Oxford: Oxford
University Press, 2005), gives a concise account of neoliberalism
as a political phenomenon. Stedman Jones's *Masters of the
Universe* is a more elaborate and precise explanation of the
development of neoliberalism in the context of the Mont Pelerin
Society and individual thinkers/actors.

60 F. A. Hayek, *The Road to Serfdom* [1944] (London: Routledge, 2001); F. A. Hayek, *The Constitution of Liberty* [1960] (London: Routledge, 2006).

61 Iain McKay, 'Proprietarianism and Fascism', *Anarcho-Syndicalist Review* 75 (2019): 25.

62 Ryley, 'Individualism', 234.

63 Murray N. Rothbard, *Man, Economy and State* [1962] (Auburn, AL: Ludwig von Mises Institute, 2009), 1025.

64 Ibid., 1024.

65 Ibid., 657, 800.

66 Murray N. Rothbard, 'The Myth of Neutral Taxation', *Cato Journal* 1, no. 2 (1981): 528.

67 McKay, 'Proprietarianism and Fascism'; Marshall, *Demanding the Impossible*, 641–2.

68 Ryley, 'Individualism', 234–5.

69 Audrey Herbert [*pseud.*] [Murray N. Rothbard], 'Are Libertarians Anarchists?' [n.d., 1950s]. Available online: https://mises.org/library/are-libertarians-anarchists.

70 Ibid.

71 Ibid.

72 Ibid.

73 Ibid.

74 Benjamin Franks, *Rebel Alliances: Contemporary British Anarchisms* (Edinburgh: AK Press, 2006), 162–3.

75 Ward, *Anarchy in Action* [1996].

76 Ward, cited in David Goodway, '*Freedom*, 1886–2014: An Appreciation', *History Workshop Journal* 79, no. 1 (2015): 238.

77 David Berry, 'Anarchism and 1968', in Levy and Adams, *Palgrave Handbook of Anarchism*, 449.

78 Ibid.

79 Richard Vinen, *The Long '68: Radical Protest and Its Enemies* (London: Penguin, 2018), 122.

80 Todd Shephard, *The Invention of Decolonization: The Algerian War and the Remaking of France* (Ithaca, NY: Cornell University Press, 2006).

81 Mikkel Bolt Rasmussen, 'The Spectacle of de Gaulle's coup d'etat: The Situationists on de Gaulle's Coming to Power', *French Cultural Studies* 27, no. 1 (2016): 101.

82 Ibid., 98.

83 Ibid., 100.

84 Ibid., 103.

85 Tony Judt, *Postwar: A History of Europe Since 1945* (London: Vintage, 2010). I am grateful to Anton Jäger and Paul Ewart for drawing my attention to critiques of Judt and the period in general.

86 Shephard, *Invention of Decolonization*, 1.

87 Frantz Fanon, *The Wretched of the Earth* (New York: Grove Press, 1963), 35. Vinen, *Long '68*, 100.

88 Ibid., 35–6.

89 Ibid.

90 David Macey, *Frantz Fanon: A Biography* (London: Verso, 2012), 276.

91 Vinen, *Long '68*, 100.

92 Ibid.

93 Fanon, *Wretched of the Earth*, 107–47.

94 Ole Birk Laursen, 'Anti-imperialism', in Levy and Adams (eds), *Palgrave Handbook of Anarchism*, 160–1.

95 Ibid., 161.

96 Vinen, *Long '68*, 125.

97 Berry, 'Anarchism and 1968', 459.

98 François Crouzet, 'A University Besieged: Nanterre, 1967-69', *Political Science Quarterly* 84, no. 2 (1969): 328–50.

99 Ibid., 332.

100 Berry, 'Anarchism and 1968', 459.

101 Crouzet, 'A University Besieged', 337.

102 Judith Friedlander, 'The Place of Philosophy at the New School for Social Research', in Michela Beatrice Ferri (ed.), *The Reception of Husserlian Phenomenology in North America* (Geneva: Springer, 2019), 88.

103 Crouzet, 'A University Besieged', 337.

104 Berry, 'Anarchism and 1968', 460.

105 'Vive les etudiants', *Freedom*, 18 May 1968.

106 Vinen, *Long '68*, 123.

107 John Vane, 'Anarchism in the May Movement in France', *Anarchy* 99 (1969): 129.

108 Berry, 'Anarchism and 1968', 462.

109 Interview with Alexandre Hebert, *Anarchy* 99 (1969): 160.

110 Interview with Daniel Cohn-Bendit, *Anarchy* 99 (1969): 157.

111 Anthony Arblaster, 'The Relevance of Anarchism', *Socialist Register* 8 (1971): 160.

112 Daniel Cohn-Bendit and Gabriel Cohn-Bendit, *Obsolete Communism: The Left-Wing Alternative* (New York: McGraw-Hill, 1968), 217.

113 Marshall, *Demanding the Impossible*.

114 Interview with Daniel Cohn-Bendit, 153.

115 Vinen, *Long '68*.

116 Julian Bourg, *From Revolution to Ethics: May 1968 and Contemporary French Thought* (Montreal: McGill-Queens' University Press, 2007).

117 Anthony Crosland, *Socialism Now* (London: Jonathan Cape, 1974).

118 Dana M. Williams, 'Black Panther Radical Factionalization and the Development of Black Anarchism', *Journal of Black Studies* 46, no. 7 (2015): 679.

119 Jeffrey Haas, *The Assassination of Fred Hampton: How the FBI and Chicago Police Murdered a Black Panther* (Chicago: Lawrence Hill Books, 2010).

120 Interview with Lorenzo Kom'boa Ervin, *Black Flag*, 206 (1995), Available online: https://libcom.org/library/interview-with-lorenzo-komboa-ervin-from-1995.

121 Ashanti Alston, 'Black Anarchism', *Anarchist Panther* (Spring 2004): 6.

122 Interview with Lorenzo Kom'boa Ervin.

123 Kom'boa Ervin, *Anarchism and the Black Revolution* in Black Rose Federation, *Black Anarchism: A Reader* (2016), 19.

124 Alston, 'Black Anarchism', 7.

125 Williams, 'Black Panther Radical Factionalization', 691–2.

126 Ibid., 691.

127 Kom'boa Ervin, *Anarchism and the Black Revolution*, 19.

128 Ibid., 21.

129 Ibid., 22.

130 Ibid.

131 Ibid., 22–6.

132 Alston, 'Black Anarchism', 8.

133 Ibid.

134 Ibid., 8.

135 Marquis Bey, *Anarcho-Blackness: Notes Towards a Black Anarchism* (Oakland, CA: AK Press, 2020).

136 Ibid.

137 Ibid.

138 Joaquin A. Pedroso, 'Black Lives Matter or, How to Think Like an Anarchist', *Class, Race and Corporate Power* 4, no. 2 (2016): 2.

139 Bey, *Anarcho-Blackness*.

140 Ibid.

141 Ibid.

142 Ibid.

143 Ibid.

144 Tanenbaum, 'To Destroy Domination in All Its Forms', 15.

145 Ibid., 13–14.

146 Clare Hemmings, *Considering Emma Goldman: Feminist Political Ambivalence and the Imaginative Archive* (Durham, NC: Duke University Press, 2018), 10.

147 Tanenbaum, 'To Destroy Domination in All Its Forms', 15.

148 Ibid.

149 Ibid.

150 Peggy Kornegger, 'Anarchism: The Feminist Connection' [1979], in Dark Star Collective, *Quiet Rumors: An Anarcha-Feminist Reader* (Oakland, CA: AK Press, 2012), 25.

151 Ibid., 28.

152 Ibid., 29.

153 Ibid.

154 Ruth Kinna, 'Anarchism and Feminism', in Nathan Jun (ed.), *Brill's Companion to Anarchism and Philosophy* (Leiden: Brill, 2018). Preprint version cited available online: https://repository.lboro.ac.uk /articles/Anarchism_and_feminism/9470303. Page references are from this PDF. Citation at p. 1.

155 Ibid., 2–3.

156 Donna M. Kowal, 'Anarcha-Feminism', in Levy and Adams (eds), *Palgrave Handbook of Anarchism*, 267.

157 Kinna, 'Anarchism and Feminism', 3.

158 Judy Greenway, 'Twenty-First Century Sex', in Jon Purkis and James Bowen (eds), *Twenty-First Century Anarchism* (London: Cassell, 1997), 170.

159 Ibid., 170–1.

160 The project, *Anarchism and Feminism: Voices From the Seventies*, can be accessed via Greenway's personal website at http://www.judygreenway.org.uk/wp/anarchist-feminist-interviews/.

161 Judy Greenway, Interview with Susan [1977], *Anarchism and Feminism: Voices From the Seventies*. http://www.judygreenway.org.uk/wp/susan/.

162 Ibid.

163 Ibid.

164 Kowal, 'Anarcha-Feminism', 265.

165 Tanenbaum, 'To Destroy Domination in All Its Forms', 17.

166 Murray Bookchin, 'Affinity Groups', in George Woodcock (ed.), *The Anarchist Reader* (Glasgow: Fontana, 1977), 173–4.

167 Judy Greenway, 'The Gender Politics of Anarchist History: Re/membering Women, Re/minding Men', paper presented at the Political Studies Association annual conference, Edinburgh 2010. Available online: http://www.judygreenway.org.uk/wp/the-gender-politics-of-anarchist-history-remembering-women-reminding-men/.

168 Ibid.

169 Bookchin, *Ecology of Freedom*.

170 Andy Price, 'Green Anarchism', in Levy and Adams (eds), *Palgrave Handbook of Anarchism*, 281–91.

171 Janet Biehl, 'Bookchin Breaks with Anarchism', *The Anarchist Library* (2011). Available online: https://theanarchistlibrary.org/library/janet-biehl-bookchin-breaks-with-anarchism.

172 Andy Price, *Recovering Bookchin: Social Ecology and the Crises of Our Time* (Porsgrunn: New Compass Press, 2011).

173 Ibid.

174 Tanenbaum, 'To Destroy Domination in All Its Forms'.

175 Murray Bookchin, *Post-Scarcity Anarchism*, 2nd edn [1971] (Montreal: Black Rose Books, 1986).

176 Brian Tokar, 'On Bookchin's Social Ecology and Its Contributions to Social Movements', *Capitalism Nature Socialism* 19, no. 1 (2008): 51.

177 Geoffrey Ostergaard, *Resisting the Nation State. The Pacifist and Anarchist Tradition* (London: Peace Pledge Union, 1982).

178 John McCormick, *Reclaiming Paradise: The Global Environmental Movement* (Bloomington: Indiana University Press, 1991), 57.

179 Mark Hamilton Lytle, *The Gentle Subversive: Rachel Carson, Silent Spring, and the Rise of the Environmental Movement* (New York: Oxford University Press, 2007), vi.

180 John Paull, 'The Rachel Carson Letters and the Making of *Silent Spring*', *SAGE Open* (July–September 2013), 1.

181 Juan Diego Pérez Cebada, 'An Editorial Flop Revisited: Rethinking the Impact of M. Bookchin's *Our Synthetic Environment* on Its Golden Anniversary', *Global Environment* 6, no. 12 (2013): 250.

182 Ibid., 251.

183 Murray Bookchin, 'Ecology and Revolutionary Thought' [1965], in Bookchin, *Post-Scarcity Anarchism*, 79.

184 Ibid.

185 Ibid., 80.

186 Ibid.

187 Ibid., 101.

188 Bookchin, *Ecology of Freedom*, viii.

189 Bookchin, 'Ecology and Revolutionary Thought', 84.

190 Ibid.

191 Ibid.

192 Ibid., 85.

193 Ibid.

194 Including a devastating critique in Bookchin, *Social Anarchism or Lifestyle Anarchism*.

195 Murray Bookchin, 'Towards a Liberatory Technology' [1965], in Bookchin, *Post-Scarcity Anarchism*, 107–61.

196 Janet Biehl, *Ecology or Catastrophe: The Life of Murray Bookchin* (Oxford: Oxford University Press, 2015), 185.

197 Bourg, *From Revolution to Ethics*.

Conclusion

1 David Graeber, *Fragments of an Anarchist Anthropology* (Chicago: Prickly Paradigm Press, 2004), 1.

2 Andrew M. Koch, 'Post-Structuralism and the Epistemological Basis of Anarchism' [1993], in Duane Rousselle and Sureyyya Evren (eds), *Post-Anarchism: A Reader* (London: Pluto, 2011), 28.

3 Ruth Kinna and Alex Prichard, 'Introduction', in Alex Prichard, Ruth Kinna, Saku Pinta and David Berry (eds), *Libertarian Socialism: Politics in Black and Red* (Basingstoke: Palgrave, 2012), 7.

4   David Graeber, 'The New Anarchists', *New Left Review* 13 (2002): 61.

5   Ibid.

6   Jackie Smith, 'Globalizing Resistance: The Battle of Seattle and the Future of Social Movements', *Mobilization: An International Quarterly* 6, no. 1 (2006): 1–19.

7   Graeber, 'The New Anarchists', 64–5.

8   Ibid., 62.

9   Ibid., 69.

10 Ibid., 67.

11 Roger Burbach, 'Roots of the Postmodern Rebellion in Chiapas', *New Left Review* 205 (1994): 113–24.

12 Ibid., 122.

13 Ibid., 123.

14 Graeber, 'The New Anarchists', 63.

15 Chapter 4, this volume.

16 'David Graeber, 04/04/2006', CharlieRose.com. Available online: https://charlierose.com/videos/10730 (accessed 25 March 2018).

17 Graeber, 'The New Anarchists', 72.

18 Ibid.

19 David Graeber, *Debt: The First 5,000 Years* (New York: Melville House Publishing, 2011); *The Utopia of Rules: On Technology, Stupidity, and the Secret Joys of Bureaucracy* (New York: Melville House Publishing, 2015); *Direct Action: An Ethnography* (Oakland, CA: AK Press, 2008).

20 David Graeber, *The Democracy Project: A History, a Crisis, a Movement* (London: Penguin, 2013).

21 Ibid., 187.

22 Ibid., 188.

23 Ibid., 188–9.

24 Representative examples include James C. Scott, *Weapons of the Weak: Everyday Forms of Peasant Resistance* (New Haven, CT: Yale University Press, 1985); *Domination and the Arts of Resistance: Hidden Transcripts* (New Haven, CT: Yale University Press, 1990); *The Art of Not Being Governed: An Anarchist History of Upland South Asia* (New Haven, CT: Yale University Press, 2009).

25 James C. Scott, *Two Cheers for Anarchism: Six Easy Pieces on Autonomy, Dignity, and Meaningful Work and Play* (Princeton, NJ: Princeton University Press, 2012), ix.

26 Ibid., ix–x.

27 Ibid., x.

28 Ibid., xii.

29 Ibid.

30 Ibid., xiii–xiv.

31 Ibid., xvi.

32 Markus Lundstrom, *Anarchist Critique of Radical Democracy: The Impossible Argument* (London: Palgrave, 2018).

33 Jacob Blumenfeld, Chiara Bottici and Simon Critchley (eds), *The Anarchist Turn* (London: Pluto, 2013).

34 Tomás Ibáñez, *Anarchism Is Movement: Anarchism, Neoanarchism and Postanarchism* (Autonomies, 2014). Available online: https://th eanarchistlibrary.org/library/tomas-ibanez-anarchism-is-movement.

35 Todd May, *The Political Philosophy of Poststructuralist Anarchism* (Philadelphia, PA: Penn State University Press, 1994), ix.

36 Ibid., 2.

37 Ibid., 3.

38 Ibid.

39 Ibid., 3–4.

40 Ibid., 12.

41 Ibid.

42 Ibid.

43 Jason Adams, 'Postanarchism in a Nutshell' [2003], *The Anarchist Library*. Available online: https://theanarchistlibrary.org/library/jason -adams-postanarchism-in-a-nutshell.pdf.

44 Ibid., 3.

45 Ibid., 4.

46 Benjamin Franks, 'Postanarchism: A Critical Assessment', *Journal of Political Ideologies* 12, no. 2 (2007): 132.

47 Ibanez, *Anarchism Is Movement*.

48 David Morland, *Demanding the Impossible: Human Nature and Politics in Nineteenth-Century Social Anarchism* (London: Cassell, 1997).

49 Ibid.

50 Chapter 5, this volume.

51 Gavin Grindon, 'Bey, Hakim (b. 1945)', in Immanuel Ness (ed.), *The International Encyclopedia of Revolution and Protest* (Hoboken, NJ: John Wiley & Sons, 2010).

52 Simon Sellars, 'Hakim Bey: Repopulating the Temporary Autonomous Zone', *Journal for the Study of Radicalism* 4, no. 2 (2010): 100.

53 Ibid.

54 Robert P. Helms, 'Paedophilia and American Anarchism – the Other Side of Hakim Bey', libcom.org. Available online: https://libcom.org/library/paedophilia-and-american-anarchism-the-other-side-of-hakim-bey.

55 Murray Bookchin, *Social Anarchism or Lifestyle Anarchism: An Unbridgeable Chasm* (Oakland, CA: AK Press, 1995).

56 Sellars, 'Hakim Bey', 84–5.

57 Hakim Bey, *T.A.Z.: The Temporary Autonomous Zone: Ontological Anarchy, Poetic Terrorism* [1991] (Brooklyn, NY: Autonomedia, 2003), 99, cited in Sellars, 'Hakim Bey', 85–6.

58 Grindon, 'Bey, Hakim'.

59 Ibid.

60 James Bowen and Jonathan Purkis (eds), *Twenty-First Century Anarchism: Unorthodox Ideas for a New Millennium* (London: Cassell, 1997).

61 James Bowen and Jonathan Purkis, 'Introduction: The Masks of Anarchy', in ibid., 1.

62 Ibid., 2–3.

63 Dave Morland, 'Anti-Capitalism and Poststructuralist Anarchism', in James Bowen and Jonathan Purkis (eds), *Changing Anarchism: Anarchist Theory and Practice in a Global Age* (Manchester: Manchester University Press, 2004), 23–38.

64 Ibid., 38.

65 Steven Kull, Clay Ramsay and Evan Lewis, 'Misperceptions, the Media, and the Iraq War', *Political Science Quarterly* 118, no. 4 (2003): 569.

66 Nader Hashemi, 'The Arab Spring, U.S. Foreign Policy, and the Question of Democracy in the Middle East', *Denver Journal of International Law & Policy* 41 (Fall 2012): 32.

67 Clifford Baverel, 'Modern Anarchism in Social Movements from the Arab Spring to the Occupy Wall Street Movement', *emulations: Revue de sciences sociales* 16 (2016): 74.

68 Dilar Dirik, 'The Revolution of Smiling Women: Stateless Democracy and Power in Rojava', in Olivia U. Rutazibwa and Robbie Shilliam (eds), *The Routledge Handbook of Postcolonial Politics* (Abingdon: Routledge, 2018).

69 Murray Bookchin, *Libertarian Municipalism: An Overview* [1991]. Available online: https://theanarchistlibrary.org/library/murray-boo kchin-libertarian-municipalism-an-overview.a4.pdf.

70 Spencer Louis Potiker, 'Obstacles to Insurrection: Militarised Border Crossings Hindering the Rojava Liberation Struggle', *Anarchist Studies* 27, no. 2 (2019): 90.

71 John L. Hammond, 'The Anarchism of Occupy Wall Street', *Science & Society* 79, no. 2 (2015): 288–13. Citation at p. 290.

72 See the essays in Torsten Geelan, Marcos Gonzalez Hernando and Peter W. Walsh (eds), *From Financial Crisis to Social Change: Towards Alternative Horizons* (London: Palgrave, 2018).

73 Goran Therborn, 'Preface: The Labyrinths and the Layers of Social Change', in Geelan, Hernando and Walsh (eds), *From Financial Crisis to Social Change*, v.

74 Joseph Ibrahim, 'The Moral Economy of the UK Student Protest Movement 2010–2011', *Contemporary Social Science* 9 (2014): 79–91.

75 Matt Myers, *Student Revolt: Voices of the Austerity Generation* (London: Left Book Club, 2017).

76 Paul Lewis and Tim Newburn, *Reading the Riots: Investigating Britain's Summer of Disorder* (London: Guardian Books, 2012).

77 Hammond, 'The Anarchism of Occupy Wall Street', 288.

78 Ibid., 289.

79 Ibid., 295.

80 Nathan Schneider, 'Introduction: Anarcho-curious? Or, Anarchist America', in Noam Chomsky, *On Anarchism* (London: Penguin Books, 2014), viii.

81 Ibid., ix.

82 Ibid.

83 Ibid.

84 Ibid., x.

85 Ibid., x–xiii.

86 r/BreadTube. Available online: https://www.reddit.com/r/BreadTube/.

87 David Priestland, 'Introduction', in Peter Kropotkin, *The Conquest of Bread* (London: Penguin, 2015), vii.

88 David Goodway, 'Freedom, 1886–2014: An Appreciation', *History Workshop Journal* 79 (2015): 233.

89 Jon Bigger, 'Class War, Anarchism and Elections', Anarchism Research Group Episode 3. Available online: YouTube at https://youtu.be/neiK3rbUo6g.

90 Ruth Kinna, 'Anarcho-Corbynism', *DOPE* 4 (2018).

91 Black Rose Labour, 'Reading List'. Available online: https://blackroselabour.uk/reading-list/.

92 Senator Tom Cotton, via Twitter, 1 June 2020. Available online: https://twitter.com/tomcottonar/status/1267459561675468800?s=21.

93 Aurelien Mondon and Aaron Winter, *Reactionary Democracy: How Racism and the Populist Far Right Became Mainstream* (London: Verso, 2020).

Index